Moonlit

a Pearl Lake Novel
Book 1&2
Moonlit Stalker

Aquila Thorne

This is a work of fiction. Names, characters, businesses, places, events, and incidents are either the products of the author's imagination or used in a fictitious manner. Any other resemblance to actual persons, living or dead, or actual events is entirely coincidental.

Moonlit Night & Moonlit Stalker

a Pearl Lake Novel

Book 1 & (2) of Pearl Lake the Series

Copyright © 2021 Aquila Thorne

ISBN: 9798763367324

This novel was previously published as One Moonlit Night by me, Tina Marie

Books in the series

Ben and Abbi: Before Pearl Lake[1]
Moonlit Night[2]
Moonlit Road[3]
Heaven in the Moonlight[4]
The Inn at Pearl Lake[5]
Lane's Destiny[6]
Tim's Bar[7]
Her Christmas Wish[8]

---

1. https://books2read.com/AQBenandAbbi
2. https://books2read.com/AQMoonlit-Night
3. https://books2read.com/AQMoonlitRoad
4. https://books2read.com/ATHeavenintheMoonlight
5. https://books2read.com/AQInnAtPearlLake
6. https://books2read.com/ATlanesdestiny
7. https://books2read.com/AQTimsbar-
8. https://books2read.com/AQ-herChristmaswish

Dear Readers

Just in a case you're joining me now, I wanted to mention a few things. The series is best read in order, although the books can be read individually, some readers might get confused. Also, I've combined the first two books of the series into one, Moonlit Night. A couple of reasons why I did that are:

1. Money is tight for a lot of people. Don't get me wrong, I need it just as much as the next person, but I too know what it's like to want to escape from the realities of life within a good book and not always have the extra money to do so.

2. The title of the second book I think might have scared a few readers off, something that was never intended. As a new writer, when I wrote these books, I never wrote them like many authors do. I didn't plot or write to reader expectation or to market.

I just simply wrote them. The characters had a mind of their own and took me on a journey as well. One that I had fun writing and one that allowed me to escape the realities of life. Something that I wish for all my readers. My books will always have relatable characters and that comedy factor with a little suspense and of course romance.

A few times I've been told to there are typos in my books. I want to mention that I am Canadian and as a Canadian; I write in British English. There may be a time or two that you happen along a word that is spelled with American English and the reason for that is I've lived all my life close to the Canadian/US border. Because of that, sometimes I switch back and forth, an example would be that I use imperial instead of metric when describing feet instead of meters and miles instead of kilometers. Other words, you might think are typos if you're living in the US would be any word that ends in 'OR', like color, honor, favor, flavor, neighbor, all those words and more, over here in Canada have a 'U' added, colour, honour, favour, flavour, neighbour and so on. Also, words ending with 'ER', theater, center, once again, here in Canada we spell them theatre, centre, etc. With that said and keeping it in mind, I welcome you to Moonlit Night, I do hope you enjoy it!

Chapter 1

Not liking the darkness that had settled across Pearl Lake, Ben Quinn fumbled with the keys to his new house, and cursed himself for not having the forethought to bring a torch with him. He had been in a hurry to vacate England, grabbing what he could as he fled. He had been successful eluding the horde of paparazzi that had followed him from his flat towards the airport, minus a few suitcases, but at least he hadn't been followed. Being a Hollywood actor had its perks, being chased by photographers wasn't one of them.

He went to reach for his cellphone in his coat pocket and groaned, remembering that it had died somewhere over the Atlantic nine hours ago. Instead, he went by feel until he was able to jam the key in the lock. Successful, he turned the knob and pushed the door open, then kicked it closed as he dumped his suitcases just inside. He felt for a light switch next to the door and was mildly surprised when there wasn't one. "To hell with it," he mumbled and started stripping his coat and clothes off as he made his way down the hall. He nudged the first door he came upon with his shoulder and sighed, "This is going to be a pain in the ass in total darkness..." Walking into the room like a blind man, Ben waved his hands in front of him, hoping to meet a source of light.

He took a guess that he was eight feet into the room when his knees met with the foot of a bed knocking him onto it. He coughed as a cloud of dust raised into the air and settled onto his bare skin. He was too tired to care and pushed himself up to stand. Yanking the dust cover back, he dropped it onto the floor, then collapsed into a heap of exhaustion onto the bed and narrowly missed hitting his head on the corner of a bedside table.

He thought to himself, as he laid there that he would never again make such a grueling journey in one day. Turning over, he smashed his elbow on the wall and cursed a blue streak. Despite being exhausted, he couldn't get comfortable. It was so dark that he had a hard time recognizing the furnishings in the room and the silence was deafening. He wasn't sure if he would get used to it. For the past few years, the backdrop of a bustling city lulled him to sleep.

He reached out a hand and felt for a lamp. Almost knocking it over, he sat up and grabbed it before it toppled to the floor. Pulling on its chain, he was relieved to find it worked as it filled the room with its soft glow. Getting up, he made his way to the kitchen where he'd dropped his suitcases and snagged his coat off the floor on the way back to the bedroom.

Ben tossed everything onto the bed then unzipped one of the cases and rifled through it. Pulling out his phone charger and earbuds, he set them down, then grabbed his coat. Stuffing his hand into the pocket, he took out his phone and connected the charger. Pulling the nightstand away from the wall, he plugged the charger into the socket then sat on the side of the bed. With phone in hand, he yawned, watching as the lightning symbol on the screen turned from red to green and wasted no time hitting the power button when it did. Laying back against the pillow, he stuffed the earbuds in his ears and swiped the screen. Tapping on the music app, Ben hit the play button and was soon lulled to sleep as the night sounds of London filled his ears.

The sun slowly crept over the trees shining on the mirror-like image of the lake as Ben searched the pantry shelves. Feeling the effects of jet lag, he needed something to wake him up. Mark, his buddy that he bought the place from had assured Ben there were dry staples in the pantry. He didn't care if it was coffee or tea, heck he would take hot chocolate even.

As the tea kettle whistled on the stove, Ben made a face when he spied a jar of coffee behind a very outdated cereal box. He wouldn't be surprised if it hadn't been there for the past five years. Shoving it aside he took the jar of coffee and unscrewed the lid. Peering into it, he gave it a sniff. "Meh," he shrugged. "It's passable." He went into the kitchen and turned the burner off then filled a mug with the steaming water. Dumping some coffee in along with sugar he stirred it with the only thing he could find in the utensil drawer, a straw.

Mug in hand, Ben headed out to the back patio and sat on a chair at the table. He'd been sitting there quietly contemplating what to do for the day, when a doe came cautiously out of the woods. Holding his breath in anticipation of her next move, he was in awe when a fawn came stumbling out on its mother's heels. Mesmerized by the pair, Ben sat there sipping his coffee in silence until they took their leave.

He couldn't remember a time when he was so content and relaxed doing nothing.

Glancing at his watch, he was shocked to see an hour had passed. But he needed that hour of peace. He felt more refreshed than he had in a long ass while. As much as he hated the thought, it was time to head into the house and unpack. But first, the rumble in his stomach reminded him that the food in the house wasn't fit for a dog, and so he sent a quick text to Mark asking where he could buy some. Picking up his mug he headed into the house and sat the phone and cup on the kitchen counter before heading into the living room. Scowling, he rolled his sleeves up as he looked around the room.

He should have taken Mark's advice and hired a cleaning crew to come in. At the time, he didn't think it would be necessary, planning on doing it all himself. But as he looked around, he regretted that decision when he realized there was dust on every surface imaginable.

With a sigh, he went into the laundry room and grabbed a broom. Sweeping the floor, he started choking on the dust within minutes. Stopping what he was doing, Ben threw open the doors and windows to clear the cloud. There had to be a better way to do this. He turned and headed back to the laundry room to grab the shop vac he saw sitting in the corner.

A few hours later, he was finishing up by mopping the floor when his stomach reminded him it needed some attention too. Patting his pockets, he glanced around the room wondering what the hell he did with his phone.

"Right!" he said, remembering he left it on the counter. Snatching it up he noticed he had four missed calls from his mum and one from Mark. He punched in Mark's number, thinking he would call his mum in a minute. Right now, food was his main priority.

Walking to the store called Mackwell's, Ben called his mum back home. It would be 10 pm in England, but he knew she was likely going mildly insane by now with concern waiting to hear from him. She was the type of mum who imagined worse case scenarios. On the third ring, she picked up.

"Oh, my goodness Benjamin Quinn, are you trying to drive your mother crazy with worry? I was just about to book a flight to Canada!"

"Hello to you too Mum," he chuckled. "How's it going?"

"Don't you dare laugh at me, young man, it's been days since you left home."

By home she meant her home. Ben had spent a week at his childhood house placating his parents. His lifelong supporter, his dad Greg, was happy that Ben was making the move. Nancy, his mum on the other hand, wanted to know every detail before she accepted the fact that her only child would no longer be making England his home. A fear she had since he started acting. Sobering up, he apologized and explained the reasons he was so late in calling her as he walked to the store.

A few minutes later he was rounding the corner to the 'downtown' of the village. "Look mum, it's getting late there. Get some sleep, please. I'll call you in a few days, okay?... I love you too, goodnight." He hung up just as he pushed the door open of the only grocer in town, as he did, he heard a bell tinkling above the door.

A burly older man was standing behind the counter while two teenaged girls sat at it drinking milkshakes. He steeled himself for the screams of recognition as all three glanced his way.

"Hey there stranger," the man said. "Are you just passing through or visiting for a spell?"

"Hi. I'm settling in actually," Ben replied, chancing a glance around.

"Settling in you say? Where might that be? By the way the name's Mackenzie Wells, but everybody calls me Mack." He thrust his hand in Ben's direction.

He took it and shook it in a firm handshake as he said, "Ben... Ben Quinn. I just bought the place on the point at the water's edge." He tilted his head in the general direction of his home.

"You don't say? Hmm... that place has been empty pretty close to three or four years now. Didn't know it went up on the market."

Ben smiled, "Ah, it didn't. A friend of mine was planning on selling it and I grabbed it up the minute he told me about it."

"Well, happy to have you here. You want a bite to eat? On the house, as a welcome to the neighborhood kind of thing. We have the best burgers and fries around these parts, won't take but a few minutes to whip it up for you." Mack looked at him and waited for his response.

His offer floored Ben. He could tell that Mack didn't know what he did for a living, nor did the teenage girls sitting at the counter. It was odd to be treated like a nobody for once. And he liked it.

"A burger and fries sound just about perfect, thanks!" He jerked a thumb towards the grocery area, "Do you mind if I pick up a few things while it cooks?"

Mack spoke over his shoulder as he headed to the kitchen, "Sure, you go right ahead. I'll yell for you when it's two minutes to being done."

Nodding his thanks, Ben grabbed a shopping basket sitting near the door and headed towards the food area, filling it as he went. Deciding to grab the rest after he had eaten, he sat down at the counter to wait for his food.

He was studying the dessert menu when he heard a soft, "Excuse me."

Ben lifted his head and turned to the teenagers, "Yes?"

"Um, ah... we just wanted to tell you we think you have a nice voice, like your accent," they giggled in unison.

"Why thank you," Ben responded with a smile, one that sent the girls into a fit of giggles again.

"And you're cute too," they tossed in for good measure.

"Girls leave the man alone, in peace. Get going home now. I know you both have chores or homework to do," Mack said, as he placed a heaping plate of food before Ben.

"Sorry about that," Mack told him, as the girls took their leave.

Ben chuckled, "It's fine really, at least they were polite about it."

"I'll leave you to your dinner. Just holler if you need anything."

Ben dug into his food, savoring every bite. He was either extraordinarily hungry, or it was the best food he had ever eaten. He was thinking it was both.

Munching on a fry, he called out towards the kitchen, "Hey Mack, can you tell me a bit about the area?"

Mack appeared in the doorway, wiping his hands on a towel. "That I can!" He moseyed over and leaned a hand on the counter, "This side of the lake is mostly a vacation retreat for the rich." He pointed at the windows and went on, "There are a few cabins up the road that away; only for summer use. People come late spring every year and stay until Labour Day then head back home. Some come and go throughout the season, and some stay year-round, but not too many. In a couple of weeks, you'll see more traffic. The lake will be a busy place. At the far end of it, there are rental cabins and a camping site, a few restaurants too. You'll hear it soon enough." Mack continued, "Keep an eye out though. They like to come to this area of the lake and cause a little havoc from time to time."

Great, that's all I need. "What sort of havoc?" Ben questioned. He could already feel the tension at the thought.

"Nothing too serious. Mostly just trespassing, cutting through the private properties along the waterfront. Although Abbi Peterson, your neighbor had a break-in a few months back. She came home after a week away to her door kicked in. Her dog was nowhere around. She found her a day or so later over at your place, huddled on the porch. They never found who did it," Mack said, shaking his head.

Almost choking on his food, Ben's brows shot up with a quick flash of anger. "Wait... what? She left her dog alone for a week?" He had a soft spot for all animals but especially dogs.

"Oh, well, she had a house sitter staying to take care of Lucy while she was away. Just so happened that she had stepped out for a bit, knowing Abbi was coming home later in the day. Abbi has since alarmed the place and has cameras inside and out to catch every angle. I can't say I blame her one bit, with her job. It can bring out the wackos if you know what I mean?"

Confused, Ben nodded his head in agreement. The way Mack made it sound; it was like he should know who this Abbi was. He hadn't a clue and wondered if he should ask. Mack must have surmised from the look on his face he didn't because he pointed to the wall behind Ben.

"Right over there is where you'll find her work."

Ben turned around to where Mack was pointing. "Oh, so she's a writer, is she?"

Standing up from the stool, he set off towards the book section. He could use a good read to pass the time. Not like he'd bother with her book, though.

She's likely some boring historical romance novelist that writes about the 1300's British royalty... the kind of book my mother would love to read, he thought with derision.

"She sure is, our Abbi. And a damn fine one too. That one right here is being made into a movie as we speak," Mack beamed, proud as a peacock.

"You don't say?" Ben murmured, a bit surprised, as he searched out the titles looking for something that caught his eye. He picked up a book that looked interesting by the front cover, not bothering to read the title. He flipped it over in his hands to see the back. A black-and-white photo of an attractive woman stared back at him. Extremely attractive, he noted. He checked the inside back cover to find the 'about the author' section and skimmed through it.

Abbi Stevens started her writing path later in life. Having started her family at the tender age of 16 with twin boys and soon to follow a girl. She felt raising her family was more important than her dream. Never giving up hope, she carried out that dream at the age of 41. Abbi hails from Windsor, Ontario Canada, where she lives with her husband and loyal companion, Lucy.

Closing it, he started to read the back cover. A feeling of familiarity came over him as he read. *Wait a minute...* Frowning, he flipped it over to read the title, 'The Jasper Killings' by Abbi Stevens.

"Uh, Mack! What did you say Abbi's last name is?" Ben asked, confused.

"Peterson. But she writes under the pen name of Abbi Stevens."

He glanced around in dawning disbelief. "Bloody hell!" he snickered.

"Something wrong, Ben?" Mack's voice filled with concern.

"Nope. Not at all." He stood there, hands on his hips, still clutching the book in one. "Ring me up, would you Mack?" He held up the book and said, "And I'll take this too."

If someone had told him a month ago that he'd live right next door to the author of the book for the movie he was filming, he'd have thought them crazy.

Chapter 2

She held the paper in her hands, not believing it for a second. Since splitting with her ex-husband, four years ago, best-selling author, Abbi Peterson was free. Free to do what she pleased when she pleased and who she pleased. *Ha! Like that will ever happen again*, she thought with a sad smile.

The split had been mutual, but it had come at a price for her. It was only mutual when she had willingly given her ex, half of her royalties for the first year. Lucky for him it was being filmed for the big screen. Otherwise, he wouldn't have gotten squat. Towards the end of their relationship, he started squandering her advance cheque. If she had stayed, she was certain without a doubt, she'd be flat broke by now.

Marrying young after their firstborns, they had grown their separate ways long before she completed the first draft of her manuscript. She couldn't hate him; he had given her three awesome kids, all adults now. Twins, Luke, and Lane, 29 and Ava, 27. For that, she'd be eternally grateful. Tossing the letter aside, she opened the cupboard to get the morning underway.

The snap of the can opener was the call of the breakfast bell for her menagerie of pets. They came flying into the kitchen in a frenzy of hair, feathers, and dust.

Each one of her five dependents held a special place in her heart. She had two dogs. Lucy, her aging cuddle bug

Yorkie, and a Bull Mastiff American Bulldog mix, who was so aptly named Brutus. She brought him into the family fold for his intimidating physique after the break-in a few months back.

They guaranteed her at the time of rescuing, that he'd know that his sole purpose in life was to protect his mistress.

He failed miserably at it. With his lopsided grin and lolling tongue forever hanging out, he was the goofiest member of their family. But he was a work in progress and being a pup of only a year didn't help matters. She had to admit though that he was getting better. He at least now knew the cats, Null and Void were not his toys to drag about and that Bird, a beautiful sulfur-crested cockatoo could indeed fly around at will. Cussing the blue blazes out of anything he met, Bird knew he was the boss of their cozy abode.

They kept her company; they kept her sane when living in such a remote area was sometimes terrifying. Terrifying because every little sound had her jumping out of her skin, thinking someone was watching her. After the break-in, things just snowballed for her. She craved her privacy to the point of being considered a recluse by many. Not anything too drastic mind you, she still socialized with the locals, but that was it. She even avoided the web as much as possible, not caring to know what was going on in the world outside her bubble.

The closest neighbor was 300 feet away. Well, would be, if anyone were living there. She was told the house had been vacant for the past four years. When she bought her property on the lakes shore, she had wanted to buy it instead. Her real estate agent, Nigel, told her it wasn't for sale. Some Hollywood actor owned it as a vacation retreat and therefore it would never be on the market. Despite the warning, Abbi told Nigel if anything changed to let her know the second it came available, and she would snag it up. She hated being so secluded, but she also didn't want any hotshot ruining her peace and tranquility.

Setting a bowl in front of each patiently waiting pet, Abbi remembered she needed to get to the store, to pick up some much-needed food and wine. The wine was a must. She had to get back to writing her book, and soon. Her agent Herb Evans had been breathing down her neck like the dragon he was, to get the next book in her series finished by the deadline, and she'd hit a brick wall. She needed to get the gears rolling somehow and the wine should do the trick. She hoped.

Taking a scoop of bird feed from the plastic container under the counter, Abbi went to the library where she turned on Marshall, her self-cleaning vacuum and dumped the seed into Bird's feeder inside his cage. Yes, she had named her vacuum cleaner. It was the only way to get the crazy bird to leave it alone. Until she had, he would attack it every time it was running. With it having a name he must have thought it was just another animal she had added to her collection.

She glanced at her desk where her laptop sat closed and noticed it had a fine layer of dust on it. Abbi looked out the windows guiltily and noticed there must be a nest outside above the one with all the crap splattered on it's surface. She decided cleaning them was more appealing than sitting down only to stare at her computer screen. How was she expected to be inspired when there was bird crap on her window?

She spun on her heel and headed to the kitchen. From under the sink, she grabbed paper towels and window cleaner and headed out onto the porch.

Standing on a stepladder, Abbi was on her third window when she heard something off in the near distance. She stopped mid swipe of her vigorous scrubbing to get a better listen and looked at the dogs, "What the hell was that?"

It sounded like a banshee screeching in the trees. Not being able to pinpoint the source, she peered towards the vacant house. Leaning from side to side, she looked through the leaves on the trees and could just see the outline of the roof in the distance. Climbing down from the stepladder, she headed for the steps to get to ground level. Maybe someone was playing rock music, that had to be it.

But her focus was on the house and not her footing, which caused her to trip on the loose board of the bottom step. Flailing about, she tried unsuccessfully to grab the railing and fell flat on her face. With an "oomph," Abbi pushed herself up, and quickly glanced around to see if anyone saw.

They didn't you fool! There's no one around for miles, she reminded herself. With a pivot, she scurried back towards the house to safety. Just as she was about to set her foot down on the cursed step, she heard laughter and froze... A horrifying realization hit her; Someone *had* saw her!

"To hell with cleaning guys, let's get out of here!" she called to the dogs. She had more important things to do than clean bird dung off the windows, like getting her butt to Mack's to see if any tourists had arrived.

As soon as she got in the house Abbi went straight for the bathroom for a quick shower. With that done she quickly dressed in a pair of faded blue denim capris, a white t-shirt, and paisley poncho. She called the dogs to go out for a quick pee. Impatiently she tapped her foot for them to pick the perfect spot while she twisted her damp hair into a bun and secured it with a clip.

Finally, they both ambled up the steps and back into the house. She slipped her feet into a pair of white sneakers, grabbed her purse and cell phone, and kissed each dog on the head.

Setting the house alarm, she tossed a quick, "Be good you two," over her shoulder as she pulled the locked door closed firmly behind her. Carefully sidestepping the bottom step, she once again glanced over to the vacant house.

"Do I dare go over there?" she muttered to herself. She decided it was better to wait and see what she could find out first before ambling up to a deserted place alone. Brutus would come with her when she did, he might be a doofus, but he did still protect her when the need arose.

PUSHING THE DOOR OPEN to Mack's store, the tinkling bell above the door announced her arrival. Every time she came in, it felt like she catapulted back in time 40 years.

"Hey Mack, how's it going?" Abbi called, walking down the gleaming hardwood floor that creaked with every step.

She sat on a barstool at the lunch counter thinking she'd grab a quick bite to eat before getting her groceries. She glanced at the daily specials written on the chalkboard on the wall behind the counter, undecided.

"Abbi! Good, good. What can I get you girl?"

She had to smile at that; she was hardly a girl anymore.

"Coffee and a toasted fried egg sandwich, please," she responded, flipping the upside-down cup in front of her over. She watched as Mack skillfully filled it with the piping hot java.

"So, how are things out at your place, everything quiet?" he asked.

Mack was an aging bear of a man. Ever since the break-in, he was like a father to her.

"Yup, it's been really quiet lately. Although I think I heard something earlier this morning," she frowned.

"What was it?"

"I have no idea, never heard anything like it before. It sounded like something was screeching."

"Well, on calm mornings like these sounds carry around the lake. It's hard to tell where it came from... likely across the water," he said, wiping the counter.

Abbi had never thought of that. She supposed he could be right; she probably was overreacting.

"I'll go get your sandwich ready, be right back," he said as he ambled away.

Abbi pulled her cell phone out and was checking her email when Mack placed a plate in front of her. "Here you go honey."

"Thanks Mack," she smiled.

"I'll be in the kitchen if you need anything. I'm up to my elbows in chicken and dumpling stew."

Abbi looked down at her sandwich and groaned. "You know I *love* that dish."

Mack chuckled, "I know you do, that's why I set some aside for you to go."

"Thanks Mack, you're a doll."

When he disappeared into the kitchen Abbi went back to reading her email. Absentmindedly she grabbed the sugar jar, added a dash then exchanged it for the little cream pitcher. The tinkling of the bell had her glancing around to the entrance to see who was coming in. "Oh my!" softly escaped past her parted lips. Her mouth gaped open as her eyes grew large.

... *And who do we have here?* she wondered before snapping her jaw closed.

Chapter 3

Abbi realized she had never seen the man that just walked into the store. Tall, broad-shouldered and muscles galore. His blondish brown hair shimmered with blonder highlights if that were even possible. Not dyed though. His hair was kissed from the sun and looked tousled as if he were out for a quick jog or had just rolled out of bed. She couldn't figure out which, but the latter brought a pleasant image to her mind.

As she started to add the cream to her coffee, she swallowed hard, not taking her eyes off him. *A man that looks that good has got to be an ass!*

She heard Mack call out. "Hey, Ben. How are you doing today?"

Hmm... Ben, is it? Abbi thought, as she looked between the two men while they exchanged small talk. She noted he had an accent... British if she wasn't mistaken; and young. Young enough to be her kids' ages. With a dreamy sigh, she thought, *well there goes that idea!* That wasn't going to stop her from getting her fill of him though.

He glanced her way. "Ah... excuse me, Miss."

Miss? Abbi was sure she was the only woman sitting at the counter. She turned her head to see just who he was talking to. *He's talking to me!*

She whipped her head back around.

A warm tingly feeling had her suddenly feeling like a schoolgirl with her first crush. She could feel the heat of a blush erupting on her cheeks. With her heart racing, she looked up at him and smiled. "Yes?"

"You..." He made a sound in his throat while inclining his head. "Err... you're spilling a bit there," he gestured to the counter.

What the hell kind of greeting is that?! Was it some kind of British slang? Slightly confused, Abbi shook her head and blinked. "*What?!*"

He stood there gazing intently at the counter. Following his stare, she saw she was still pouring cream into her coffee. She pulled back and said, "*Oh my god!*" just as the cream and her overflowing coffee was making its way towards her lap.

Standing abruptly, her legs tangled around the stool, tripping her up. Helpless, she felt herself falling backward.

Good Lord! I'm going to fall ass over teakettle in front of a perfect specimen of God's gift to women... albeit a young one, but a perfect one. She braced for the impact of the floor that never came. Instead, she felt her back meet a chest of steel. Strong hands righted her to a standing position.

Somehow her beautiful paisley poncho had a mind of its own, thinking it would be better suited as a veil. The back of it had flipped over her head and covered her face.

Abbi stood for a moment, not knowing what she should do. What she did know was that at that very moment the floor could open and swallow her whole, and she'd be completely fine with it.

She felt herself being turned around. Felt her newly fashioned attire being lifted and flipped back down her back. She fixed her eyes on the floor. A firm, but gentle hand lifted her chin and Abbi had no choice but to look in his searching eyes, eyes filled with genuine concern.

"Are you okay?"

She should have just nodded and kept her mouth shut. But oh no not Abbi Peterson. She said the first thing that popped into her head.

"You smell really good."

Mortified, she quickly spun on her heel and rushed herself to the ladies' room.

Walking to the counter, Ben sat and tugged up his sleeves. "Can I get a coffee, Mack, please. And, ah... I'm curious," he squinted, tilting his head. "Is she always like that?" he chuckled.

Cleaning the spilled cream off the counter and floor, Mack laughed. "Pretty much. Normally, not that bad though."

His laughter grew in momentum.

"She's a little klutzy from time to time."

Mack was snickering and snorting, full out belly laughing at this point. "But I never...I've never seen her like *that* before." By this time Mack was bent over smacking his knees, as cackling laughter erupted past his lips.

"Ooh!" he sucked in a breath, wiping tears out of his eyes as he walked into the kitchen to retrieve Ben's coffee.

"YOU IDIOT!" ABBI TOLD her sodden reflection in the mirror over the sink. For the tenth time she splashed cool water on her face, hoping it would remove the humiliation from her face. She grabbed a fistful of paper towels and blotted her at the water droplets on her skin.

Of all the things one could say to a person upon being asked if she were all right, she just had to say, 'You smell really good'... *What the hell is wrong with me?* she thought sourly, scowling at herself in the mirror.

She glanced at her watch. Fifteen minutes had gone by since she made her escape to the washroom. With one long last look in the mirror, she turned the doorknob, praying that Ben had left.

Rounding the corner, she spied him sitting at the counter. Stopping in her tracks, she took a deep breath, intent on walking right up to him to apologize and thank him. Chickening out, instead, she veered off to the pet aisle. Calmly, she selected a few tins of dog and cat food and searched for the birdseed. Grabbing a few boxes of those, she walked to the snack aisle. Bird just loved peanuts in the shell and if she didn't get him any, he'd cuss at her for days. Next was a bottle of the bubbly. Abbi selected one, thought better of it and grabbed two more. She needed it after today.

With thoughts of getting drunk this afternoon she juggled her findings and realized she could no longer avoid Ben. As she headed to the counter to pay, out of the corner of her eye she saw him get up and start walking towards her. Keeping the counter in her sights, she prayed that the third bottle of wine stayed in her firm grip. She could picture it now, the bottle slipping from the death grip she had on it, crashing to the floor. If it did, she hoped it would just smash. Knowing her luck it wouldn't, she'd end up stepping on it and off it would carry her like a rolling log on water.

"Hey. Here, let me help you," his deep voice interrupted her thoughts. Not waiting for a response, he took the items, settled them on the counter and casually leaned against it. Folding his arms across his chest he waited for her. Abbi made her way to it slowly. As she approached, he straightened, taking a step towards her with his hand outstretched.

"I'm sorry. I haven't properly introduced myself," he said as he gazed into her eyes.

Abbi had always had an issue making eye contact. She didn't like it. It always made her feel like someone could see her soul and she avoided it at all costs. But try as she might, she couldn't look away.

"I'm at a slight advantage here. I know your name is Abbi, but you don't know mine. I'm Ben Quinn."

The way her name rolled off his tongue had her weak in the knees. *Damn that British accent!* Abbi couldn't tell if he was being nice or just plain sexy! The only coherent thought that echoed through her mind was, *this guy is trouble.*

She licked her suddenly dry lips. She couldn't for the life of her look at anything but his green eyes.

Not wanting to be rude, Abbi took his hand and murmured, "Pleased to meet you."

Okay. Now she felt silly. She did not just feel a jolt as if she stuck a fork in a wall socket.

Funny thing when looking into someone's eyes, you can read their reaction. Because in his eyes, she saw it too. As one, they jerked their hands back just as Mack came walking up to the pay counter.

"Mack... um... can I... get... ah...." *Jesus Abbi, spit it out,* her mind screamed. "Get a coffee to go with this, please?" she rushed on, breathlessly.

"Sure thing, Hun. Gotta make a fresh pot. Decaf, right?" Mac called over his shoulder as he went to get it.

She nodded rapidly. "Yes please."

"So, I guess I'll see you around then," Ben said, looking at her.

"Oh, are you here for the summer?" she asked, slowly recovering from her shock.

"For now," he pursed his lips. "I haven't decided on the long term yet. Will have to look the place over, make sure I can get it ready in time for winter if I stay. I like the fact that it's so isolated but then it isn't, you know what I mean?"

Abbi nodded. "I do. That's what drew me to the area myself. The views are spectacular all year round. It's really quite lovely."

"I agree with you about that, the spectacular views that is. They are beautiful," he added softly, looking her up and down appreciatively.

Oookay.... It's not the accent. Abbi had to bite her lip to contain herself. She turned her head away quickly to stifle a smile. *Girl, get a grip! He's a young'un* she thought, tapping the counter.

"Mack!" her voice cracked. "You got that coffee ready yet?"

"Yup! Just pouring it now," he returned.

Taking a deep steadying breath, Abbi turned her head back to Ben. "Well, it was nice meeting you, enjoy your stay."

"I'm sure I will, thank you," he responded, a soft smile tugged the corners of his lips as he went back to his waiting coffee.

"So, I see you met Ben. Seems like a nice enough fellow," Mack said as he rang up her items. "You two seemed to hit it off."

"Yes. We did... meet that is." Abbi could feel her face turn hot as she fumbled in her wallet for the cash. She mumbled her apologies as she thrust the bills at him, knowing Mack was always short of coins.

"At least you won't be all alone out there now." He handed her change to her.

"What do you mean by that Mack?" she asked, looking down as she concentrated on stuffing the money in her wallet.

Considering it was just her place and the vacant actor's house... her hands stilled. *No way!*

She craned her neck to look at him. *So, he's the actor who owns the place.*

"Hmm, well, it's about time he came and did something with it instead of letting it sit there to rot away," Abbi responded with a little more annoyance than called for. She zipped up her wallet and was slipping it into her purse when Mack added more salt to the wound.

"Oh no, that's not him. Ben, bought it from the actor."

Without moving her head, Abbi glanced up. One brow arched as she looked at Mack, then she turned her attention to Ben, giving him a sidelong glare. Her annoyance turned into rage. Ben must have been watching her, for he gave her a quick smile and a wave of his hand.

Resisting the urge to shoot him the finger Abbi turned her attention back to Mack. "I have to go now," she spoke in a rushed monotone.

"I stuck the chicken and dumplings in the bag for you," Mack said as she grabbed her bags from the counter and turned on her heel.

"Right. Thanks. Bye, Mack."

In the few steps it took to reach the door, she was mentally cursing out her real estate agent. Shoving the door, she discovered her escape was blocked. No matter how hard she pushed and shoved, the door would not budge. Turning to Mack, she made a desperate sound in the back of her throat.

"Uh, Abbi. You've got to pull the door open, towards you, Hun," he supplied.

She closed her eyes. *How many times must I embarrass myself in front of this man today?* Tossing one last heated look behind her before exiting, Abbi shot Ben a quick huff and out the door she went.

Ben barked out a laugh. "She is certainly entertaining, isn't she?"

Mack cackled in response, "That she is, Ben my boy, that she is."

Chapter 4

Abbi was fuming as she walked home and debated on stopping to call Nigel to find out what the hell happened. She was close to tears; she was so mad. He knew she was interested in that place and settled for her own. Yes, she had made her house a home over the years, adding her personal touch to it, but that wasn't the point!

She stopped, dropped her bags, and fumbled in her purse for her phone. Agitated beyond belief, she scrolled through her contacts until she found Nigel's number. She stabbed his name with her finger, as she did, she was picturing it was him. He picked up on the fourth ring.

"Nigel. Abbi Peterson here," she said testily.

"Abbi, darling! It's so nice to hear from you. What can I help you with?"

"If I recall, I asked you to tell me the second the house on the point came up on the market," she bristled.

"Let me just pull your file up here. Okay, let's see," he mumbled to himself, reading the notes.

Her mind strayed to her encounter with Ben. How strong his arms felt, how gentle his touch was on her chin. *Stop it! He's a kid for Pete's sake.* Besides, she was mad at him for buying her house!

"Ah-ha! Here it is. Yes, you said that you would take it the second it came up. Money wasn't an issue and full asking price would be the offer. It's all here, yes!"

"Just what I thought. Can you tell me then why you didn't call me about it?"

"Whatever do you mean, my dear Abbi? It never was on the market..." he sounded confused.

He was either lying or he didn't have a clue. He stood to lose a nice hefty commission on the sale of that place, so, he had no reason to lie about it. Now she felt terrible how she talked to Nigel. And especially how she had treated Ben. Drained, as the fight left her, she felt exhausted.

"Never mind Nigel. I'm so sorry. I must have been mistaken. You take care."

She supposed it wouldn't be so bad having someone close by she thought as she disconnected the call. She just wished they had been old and crotchety instead of, well, Ben.

Pushing that thought to the back of her mind, she picked up her bags and continued home. Ten minutes later she was looking at her house, admiring the sparkling windows from their earlier scrubbing. She would do the rest tomorrow she decided when she spied something odd. All her animals were sitting in the bay window, including Bird. In the middle was Brutus, howling his fool head off.

"Good Lord, I wasn't gone that long."

She bounded up the steps and fumbled with her keys. Finally, she got the door open and all of them rushed at her as if they hadn't seen her in days.

Turning off the alarm, she hurried into the kitchen and set the bags down as the dogs danced around her legs. Lucy, in her quiet demeanor, pawed the air and Brutus yipped with excitement, both communicating their need to go outside.

"Come on than!" she said, walking through to the living room at the back of the house with the dogs following on her heels. She loved this room the most. The massive stone fireplace drew the eye to the room from the kitchen and windows on either side and along the outer walls gave a view of the lake from all directions. She opened the French doors that led out onto the covered back porch and taking a seat on a lounge chair, she waited for the dogs to finish their business.

Glancing at her watch, Abbi noticed how close to dinnertime it was, her favorite time of day. Shortly after, the sun would start its descent, painting the stillness of the lake with its reflection of orange and reds. The loons would soon be out on the lake, too. Their haunting wail echoing, calling to each other, sending shivers along her spine. She loved it.

Cries of a dog in peril interrupted her musings. Her first thought was Lucy and Brutus! Panic had her jumping out of her seat and racing down the steps as she called to them. Abbi was relieved to see them standing at the water's edge, both staring intently towards the beach across the lake. Her relief was soon replaced with concern when Brutus started howling, a mournful cry, something he'd never done before.

A chill ran along her spine as she approached the pair, the kind you get when someone is watching you. Nothing appeared out of the ordinary to Abbi as she gazed to the shore across the way. It was deserted, as it always was and far as she knew it was just vacant land.

Wait... is that a flashlight in the woods?

Her eyes started to sting from staring for so long, as far as she could tell there was nothing there. It must have been her imagination or headlights from the road beyond. Still though, something was out there and hurting by the sounds of it.

Abbi was tempted to get in her car and search for the injured animal. But like earlier when Mack had mentioned the sound carrying around the lake, it would be futile to do so. She could look for days and never find it in the dense trees. With a sad sigh, she set off for the house.

"Come on guys. Let's get you some food."

Both came trotting behind her. Halfway to the house, Brutus shot past her, a low growl emitting from his throat that turned into crazed barking as he got closer to the house. Someone was on her porch, sitting in the chair she had earlier vacated.

"Brutus! Come!" she ordered.

Of course, he didn't listen. She envisioned him attacking whoever it was when silence descended. She started to run with Lucy barking at her heels.

Reaching the bottom step, she stood there a moment in disbelief. Her 'watchdog' was lying flat out on his back, legs stiff in the air, groaning in pleasure as he was getting the mother of all belly rubs by none other than— Ben.

Lucky dog, she thought fleetingly. *Damn it, stop that!*

"Hey Abbi," he said in his deep accent.

"Hi, I see you've met Brutus," she nodded towards the puddle she called a dog. "As you can tell, his bark is worse than his bite. This here is Lucy," she said, glancing down. "She's shy with strangers."

"Yeah." He snickered, "He's a tad intimidating. For a minute there I was thinking I was in for it," he said, crouching down to greet Lucy. Glancing up at Abbi, he said, "I thought I would pop by to see how you're doing."

"I'm fine," she mumbled wishing to never relive that moment again. Her embarrassment turned to shock when she saw Lucy was glued to the spot by her side. Normally when meeting new people, she would tuck her tail and cower away to hide until the person left. But not with Ben. The wiggle of her back end told Abbi that the tiny dog was in love.

"Hello Miss Lucy. Now, aren't you a sweet one," he said softly, stretching out a hand for her to sniff. He was granted a small lick and a vigorous shake of her butt. She scooted closer to put her tiny paws on Ben's leg to get better leverage and promptly smothered him in kisses.

Abbi gaped. "Wow! That's amazing. She really likes you."

That sounded extremely rude to her own ears. Back peddling she waved a hand, "Don't get me wrong. Not that you're not a likeable person, but since the break-in, she hides when anyone comes to visit."

Glancing up, Ben sighed, "Right. Mack told me about that. I can only imagine how that must have affected you." Looking down, he added, "And Miss Lucy here. He mentioned she was missing for a day or so?" he questioned, continuing to pet both dogs at the same time while looking up at her.

Abbi wrinkled her brow. She hated thinking about it.

"Yes. We... as in me and the police..." *Wait. Why did I feel the need to explain that?* She shook her head and continued, "... figured she must have darted out the door when they kicked it in. I thought I lost her for good."

Shivering at the memory, Abbi waved a hand towards the bush lot at the side of her house. "I found her two days later, on your porch, huddled in the corner." She shivered at the memory. "She was muddy, her hair matted with leaves and sticks."

Ben must have thought she was catching a chill. With one last pet to both dogs, he said, "It's cooling down a bit; I don't want to keep you." Standing up he added, "Oh, I almost forgot. I've brought over a little something for you," he turned and reached beside the chair producing a bunch of wildflowers.

"Oh!" She felt that all too familiar warmth spread across her cheeks whenever she was with him. "They are beautiful. You didn't have to do that." She reached out to take them, inhaling the scent. She'd never received flowers before for no reason, not even from her ex.

"There is a field of them just on the other side of my house. I thought you might enjoy them after the day you had," he grinned, stuffing his hands into the pockets of his jeans.

"Please, don't remind me," she said with a laugh, admiring the flowers. "Um, I was just about to get the dogs their dinner. Do you want to come in for a coffee? I mean... you don't have to if you need to be going. I completely understand."

She should have just let him take his leave. She didn't want to encourage him. But honestly, she didn't want to be alone after revisiting the memory of the break-in. Not waiting for his answer, Abbi walked through the open doors, the dogs trailing behind her.

"Yeah, I'd like that," he nodded and smiled, following the three of them in.

Abbi went directly to the kitchen counter to fetch a vase from under the sink. She busied herself putting water in it, and then the kettle. "I only have instant is that okay?" she looked over her shoulder as she placed it on the stove to boil.

"It's fine it's all I have to drink at my house," Ben responded glancing around.

"Perfect, I'll just get these in some water, then I'll get the animals' food ready." She placed the flowers in the vase and began to arrange them.

Animals? Ben thought. He only saw the two dogs drooling patiently, at the mention of food. "If you like, while you do that, I can feed them."

"Would you? That would be great." She smiled her thanks. "The tins are in the drawer to my left. On the left are the dogs' and the cat tins on the right are for Null and Void."

Abbi finished arranging the flowers, walking to the dining table she carefully set them in the middle of it.

"There," she softly said, still touched at his thoughtfulness.

Ben squinted his eyes. "Did you just say, 'null and void'?" he asked, not sure if he heard her right.

She put a hand on the table, leaning; she smiled and nodded. "Yeah, I did. When I got them, the contract from the breeder, said it would be null and void if they were to go outside. Keeping them inside is nearly impossible."

He laughed. "Did you send a picture of them enjoying the sunshine in the yard?"

"I did! They weren't impressed," she grinned.

She went back to the counter and gathered cups, coffee, and sugar on a tray. She noticed Ben standing at the opened drawer. Smiling at him, she said, "The can opener is in there too. They each get a can, except Brutus, he gets two. Under the counter, in the big plastic tub, are peanuts in the shell, only one scoop. Their dishes are all in there as well."

Shut up now Abbi, she told herself. She was babbling and knew it; he didn't need such explicit instructions. But hell, she was nervous!

Opening the fridge, she took out the cream and gathered some containers of cleaned vegetables she always had on hand and a package of kielbasa. Hands full, she closed the doors with her hip and as she did, she glanced at him to apologize, but he spoke first.

"Okay, got it. But, um," he scratched his head, "which one of them gets the peanuts?" He looked at her with a puzzled look.

He looked so confused she couldn't help but laugh at him, "I'm so sorry." She dumped the food on the counter and started to flip open the lids. "I kind of rattled it off to you, didn't I?" she said. As she arranged the brightly coloured edibles in neat stacks on a plate, she looked at him.

"Yeah... a bit," he chuckled. He scooped the contents into the bowls and with a flourish, he presented the dogs with their dinner along with a scratch on their heads.

Just as she was dumping a generous heap of crackers in the middle of her veggie arrangement, she heard Ben say, "Why, helllloo there, you beautiful beast."

She jerked her hand in response to his glorious words and crackers flew. Not one to let good food go to waste, Brutus caught each one before they hit the floor. Abbi smacked the box on the counter and wiped her brow, *damn it's getting hot in here...*

"Did you—"

"Um, nope, um... we do that all the time," she nodded her head slowly. The reality was, she thought he was talking to her. She didn't think of herself as beautiful or a beast but then she heard the "meah" only Null could create.

Relief flooded through her, and she hurriedly said, "That would be Null. And you're right he is a beast."

He was a giant cat, with beautiful long jet-black fur, except for the dusty grey mane around his neck. His piercing golden eyes looked like marbles with flecks of green throughout. He was much larger than Lucy, but gentle as a kitten. "And that is Void," she motioned, as he waddled his way to his food dish.

He was smaller than Null, identical in every way, but solid with short stubby legs.

The kettle began its shrill whistle and Abbi rushed over to remove it from the burner.

"Oh! Almost forgot... the peanuts are for Bird," she said, as she turned the stove off.

Bird? Ben cocked his head. "What the hell is that screech?" He had watched Abbi shut the kettle off, so he knew that wasn't it.

"Oh, shit! Hit the deck!" Abbi yelled, as she motioned with her hands for him to get down.

"What... why?" Instead of heeding her warning, Ben stood there confused. Is she off her meds? he thought fleetingly before he noticed the screech was a shriek. It was louder now, followed by, "Asshole! Get out of my house!"

No time to waste. Ben dropped to the floor, just as the bird swooped to where he had stood a second before. He glanced up from his spot on the floor, just as a huge slobbery tongue swiped across his face.

Brutus grinned at him with complete adoration. Laughing, Ben rolled onto his back, scratching Brutus on the belly while they both watched Abbi take after his attacker.

"Bird! You get in your cage! *Now!*" she yelled, clapping her hands as she chased Bird around the house. When that didn't get the result she wanted, she started flapping her arms about as if she was the one trying to take flight.

"Piss off!" Was the response she got as Bird cackled about the room.

She ran and slid to a stop at the counter, grabbed a scoop of peanuts and called out sweetly, "Oh look, Birdy Look what I have for you!" as she headed to the library and his cage. Dumping the contents into his dish she stood and waited as he landed on top, swung down by his beak, and made a perfect landing on the perch inside.

Promptly she closed the door as he squawked innocently, "I love you."

"Yeah, yeah. I love you too, but stop being such a bugger, will you?"

She rushed back into the kitchen to see Ben still lying on the floor, eyes closed and shaking. *Oh, my goodness! Did he hit his head?*

She knelt at his side. "Ben?" She called out softly, nudging his chest. His hand snaked out, grasping her wrist lightly he pulled her towards him as he opened his laughing eyes.

"Please, join me down here," he said, tugging her closer as he laughed uncontrollably. "I dare say, you have a... err... lovely ceiling." His laughter was contagious and the relief she felt knowing he was okay she joined him, giggling as he tucked her at his side. "Here," he said, putting an arm out to cushion her head as their laughter finally calmed to an occasional chuckle.

"Ah man. That felt great! I needed that Abbi. Thank you for that." He glanced at her, searching her face for a reaction. "I have to say, I've met a lot of women in my line of work, but never one as remarkable as you," he murmured, gazing into her eyes.

She knew that look; the look of one that was about to pucker up their lips! Should she let him? No, she couldn't, she was too old for him to let that happen! But a part of her wanted him to.

She wanted to throw caution to the wind and to hell with what was right or wrong. For once in her life, she just wanted the moment to happen and not analyze it. She watched as he came closer, inch by inch. Closing her eyes for fear of them going crossed, she waited for the moment their lips met.

She felt the lightest brush on her... *forehead? What the hell was that?*

Her eyes snapped open, meeting his. She shouldn't have done that. Because when she did, she saw the fire of desire in them.

"Please, forgive me. But I've wanted to do this since the minute I saw you." He gently grabbed her jaw. Guiding her face towards him, he held it as if it was a lifeline. Their lips met... softly, like the touch of a feather... tenderly seeking. A sudden shriek from Bird brought Abbi to her senses. Breaking off the kiss, she grabbed his hand that still held her face and rested her forehead on his, catching her breath. She didn't know what to say to break the silence. Ben did so for her.

"How about that coffee now?" He murmured.

Good. Lord. His voice just then nearly had her jumping his bones. Instead, she broke out into a grin, "Yes, that sounds wonderful."

THEY SAT OUT ON THE back porch with their drinks in hand. The plate of food on the table between them, both dogs lying at their feet. Neither one mentioned the kiss, and for that Abbi was thankful. It was bad enough that she couldn't stop thinking about it, but it would have been terrible if he mentioned it. That was something she needed to process in her mind, alone.

"So, the other day when I was at Mack's, he mentioned that you're a writer. I bought a copy of your book." He paused, selecting some cheese and meat, stacking them on a cracker. Taking a bite, he chewed thoughtfully. "I have to say,

I'm impressed with the writing. You did very well for it being your first."

Blowing on her steaming coffee, she nodded in agreement.

"Thanks. I am surprised myself. I started it after my daughter moved out. Empty nest syndrome got to me... just a tad." She laughed at the memory.

"Good, for you. Well, not the empty nest part," he said. "It explains why it's so dark though."

"It wasn't easy. What, with my marriage crumbling and work, it was hard to find the time, but I'm happy I did." She was happy. Something she hadn't been in a long time. She had almost forgotten what it felt like. "As for it being dark, it was a dark time in my life. I guess you could say I poured my heart into that book."

"Well, it shows."

She took a celery stick from the plate. Swirling it in the dip, she popped the end in her mouth, biting it off. Chewing, she said, "I love this time of day. Have you heard them yet?" She asked, motioning towards the lake with the celery.

Bringing a stacked cracker to his mouth to take a bite, he stopped midway. "Pardon? Heard who?"

Just as the words left his mouth, a haunting wail came across the lake. It was almost dusk, the sun almost hidden from sight. "Bloody hell! What was *that?*"

She looked over at him and laughed. Ben hadn't heard the loons yet, clearly. She smiled. "That my friend is a loon. Listen, you'll soon hear its mate." She watched the play of emotions cross his handsome face.

"That is so hauntingly beautiful," he remarked in amazement.

"Isn't it though! The first time I heard them, it brought tears to my eyes. They sounded so sad."

"Do they do that all the time?"

"Sadly, no. Only from mid-May to mid-June usually. They're early this year for some reason," she replied munching on a carrot stick.

They fell silent, just sitting, listening to the marvel of Mother Nature.

When darkness fell, Ben held out his hand. "Abbi?"

Shyly, she reached for it, feeling the warmth radiate from him as he rubbed the back of her hand with his thumb. Tonight, she had stepped out of her comfort zone. She had thrown caution to the wind and just lived for the moment. Tomorrow was another day, another day to do the right thing, the proper thing. But tonight, there they sat, hand in hand, listening to the haunting songs of the loon.

Chapter 5

Ben awoke to sunlight streaming across his face. "I really ought to get some window coverings," he said aloud as he reached for his cell on the bedside table. He squinted, trying to focus on the time... 6:58 am. He groaned when he noticed the exuberant number of notifications on his social media accounts. He placed it on the table, face down. He didn't want to deal with that right now. Stretching the kinks out of his neck and back, he clasped his hands behind his head. He felt like going back to sleep, but with that sunlight, he couldn't.

His mind wandered to thoughts of Abbi like it did every day... all day, since he met her. It had been nearly two weeks since he last saw her.

His lips broke out into a smile at the thought of her. She was remarkable. She was shy; he had noticed from the start. But she was also sweet, caring, smart, and funny as hell. She had him in stitches without even trying. She was a klutz, and he was falling for her.

He laughed, thinking about the first day they met at Mack's place. It felt like he had known her for years. But most importantly, she was real. She let her natural beauty shine through without even realizing it. She was unlike the women he had met in his chaotic life, the fake ones, the ones that were only trying to hook their claws into someone in his position. She hadn't even asked him what he did for a living, nor did he offer. With a sigh, he glanced towards the window, looking at the trees beyond. His expression softened. No, she was nothing like that. She was a breath of fresh air. She was special. He thought about the kiss. Never in his life had he kissed a woman on the first day of meeting her. It was like he was drowning, and her mouth was his only lifeline. The only way to describe the feeling was a need. He needed to taste her lips, to feel them under his own. It scared the hell out of him. To be honest, *she* scared the hell out of him. The way she made him feel so alive was something he realized he hadn't felt in an awfully long time.

He wanted to get to know her better if she'd let him. He wondered if she'd go with him shopping to get something to cover the window.

On that thought, he tossed the covers aside and threw his legs over the edge of the bed and stood there naked with the sun shining on his body. *Yup, need to cover that window for sure!* All he needed was the paparazzi finding out where he lived. He and his peace and quiet would be gone from Pearl Lake in a heartbeat.

ABBI STEPPED OUT OF the shower, groping blindly for the towel hanging on the rack. Leaving the bathroom, she went to get dressed. Taking a quick look out the window, she figured it would be a repeat of yesterday, another sunny, beautiful day. Dressing in jeans and an old plaid work shirt, she headed to the kitchen for a cup of coffee.

"Good morning my lovelies," she called out to her brood. A stampede of paws broke the silence as she turned to ready their food.

Setting their dishes before them, she took some feed to Bird. He squawked his displeasure of being locked in all night. "I'm sorry. How could I forget to let you out again?" She crooned to him while opening his door.

She knew exactly how she could forget... Ben.

Ever since meeting him, her mind was in a fog. It was a wonder she remembered to do anything. Two weeks had passed since the night he had shown up on her back porch. After they sat listening to the loons, they had talked about their lives.

She told him about her kids, her divorce and what she had done with her life until this point. He talked about his parents and growing up in England.

She was disappointed when he said he should be going. She walked him through the house to the front door and stood on the porch to say goodnight.

At the same time, they reached towards the other for a hug. She didn't want to let go when he'd brushed his lips against hers. It felt good just being held. Letting him go felt like he took a piece of her with him. She had sat down on the top step watching him walk away, sitting in the moonlight long after he'd gone home.

With her fingers to her lips, she remembered what it felt like when he kissed her. Even now it made her blush and her stomach tingle.

Strange, she had never felt that way before, not even with her husband when they started dating. Shaking her head to clear her mind, she picked up the animals' dishes and placed them in the dishwasher.

She tugged on a pair of garden gloves, and called out as she went out the back doors, "Lucy... Brutus, you two coming?" The dogs took off running across the yard as she made a beeline to the garden shed. Unlocking the door, she opened the doors wide, and she stood in disbelief and groaned at the mess. "Why did I leave it in this condition?"

"HEY BOY. HOW ARE YOU doing today?" Ben asked as he stroked the dog's head. "And just where is your mistress?" he asked, looking into the wise eyes. He'd knocked on the front door but there was no answer. He found it odd of her to leave without letting Brutus in. A tiny bark announcing Lucy's arrival had him looking to the side of the house.

Ben looked at the hulking dog beside him. "She's out back, is she?" He was rewarded with a 'woof', as he bounded down the steps with Brutus by his side.

Following the dogs, he made his way to the backyard. He glanced at the chairs that Abbi and he sat in and found them empty. He scanned the deserted yard. *Where the heck is, she?* He called out her name with no response.

Heading to the water's edge, Ben started thinking something had happened to her. He was just about to pass the garden shed when a missile was launched in his direction.

"Whoa!" he ducked, narrowly being hit by a life preserver.

Abbi jumped, dropping a shovel with a clatter. "Sweet baby Jesus! You scared the crap out of me!" she yelled.

Ben laughed. "Sorry about that. I wasn't expecting projectiles coming out of the garden shed." Bending, he picked up the preserver. "What are you doing with all of this stuff?" he asked, gesturing at the ground.

"Well, I intended on cleaning out the flowerbeds today and came in looking for a rake." She motioned with her hand at the floor. "I found this mess." She glanced around. "I have yet to find the rake."

For the first time since his arrival, she looked at him. *How do you look so damn good first thing in the morning?*

The light breeze had teased his hair and Abbi had to fight the urge to run her fingers through it. Her mouth, suddenly parched, she licked her lips and asked, "Do you want a drink or something?" That was a mistake. His eyes at once went to her mouth.

"Um…" Ben cleared his throat. "Any chance there is a larger town nearby?"

"What? Oh. Yeah, there is, yes." Abbi took the preserver from him and hung it on a nail.

Ben started gathering empty planters where she had tossed them on the ground and brought them into the shed, stacking them neatly against the wall.

The earthy, woodsy scent of his cologne had her closing her eyes, recalling what it felt like to have his arms around her, his hand caressing her face as he kissed her. She needed to get out of there. Now. Before she did something stupid, like, sniff him like the dogs did. While his back was turned, she darted out the door.

"Why? What did you have in mind?" she questioned, taking off her gloves.

Glancing around to where she was last standing, he did a full circle before he spied her outside the shed. With a grin, he replied, "Actually. I was wondering if you would go shopping with me... grab some lunch if you like. I'll do the driving if you will be my navigator."

She hesitated. Her mind was already calculating the time it would take to get to Springbank and back. That would mean a 45-minute drive one way... sitting near him. Alone. No more than five hours, she figured. Could she do it? Despite the feelings she had when she was around him, it was not to go any further. She had already decided that. She needed to distance herself from him as she was getting attached and fast, which was something she couldn't allow.

"What is it you need? Maybe Mack has it in stock," she offered as a solution.

"I checked there, and he doesn't carry the size I need."

Her brows shot up in surprise. She nodded her head. The faster she did, the higher her eyebrows rose. "Oh!" she said, a small gasp escaping past her lips, her mind in the gutter.

Ben shot out a bark of laughter, "Blinds, Abbi! I need blinds or curtains for my bedroom. The sun is so brilliant in the morning, and I find I rather enjoy sleeping past 7 am. Plus, I sleep naked," he casually stated. Lowering his voice to a murmur, he added, "Who knows who is out there... someone could be watching me."

He grinned when he saw the blush rise on her face.

"Nope! You're right. Mack doesn't have those, that's for sure!" *Good Lord, I have a one-track mind around him...* She shook her head to clear her thoughts. "Okay. Um... let me change and we can go." She turned to call the dogs as she headed towards the house.

Catching her hand, Ben turned her around to look at him.

WHY is he so flipping handsome and why couldn't he be older? she thought as she scanned his features.

"Honestly, you look perfect just the way you are," he murmured, gazing into her eyes.

"That's sweet of you to say, Ben. But I need to get out of these dusty clothes," she said, wiping her sweaty palms on her jeans.

He brushed her cheek with the back of his hand. "You have a bit of smudge here," he mumbled.

She needed to haul ass before she broke her promise to herself and jumped him. She ended the eye contact and backed slowly away. "I'll go get ready."

"Right, I'll just run and get my car. Be back in five minutes," he told her, sprinting off.

Chapter 6

Ben sat in the car waiting for Abbi to appear from the house. Checking his email, he opened one from the director of the film he was working on.

"Hey Ben, hope all is well with you and you're enjoying your time off. Just wanted to let you know, filming is pushed back. Won't need you for a bit.

It will probably be another month or more before we get set to shoot your scenes. Because of the torrential downpours we have been having on set lately, we need to wait for some dryer conditions here before we get back up and running. Will be in touch, -Tony."

He wasn't disappointed. Normally he'd be itching to get back to filming. The break from it all was agreeing with him, he had to admit.

A flash of colour caught Ben's eye. Looking up, he saw Abbi coming down the steps of her house. His breath hitched in his throat at the sight of her. Quickly he opened his door, got out, and met her halfway down the walk. Taking her hand, he guided her to the passenger side and opened the door.

"My lady, your chariot awaits," he bowed, as she plopped down on the seat, buckling her belt.

She giggled to herself. *My lady? Oh, I like the sound of that; Stop that Abbi!*

Wiping the grin off her face she looked up at him and said, "You didn't need to do that... open my door, I mean."

Looking down at her, he smiled, "I know, but I wanted to." Closing the door with a soft thud, he went around and settled himself behind the wheel, snapping his seat belt in place.

He started the car and looked over to her questioningly as he backed out onto the road. "So, where are we off to?"

"Oh right, I completely forgot you don't know your way around. Do you have GPS? I can just punch it in if you like," she offered.

He nodded at her and tapped the display screen on the dash to bring it up. They headed towards the hill that would bring them to the 'downtown core' of the village and then turned right. "So, this road takes us around the lake, does it?"

"Yes. Just after the bend, we will be right across from my place," she responded. Glancing out at the scenery as it streamed past, Abbi was content sitting in the warm sunshine. She felt like she could take a nap her eyes were so heavy. Feeling her head nod off, she jerked herself awake.

"Hey there sleepyhead."

Turning to look at him, with sleepy eyes she mumbled, "Sorry, I think I nodded off for a second."

He glanced at her for a moment before looking back to the road. "Yeah, you did," he chuckled, "for about twenty minutes."

Her eyes grew large. "Impossible," she said in disbelief. "I hate falling asleep in a car. If there's going to be an accident, I want to be awake."

He looked at her and laughed before putting his eyes back on the road.

She then noticed the skin around her mouth felt tight, as if she had a face mask on. *Almost as if I had drooled? Nooo!* She giggled silently at the thought. Tentatively she touched the corner of her mouth with a fingertip and was horrified to learn that she had indeed slobbered out the side of her mouth. Thankfully, it was on the opposite side of Ben. *Wait. Did he see it? Is that why he was laughing?* Using the water bottle, she always had on hand, she took a tissue from her purse, wet it, and wiped her mouth.

She noticed Ben looking at her with a raised brow as she vigorously wiped the dried spittle.

"Oh, this." She held up the tissue with a nervous laugh. "Um, I need to wake up. This always does the trick," she said as she made the excuse, and cringed inwardly at the thought of wiping her face with back washed water as she dabbed at her forehead. It was her own back wash but none the less it was still gross. Stuffing the tissue in her purse, she leaned back in her seat and took a swig from the water bottle. As she did, she stared at his hands on the steering wheel. She noted how tanned and strong they looked. *Yet... so gentle.* She remembered his touch and it caused her to squirm in her seat. Heaven, help her... she felt like an antsy child on a long car ride.

"Do you need to make a pit stop Abbi?" he asked, looking over at her.

She whipped her head to face him.

"What... why?" she blushed knowing he saw her squirm.

"You just seem a bit... agitated," he said. "I wondered maybe you needed a rest... or something." He was too polite to ask if she needed a toilet.

Her eyes glued themselves to his profile. "No. No. I'm good," she said biting her lip.

He reminded her of a Greek god, one from the movies, *not the statues*, she thought with a silent snicker.

Her eyes were drawn to his lips... so soft, she remembered. His chin and jawline were strong and chiseled, like the rest of him and his nose was perfect. A bit of a flare at the nostrils, she noted. And his dancing, green eyes that sparkled when he was excited reminded her of the tender growth of new ferns. His forehead... *Wait*. She just noticed the ball cap that he was sporting. *He wasn't wearing that when we left? Was he?* She wrinkled her brow in thought.

He could feel her eyes upon him, studying him and he rather liked it. Not wanting to break her perusal of him, he remained silent.

Abbi pointed to his head, "Um... where did the hat come from?"

"This?" he pointed to it too, glancing at her. "Ah... yeah, I put it on while you were napping."

"Oh, okay." She nodded, thinking it odd. "So, what did you say you do for a living again?" she asked, her brow furrowed as she tried to recall if he ever mentioned it.

She saw his hands tense on the steering wheel.

Did I touch a nerve? Wait... am I in a car with my stalker, she thought in a moment of panic. Ever since her book shot to number one, she had someone constantly messaging her. At first, she responded. She enjoyed interacting with her readers but soon had to stop. The kind messages had turned threatening.

The very reason she had moved to such a remote place was that they started sending packages to her home address, not through her book agent. *Did he find me?*

"I uh... I didn't." He cleared his throat. "Say that is..."

Should I tell her? It wasn't that big of a deal. But he liked her too much for her to treat him differently when she found out.

"Okay...?" she trailed off, darting her gaze out the window. *If he is, how would anyone ever find my body in the middle of all these trees?* She was a goner for sure.

Ben noticed the change in her. *Is that anxiety, I detect, or nervousness? Maybe she did need to use a washroom this time?*

Removing his right hand from the steering wheel, he reached to take hers and felt her jump.

It only took a quick glance at her face and Ben knew something was wrong.

"Hey. Are you okay?" he asked, concern filling his voice as he pulled off to the side of the road. Shifting the car into park, he killed the engine and said, "Abbi, look at me." He carefully reached out, turning her face towards him and saw tears forming in her eyes. Fear stared back at him.

Ben dropped his hand, worried about scaring her more.

"Tell me what's wrong. Please," he begged.

She dropped her gaze and stared at her hands in her lap.

His eyes followed her line of vision and saw her clenched tight fists.

"If I tell you what I do for a living, will you promise to tell me what's wrong?" he asked.

She glanced at him and gave a sharp nod.

"Okay. But first, I have something else to say... the real reason I haven't mentioned to you what my day job is. Will you promise to listen without interrupting me?"

He gave her a sidelong glance. "And after considerable consideration, weighing all the pros and cons, give me an answer?" he asked, holding his breath.

Intrigued now, Abbi replied in a small voice, "Yes, I promise." Despite her anxiety running at an all time high, her gut was telling her she could trust him, but her mind was screaming, run.

Unbuckling his seat belt, he turned towards her in his seat. He wished she'd do the same. He so desperately wanted to reach out to pull her towards himself, but he didn't dare touch her any more than he already had. He could see her jumping out of the car if he tried to do so. Instead, he asked her, "Will you look at me, please?"

She half-turned in her seat towards him, eyes fixed out his window, past his shoulder.

Better than looking at her hands, he thought.

With a sigh, he began. "The real reason I haven't told you what my job is... is that I don't want your opinion of me to change. I didn't want you to treat me differently," he mumbled.

Her mind raced. *What kind of work could he possibly do that would make me do that?* Glancing at him now, she watched his features change with worry... *a hitman or a... porn star? Likely the latter.*

Taking a deep breath, he continued. "Abbi, I like you. I think... or hope you feel the same about me."

He glanced up through his lashes to see her reaction. "What I feel when I'm with you...."

Nope, not gonna happen. She started to shake her head and just as she was about to speak her thoughts, he held up a hand.

"Please, you promised to hear me out," he reminded her.

"Sorry," she muttered, crossing her arms over her chest.

"I've never felt this way about anyone before, ever. I want to see where this will take us... if you'll let it."

She knew she promised to wait, but she just had to say something.

"I'm flattered. Really, I am Ben. But don't you think I'm a bit too old for you? I mean, I don't even know how old you are, other than you're close to my kids' ages. You're young and yes..." she nodded her head vigorously, "...I admit, incredibly attractive, but don't you want someone your age? Or do you even know what you want?"

"I'm thirty-six, I'm not one of your kids. I'm a man and yes, I most definitely know what I want and that is you," he breathed, looking deep into her eyes.

She couldn't help but snort out a laugh. He was so serious! Warning bells went off, as Ava's laughing voice echoed in her mind, *'Watch out for those gigolos, ma. They will be after your money!'*

With the sudden flash of anger, she realized there was only one reason he *could* want her, and that was her money... Ava was right. He was a gigolo, a gold-digging gigolo. She would *not* have a kept man in her life.

Now, what is wrong with her? Ben inwardly groaned as he noted the anger flash in her gray eyes. "Look," he said, taking her hand in both of his. "Age makes no difference to me. My mum is five years older than my dad, if that makes you feel better," he offered.

Her brows shot up. Well now that would make sense. Why would it bother him when he grew up with it? "I guess that helps... a bit."

Biting his lip, he kept the sudden grin from appearing too triumphant when he noticed her features softening.

Good lord! She averted her eyes quickly. He wasn't helping when he looked at her that way. She felt a quick tightness where she had no business feeling! She couldn't let him gloat like that.

"I said a bit," she said, crossing her legs to make the sensation go away. It was not working dammit! Pausing, to do the math she added, "But I'm still older than you by four more years than your parents." She felt the need to point that out.

"Aargh...!" He threw his hands up in frustration. "*Woman!* I don't *care!*"

Giving him a sidelong glance, she sighed. "Well, maybe I do! I can't promise you anything, but I will think about it. I'll think about us... I mean, you...and me that is." *Wait, what the hell did I just agree to?* He was a gold digger. How the hell was she going to get out of this one? "Okay, now tell me about your job?" *This shall be good*, she thought giggling softly. *He thinks he can pull the wool over my eyes! Yeah right, I wasn't born yesterday!*

With more confidence than he felt earlier, he simply said, "I'm an actor. Currently production is shut down for at least a month and a half because of torrential downpours," he recited Tony's email. He watched her for a reaction.

She was shaking. *Was she cold?* He realized that wasn't the case when the shaking turned into bubbly, snorting, laughter.

"Ooh, that's a good one, Ben! I must give you an 'A' for effort. Honestly, you don't have to lie. I know you're a gigolo and only after my money." She burst into a fit of laughter.

"What? Wait. What?! You think I'm a gigolo? How?" he asked, a bewildered smile tugged at his lips.

"Well, yeah, because it's the only explanation I can think of why you would want to be with me," she said, wiping away her tears from laughing.

"Abbi, honestly... I'm not lying. As a matter of fact, the movie I'm filming, in which I have the leading role, is The Jasper Killings."

The look on her face was priceless to Ben. To say he dropped a bombshell on her was an understatement. He quickly coughed to cover the chuckle that was about to burst forth from his lips and buckled his seat belt.

"Right than... shall we be off?" Tossing a grin her way, he started the car, put it into gear and steered it back onto the road.

Chapter 7

Abbi's mind raced with his admission. Recovered, she finally said, "It just can't be. Your name wasn't on my list of actors."

Glancing over, Ben noticed the baffled look on her face before switching his eyes back to the road ahead. "Yeah? Tell me something, Abbi. What name was on the list for the leading male?"

Rummaging in her purse, she found her cell phone. Opening her email, she searched for the director's name mumbling, "Tony" repeatedly, as she scrolled through countless messages.

"Sullivan," Ben supplied, just as her eyes landed on his name.

Glancing at him, she told herself anyone could know the director's name. She opened the email and read it to him.

"Hello Abbi, Tony here, I have the list of actors I think would be perfect to do your story, The Jasper Killings. Please let me know if they are acceptable to you.

Detective Sue Martin- Joy Summers
Detective Ethan Fields- Ben Everett
Captain James- John Page"

She, of course, had approved without bothering to look the actors up.

Stopping at a red light, Ben interrupted her recitation of names. "Abbi, enlighten me for a second." He paused looking over at her. "What name do you use to write under... your pen name, I believe it's called?"

"Abbi Stevens," she supplied, blinking blankly. "What does that have to do with this?" she gestured with her phone.

A honk from behind, had Ben looking to the rear-view mirror, he did a double take and squinted, noting the finger that was currently being waved in his direction.

Stepping on the gas, he said off-topic, "I thought all Canadians were polite." Signaling to turn into the mall parking lot, he continued, "Anyway, back to your question. It has everything to do with your list there."

Parking the car, he shut the engine off and turned in his seat than inched closer to her. Her eyes were drawn to his mouth. His lips mesmerized her as he drew closer, his tongue darting out to wet them. His mouth was now a hair's breadth away from hers. She closed her eyes, melting on the spot for the touch of his kiss.

"It's simple, really. I don't use my real name for business purposes either," Ben murmured.

She could feel the warmth of his mouth so close to hers now. Suddenly, air rushed in place of his heat. She heard the soft thump of the door and sprang her eyes open.

"Ooh! That man is impossible!" she yelled, stamping her feet on the floor in frustration.

Coming around to Abbi's side of the car, he could hear her going off, which made him quite satisfied. Ben smiled sweetly at her as he opened her door, offering his hand to help her out of the car. "Shall we grab something to eat first before we shop?" he suggested.

"Fine by me," she retorted as she took his hand.

He had so desperately wanted to kiss her, but he didn't want to pressure her. He hadn't planned on teasing her like that, but it was a spur-of-the-moment decision. He honestly didn't know if he could stop if he'd started. Shutting the door, he set the alarm and off they went inside.

Not wanting to show him how hot and bothered she was by that little stunt, she cheerfully said, "I know a great little restaurant, shall we go there?"

"Absolutely." He offered her his arm. "Lead the way," he said, smiling as she took it.

ABBI TOOK HIM TO A little restaurant called Sneaky Sam's. Finding a booth, they slid in opposite sides across from one another. The waitress was a young pretty redhead named Katie, according to the tag on her shirt. As she greeted them, she sat a pitcher of water in the middle of the table, then handed each of them a menu as she prattled on about the specials of the day.

"Can I get either of you anything to drink while you look over the menu?" Katie asked, placing a hand on Ben's shoulder, caressing it.

"Water's good for me," Abbi responded. She caught the quick flash of annoyance on Ben's face as he leaned back in his seat, breaking contact.

"A ginger ale, please," he answered politely.

Abbi suddenly felt sympathy for him as he sat there, looking at the menu. She wondered if the girl had recognized him. No doubt he put the hat on to conceal his identity.

"Hey." She leaned forward, reaching for his hand. "Are you okay?" She searched his face.

He glanced up, a smile breaking on his face. "Yeah, I am now." He winked at her as he turned his hand over to hold hers.

"How about we split an order of poutine?" she asked, with a grin.

He made a face. "That doesn't sound very appealing."

"I promise you; you won't regret it."

"Whatever you want is fine with me." His eyes twinkled as he stroked the back of her hand with his thumb.

Katie returned to take their order. Looking at Ben, she gave him a dazzling smile. "Are you ready to order?"

Ben glanced up at her. "Yes, actually... we will share a.... what was it again?" He turned his head towards Abbi with a quizzical look and was met with a blank stare.

Abbi was too busy concentrating on the sensations his thumb made across her skin. He enchanted her, made her insides melt with just the sound of his voice. She resisted the urge to launch herself across the table.

"Abbi!" Ben tugged at her hand, snapping her back to reality.

She saw him looking at her. His brows raised in a questioning look.

"What?" she asked, a little too loudly.

He snickered softly, asking again what they had decided to order.

"Oh! Poutine," she replied, looking at the waitress with a smile.

"Perfect. I'll get right on that," Katie responded walking away with a fake smile pasted on her lips.

Abbi had to let go of his hand; she couldn't concentrate otherwise. She took a sip of her water and carefully sat it on her napkin. "Can I ask you a question, Ben and you answer me truthfully?"

"Absolutely. You can ask me anything."

"When we were in the car having our little roadside chat, you said you didn't want my opinion of you to change. Why is that?"

Needing a distraction, she grabbed the dessert menu from behind the salt and pepper shakers, scanning it with indifference.

"Usually, a handful of people I meet, change their whole demeanor towards me when they find out who I am," he sighed, leaning back in his seat. "Normally, it doesn't bother me, sometimes it's useful, I will admit," he said with a chuckle.

"Fair enough," she nodded. "So," she paused. "Um, does that happen often when you meet... women?" she asked, turning her attention to straightening her utensils.

She didn't want to know how many past lovers he had... more than she cared to know; she bet. That would be a major turnoff.

Ben noticed how she avoided looking at him. "Well, most women know who I am, or they soon figure it out. Either way, they are only after one or two things... sex or money. I stay clear of them... usually."

Her head snapped up at that admission, one brow arched, their eyes met, and he grinned at her.

"I thought that would get your attention," his eyes danced.

"Hey, it's not my business how many..." she gestured with her hand. For the life of her, she didn't know what word to use. Floozies, flakes, tramps? "...f...f... flings, you've had," she stammered out.

"Abbi, when I was in my teens, I had the usual one or two-month relationship, but never anything serious. My last one was six years. We started dating before the fame hit." He could tell she was mentally counting the years. "I found out she had been seeing someone behind my back. I was off shooting a short film when it happened. She begged me to work it out. I refused. Shortly after, we went our separate ways and three years later I made it in Hollywood," he trailed off.

Finding out he had been cheated on was a blow which he didn't think he would recover from. That's when he threw himself into his work.

"You mean to tell me she cheated on you?" *Was she nuts?*

He couldn't answer as Katie brought their food. "Here you go, guys." She sat the plate in the middle of the table. Katie handed Ben a napkin with a longing look and said, "If there is anything, and I mean anything you need, just call me."

Abbi needed him to continue telling her what happened, he wouldn't do that with Katie standing there. "Yup!

We're good, thank you, Katie!" Abbi called out. *Be on your way…*

With a huff, Katie gave her a rude look before walking away.

Ben pointed to the plate. "What in the world is this concoction?" he asked in wonderment.

"It's a delectable dish of French fries; that's chips for you Brit's… topped with cheese curds and smothered in gravy." She grinned, popping a stringy cheesy forkful into her mouth.

Picking up his fork, he took a stab at the plate, unsure if he was brave enough to try it.

He went for it.

Abbi watched his face for a reaction. Oh, yeah! There it was the look of one who just tasted a little piece of heaven on earth. "You like?" she asked.

"Wow!" he blinked rapidly. Taking a few more mouthfuls he picked up the napkin Katie left, wiping his mouth before answering Abbi's question. "This is amazing!"

"Right? I told you! Um… What's that?" she asked, pointing to the napkin.

"Did I miss something?" Thinking he had gravy on his chin, he gave it a wipe.

"No, not your face, it's perfect… I mean perfectly clean," she recovered quickly. "I meant on the napkin."

Ben turned it over to where she was looking. Frowning, he smoothed it out. Making a sound of disgust, he showed it to her.

Anger filled her at Katie's audacity. For her to write that Ben could find a better woman was one thing; Abbi wasn't about to argue with that, but to leave her phone number too?

"Why that calculating little witch!" Anger rose with each word. "I'm leaving them a bad review on Yelp," she said indignantly, whipping out her cell phone.

"Abbi." Ben put his hand on her arm. "It's fine. I'm used to it. It's not the restaurant's fault."

"You're right, but it's still not very professional of her to try to pick you up either." *God, no wonder he wanted to escape if this was the norm.*

"Let's just finish up and get out of here?" he suggested.

She nodded in agreement.

"And to answer your question from earlier..." he paused. *Thank you, baby Jesus.*

"Yes, my ex cheated on me. Had been for some time. Three years later, it made me the man I am today." Taking her hand in his, he turned it up and placed a soft kiss on her palm. A groan escaped past her lips as she saw the desire spring to his eyes. His breath heated the skin on her wrist as he murmured. "And I've been celibate ever since." He then placed his lips on her pulse and felt it racing against his mouth.

That did it. Abbi had to get out of there now. "Let's leave, shall we?" she suggested, gathering up her purse.

Taking his wallet out, he placed a couple of twenties on the table.

Abbi had one thing to do first. Taking a pen out of her purse she took the napkin and wrote... '*Sorry sunshine, He's taken!*'

She didn't mean it, sort of. But Katie didn't need to know that! She looked at Ben, swallowing hard as she gestured to the napkin, feeling the need to explain, "Um, well... you know... not yet."

Standing with a huge grin, he held out his hand. "Ready?" he asked. Nodding, she reached for his hand.

Chapter 8

Walking hand in hand through the mall, they headed to the nearest department store.

Abbi caught the glances thrown their way as they went down the main aisle to the housewares department. All the women, young and old, glanced at Ben as they passed by.

She looked at him out of the corner of her eye, just to see if he noticed. He was oblivious to it. The self-doubt she had been feeling all along reared its ugly head once again. Who was she kidding? She couldn't entertain a relationship with him, he'd find someone else, more youthful, more attractive.

She swallowed at the sting that suddenly appeared in her throat. *This can't happen.* Reluctantly she let go of his hand.

When he looked at her, she pasted a cheerful smile on her lips and bounded towards the blinds. "What colour were you thinking of?" she asked looking at the boxes that stood upright in a row.

When he went to put an arm around her, she side-stepped away to the curtains.

"Or would you rather some room darkening drapes?" Thrusting them in his direction, she blocked him from seeing her face. "Here, see what you think."

Something is off with her. Taking the curtains by the bottom, he gently pulled them down, along with her hands. Noticing a single tear rolling down her cheek, he took her face in his hands. Tenderly he wiped the path with his thumb. "Abbi, what's wrong?"

"Um, nothing... nothing at all," she quietly said. "I just have something in my eye."

His brows shot up. He didn't believe her for a second but said nothing.

She took a shaky breath as her face scrunched up. His kindness was her undoing.

Ben's heart went out to her. Clearly, something was wrong. Whatever it was, her tears tore him up inside. He took her in his arms and held her as he stroked her hair. He could feel her body wracking, with silent sobs. "It's okay," he whispered against her ear. "Whatever it is, we will work it out together."

No longer able to endure his kindness, she shook her head and pulled away from him. He didn't understand and never would. Taking a deep breath, she gave him a watery smile. "I'm fine. Ah... did you decide which you want? Drapes or blinds?"

Looking at the wrinkled curtains clutched in her hands, he chuckled. "I guess these are as good as any."

"Oh." She sniffed. "I'm sorry. I didn't realize I was still holding them. I'll pay for them."

"It's fine. I rather fancy black anyway. Come on, let's get home. You have your pets waiting for you."

Giving a nod, she allowed him to take her hand, guiding her to the checkout. Halfway there, Abbi noticed a stunning young blonde making a beeline for them... one of the same girls eyeballing Ben earlier. No doubt she was making laps around the store in search of him.

"Excuse me, but aren't you, Ben Everett?" the girl asked, with a dazzling smile.

Ben stopped in his tracks and took a step back. "No, I'm sorry, you must be mistaken."

Abbi could feel the tension radiating off him.

"I'm sure you're him. I've watched all your movies and I think I would know," she said, twirling fingers in her hair.

Ben glanced back at Abbi, his grip tightening on hers.

"Come on, let's get out of here," he whispered tugging her hand.

Abbi could see the urgency on his face and nodded.

Turning back around, Ben saw the blonde was now blocking their path. *Great, just what we need*, he thought. "Look, I'm not him. So, I'm not sure what you want with us at this point. Do you mind moving aside so we can pass?" he asked politely.

"I mind," the blonde responded. "... and who is she, your mother?" she asked, snidely.

That did it! Abbi's eyes flashed daggers. Dropping Ben's hand, she rolled up her sleeves and took a step towards her target. Only to be stopped when Ben's strong arms came around her waist.

"Ben!" she hissed softly, kicking the air.

"I can't let you do that Abbi," he murmured, chuckling under his breath.

"Put me down!" she yelped

He did, after pivoting on his heel and placing her in the opposite direction.

"Let me handle this," he said, dropping a quick kiss on her lips before turning around.

"What's your name?" he asked the blonde.

"Claire," she said with a toss of her hair and a jubilant smile.

"Claire... right. You see this lady you insulted..." He wrapped his arm around Abbi's waist. "... not that it's any of your business... is my girlfriend."

Claire snorted in derision. She was about to say something when Ben held up a hand. The anger in his eyes effectively shut her up.

"Even if I were Ben Everett... which I'm not, what makes you think I would ever be interested in someone as superficial as you?"

Claire looked like she was ready to scream her head off, Abbi noticed with a tiny smirk.

Tossing her hair, the girl turned around and stalked away without a parting word.

Looking at Abbi, Ben smiled. He moved his arm from around her waist to her shoulders and leaned towards her. "Come on love," he murmured as he planted a kiss on her brow.

Dear God, it's going to be so hard to tell him I can't do this, she thought as they went to pay for their purchase.

GETTING TO THE OUTER doors of the mall, they were met with a downpour. *Perfect. It matches my mood*, Abbi thought, frowning at the sky.

"Wait here and I'll get the car," Ben called, as he dashed across the parking lot.

Abbi stayed put and sighed as she wondered how she could bring up the topic of them. That there was no way she could do what he asked of her. The two incidents hit home today. Two pretty girls in one day, flirting with him. She'd forever live-in fear of never being able to compete with all these women.

BEN RAN TO THE CAR, laughing to himself as he went. He couldn't believe Abbi was going to hit that girl. He adored her when she was spitting mad, but he had to stop her. Causing a scene and Abbi getting arrested for assault was not something either of them would want to deal with. The way people took videos of everything, it would have been on the Internet faster than it took him to put the girl in her place.

Unlocking the car, he jumped in, started the engine, and drove the short distance to the mall entrance where Abbi was waiting. Ben leaned across her seat and grabbed the handle of the passenger door and waited for her to get closer. As she exited, he saw a man appeared from out of nowhere bump into her.

Startled, Abbi glanced up.

"Oops, sorry!" she said as the man steadied her. Immediately her eyes were drawn to the hands on her arms. *That's odd. Why would anyone be wearing winter gloves in this kind of weather?* She looked up at him and frowned... *and a winter hat and scarf?*

"No worries," he responded, holding on to her a little too long for her liking.

Annoyance flared in Ben as he watched the scene unfold. "Okay bud, you can let her go now." He could see how uncomfortable Abbi looked. He reached for his door handle, intending to intervene just as she backed away and skirted around the man. He shoved the door open for her to plop right onto her seat.

"Wow!" Abbi said slamming the car door. She hurriedly took a fistful of tissues from her purse and wiped the water from her face. "This rain is crazy!" she said, now trying to unsuccessfully sop the water from her hair with the same tissues.

"Who was that?" Ben asked, reaching in the backseat.

"Who?" Abbi looked around. "Oh, you mean that guy? No idea, he came from out of nowhere and just about plowed me down."

"I saw that," he said. "Looked kind of suspicious to me." Producing a towel from the back seat, he held it out for her to take. "Here, use this."

"Yeah. He did seem a little... off." She sent a disgusted look at the towel.

"What?" he laughed, pulling away from the curb. "It's clean, don't worry."

"Thanks," she mumbled taking it.

She leaned back and stared out the window as she towel-dried her hair, watching as the countryside replaced the city view. Abbi was debating on how to bring up being just friends when she realized he was pulling off to the side of the road. Dropping her hands to her lap, she turned, looking at him quizzically.

"I can't see out the windshield. I think it's because I'm still wet myself," he told her.

She watched him remove his seat belt, followed by his jacket. Her eyes grew large when as if in slow motion, she saw him reach for the hem of his shirt. She had no choice but to watch as he removed it. She did have a choice, but her eyes had other ideas.

With each inch it revealed his smooth muscled torso. A narrow line of hair traveled down from his navel, disappearing below the waist of his jeans. She swallowed hard. *Good Lord, he had to have heard that.*

Ben's skin looked as if it were made of satin. She watched in awe as goosebumps rose on his stomach. Resisting the urge to smooth them away with the heat of her hands, Abbi twisted them in the towel on her lap. It was the only way she could restrain herself from reaching out to touch him.

Fighting with herself to tear her eyes away, they travelled onward. To his wonderfully defined chest, then his eyes... *Oh my gosh. No!* He caught her staring. For the life of her, she couldn't look away. The heated look he tossed her way made her insides flop, tingle, and tighten.

I don't want to stop this attraction, she thought to herself.

Ben reached over to take the towel off her lap. He chuckled when he had to give it a hard tug to free it from her grip.

Drying himself off, he said, "You never told me what upset you so."

"Huh?" For the life of her she had no clue what he just said. "What did you just say?"

"On the way up." He reached in the back seat and grabbed a t-shirt. Pulling it on, he said, "You seemed terrified of me. I thought I must have done something to upset you like that."

Abbi sat transfixed until his head popped through the neck hole, and he looked at her.

"Well?" he raised a brow waiting for her response.

She remembered now and didn't want to talk about it, but he had the right to know. Looking down at her hands, she took a deep breath. "Before I moved here, shortly after my book started getting noticed, I would interact with my readers. I don't call them fans... I mean, I'm not famous by any means."

She glanced over at him. He sat there, one hand dangling over the steering wheel, the other on the gearshift. He watched her intently, listening to every word.

She blew out the breath she was holding.

"I would talk to them on social media and answer mail when I could. At that point, I started writing another novel, so I didn't have a lot of time. There was this one guy that was overly chatty."

She took another glance at him. He was thoughtfully rubbing his chin, watching her, waiting.

"So, kind of like what you're doing now?" he smiled. He could tell from her actions she didn't want to talk about it, but he didn't say it. He needed to know what happened.

She smiled then made a face. "Yeah, I'm sorry. This is just really hard to talk about."

"Take your time."

"Okay, so being busy I couldn't respond as quickly as he wanted me to. He started acting possessive, as strange as that sounds. He talked as if we were dating." She touched his hand for emphasis. He took the opportunity. Turning his hand over, he laced his fingers with hers.

She gripped his hand tightly, her knuckles turning white.

"He started sending letters and packages to my house. When I ignored him, they became threatening..." She stopped, tears spilling from her eyes.

Ben spoke softly as he leaned over and turned her face toward his. "There was more to it, wasn't there, Abbi?" He looked into her eyes. "Tell me sweetheart. What did he say?"

"He said, that if I didn't start talking to him again..." She stopped. Swallowing the lump in her throat, she continued, "That he'd use me, abuse me and bury me."

Sadness and anger filled him with her words. Gently he pulled her towards him as she collapsed against his chest, sobbing. "God, Abbi. I'm so sorry you went through that."

With tears forming in his own eyes he said, "Shh, It's okay, I'm here now." He soothingly stroked her hair then pulled back only long enough to look down, kissing her tears away. "I won't let anyone hurt you."

Abbi had never felt safer than she did at that very moment. His soothing touch made her want more. Her lips sought his, softly at first, then with more urgency. He laid his hand against her jaw. Wrapping his fingers around the back of her neck, he tilted her chin with his thumb, breaking off the kiss.

"Are you sure?" His eyes burned with desire.

At her quick nod, he brought her closer, his lips brushing softly against hers. At her soft moan, he deepened the kiss. Their tongues seeking and tasting, dancing softly against one another, a ritual between man and women since the beginning of time.

He nipped her bottom lip tenderly, his tongue soothing the sting.

Her soft whimper brought him back to reality, to where they were at this very moment. He tore away from the softness of her mouth and rested his forehead against hers.

"Ben?" She called to him on a breathy sigh, causing a smile to form on his lips.

"Yeah?"

"Take me home... now, please. I need a change of underwear and a shower, and oddly, I feel like smoking a cigarette."

He wailed with laughter as he pulled away from her heat and started the engine.

Abbi started giggling. She felt spent, as if they had just taken a tumble in the sack. She had never felt like that from a kiss. She could swear she had been on the verge of an orgasm. Either that, or her window had been down, and the seat was wet from the rain. She wanted to think about that for a bit and softly smiled.

For a few moments in time, they had been one; she thought crazily... not by body, but by mouth. She'd hold off for now on telling him this wouldn't work. For now, she was just going to enjoy the feelings that this man had awakened in her... feelings she hadn't experienced before.

Chapter 9

Abbi was sitting there with a soft, satisfied smile on her lips as they drove towards home. Her mind drifted to the preparations of the upcoming holiday, May 24th. In a few weeks, her kids would come up for the long weekend. Her brow furrowed at the thought.

Should I invite him?

She glanced at their clasped hands and worried how her kids would react to him. She knew Luke would be fine, but Ava and Lane... Well, that would be another story entirely. She knew if they disapproved, they would tell her and Ben. She pictured the encounter in her mind, and it wasn't pretty.

They were coming out of the bend that would take them back to their side of the lake when she felt him lift their hands. Bringing them to his mouth, he softly kissed the back of hers.

She glanced towards him to see him looking at her. Smiling at him, she turned her attention back to the road. A flash of black suddenly darted across the front of the car headed towards the lake.

"Ben, look out!" she shouted, clenching his hand while bracing her other on the dashboard.

He slammed on the brakes, the car coming to a rocking stop.

"What the hell was that?" he asked, searching the road.

She pushed her door open. "I think it was a dog," she tossed over her shoulder as she got out. Ben soon followed suit, joining her at the edge of trees that lined the road. He started whistling.

"Shh! Be quiet. It could have been a bear," she whispered, looking around with concern.

"A bear?" His brows shot up. "Huh," he replied, thinking his mum might have been right when he mentioned moving to Canada.

She looked at him. "Well, it is uncommon, but not unheard of. Come on, let's get going," she urged, walking back to the car. "Judging by its size it would be a cub. That would mean Momma isn't too far behind," she said hurrying back to the safety of the car.

"That's the size of a cub?" he asked in amazement as he got back in. At her nod, he blew out a breath, "I'd hate to see its mother."

Abbi looked at him and noticed the grip he had on the steering wheel as he drove through the village. "That's nothing. Grizzlies are a lot bigger yet."

"Good lord, my mother was right," Ben mumbled under his breath.

She burst out laughing at that and laughed even harder when she saw the look on his face.

"Mothers usually are!" she patted his arm with a giggle.

"Okay, change of subject," he chuckled, pulling into her laneway. Setting the shifter to park, he looked at her. "Do you have any plans for the rest of the day?"

"Nope. Just the usual feeding of the brood." She motioned to the window where they all stood watching them.

He glanced at the house, a smile forming on his lips. "Right... right.... I don't think they would let you forget," he laughed. "After that, would you like to come over and give me a hand with the curtains?" He deliberately put his head down and lifted his eyes to hers.

She couldn't resist him when he gave her that look.

"I can throw something on the grill, make a salad of sorts. It's the least I can do, seeing how you broke your plans today for me," he said hoping to sweeten the deal as she climbed out of the car.

Abbi shut the door and leaned her arms on the open window and looked at him. "Sounds good to me. Just let me feed these guys and I'll be over. An hour sound good to you?"

"That's perfect." It would give him just enough time to clean up a bit.

She stood and walked away, as she did, she sent him a shy wave as she headed towards the house.

Returning it, he sat a moment and wondered how in such a short time she had become so important to him. "Get a move on Ben," he said to himself. Time was ticking and he had a mess that needed cleaning before she came over.

"HEY GUYS!" ABBI CALLED to her critters. Each one clamoring for her attention. Even Bird was excited to see her, landing on the dead tree that acted as a perch by the door.

"Come along," she said to the dogs as they followed her to the back door to relieve themselves. The sun was making an appearance once again, so she left the doors open while

MOONLIT NIGHT

she returned to the kitchen to ready their food. The cats moseyed over to eat; she sat the dishes on the floor just as Lucy followed by Brutus entered the living room.

"Bird, here's yours sweetie," she said, dumping his feed in the bowl on the dead tree. She then went to her room to change into some sweats and a t-shirt. She grabbed a hoodie, just in case it cooled off too much, and tied it around her waist.

Returning to the kitchen, both dogs were finishing up their food as Abbi made her way through the living room to close and lock the French doors. After today's admission to Ben of what happened in the past, she felt uneasy about returning to an empty house after dark. She flicked the switch for the light sensor that would flood the yard upon her return.

"Lucy, Brutus, you guys want to go for a walk?" They yipped and cried in response. "Good, let's go see Ben, shall we?"

She had to laugh as Lucy whined, and Brutus bounded to the door, impatiently pawing it, and only paused long enough to look at her as if to say, 'come on lady'. She bent over to pick up Lucy, giving her a soft kiss on the head, she said, "Your boyfriend awaits."

Grabbing her cell, she walked over to the alarm to set it and double checked to make sure the door was locked before she closed it with a soft thud.

BEN TOOK THE CURTAINS out of the bag. From the back seat, he took his wet clothes and towel and stuffed them into it as he did, he cast a critical eye on the rest of his items laying there. Damned if it didn't look like he was living out of his car. He really should take them into the house too but was pressed for time.

Funny how Abbi never even commented on how his back seat looked like a dresser drawer. Any other woman would have criticized him for it. He would collect them up tomorrow, he decided as he climbed out of the car.

Taking the steps two at a time, he reached with a jangle of his keys to unlock the door and noticed something bunched up on the porch chair. Picking it up he held it and turned it around in his hands. A jacket... It wasn't his. Ben frowned looking around for a car he knew wasn't there, then heard footsteps coming from the side of the house.

Dropping the bag and curtains, he tossed the jacket on the chair and took angry strides towards the intruder. "Hey! Get the hell off my property... *whoa!*" Rounding the corner, he almost collided with a tall, dark-haired man.

"Hey! Benny boy. How's it hanging?"

Immediate relief washed over Ben. Only two people dared to call him that, his father and Mark.

Ben grinned widely.

"Mark my man," he said giving him a hug. "It's great to see you." Turning around, he motioned for Mark to follow.

"Place looks good!" Mark commented as they headed to the door. "I had some time off, as you know, and thought I would come and see how you're settling in." He bent over and picked up his jacket while Ben unlocked the house.

Ben shrugged. "It's been good. I should have taken your advice and hired a cleaning crew," he laughed. "But it's all good now," he said pushing the door open. "Come in. Make yourself at home."

He looked at Mark as he went to dump the wet bag of clothes into the washer and mentally cursed the man's timing. Adding some soap, he set the controls and walked back into the kitchen straight for the sink. "Where's your car?" he asked, stuffing dishes haphazardly into the dishwasher.

"Up the road a bit. I'm staying in the cabins there for a few days. Turned out nice after all the rain so I decided to walk here," Mark said. Pulling a stool out from the center island, he sat.

"Nice. Hey, do you want a beer?" Ben reached into the fridge not waiting for an answer from him.

Mark gave him a serious, questioning look. "Uh, buddy, you don't have to clean up on my account," he chuckled, motioning to the dishwasher.

Ben produced two frosty cold ones. Passing one to Mark over the island, he popped the cap on his and took a long swallow before answering. "I'm not. Abbi will be here any minute," he wiped his mouth with the back of his hand.

"Abbiii," Mark drawled out her name. "I like the sound of that."

Setting his bottle on the counter, Ben turned away to wipe the sink down, his brow furrowed in thought. That was the problem, Mark liked the sound of any woman's name; he was known around Hollywood as a ladies' man. He wasn't the type for a long-lasting relationship. At all.

"So, what does this Abbi look like?" Mark asked, fiddling with his beer cap.

Grabbing his beer, Ben tossed the rag into the sink and leaned back against the counter. "Um. She's nice." His eyes softened at the thought of her, a slight smile on his face. "Funny as hell, sweet, beautiful... you know what I mean?" He asked not really wanting an answer.

Mark could see the reaction on Ben's face as he talked about her.

"You got it bad, don't you bud?" he grinned at him.

Ben wiped his mouth and nodded, "Yeah. Is it that obvious?" he demanded.

At Mark's nod, Ben felt the need to explain. "Stupid thing is, I've only known her for a couple of weeks. And been in her company three times. I can't seem to control myself around her... even kissed her already for God's sake! That's not like me..." he flung an accusing hand at Mark, "that's something you'd do."

"Taking lessons, are you?"

Mark had to laugh at Ben's flustered state. Ben was never the guy to approach a woman at all. And to kiss one so soon? Mark found it funny as hell to finally see his friend shaken so much over one.

"Just do me a favor? Don't come on to her, alright?"

"I don't know man. You know I can't help myself," Mark laughed.

Raising his brows, Ben said quietly, "I'm serious." He shoved his hand in his hair, "Abbi is different. I've never been this attracted to anyone so quickly. Truth be told, she scares the hell out of me."

"Why would she?" Mark questioned, all joking aside.

Ben let out a sigh. "She's wary.... very wary." Pausing, he wondered if he should go on. He wasn't sure how his friend would react. Not that it mattered to him, he was being truthful with Abbi when he told her age meant nothing to him. "She's older than me."

Mark shrugged, splaying his hands out, "Okay... so what's the big deal?"

"By nine years," Ben supplied, watching his reaction.

"Pfft! nine?" Mark waved his hand. "That's nothing! When I was twenty-five, I dated a woman who was fifty, age means nothing."

Ben tapped himself on the chest. "That's what I said. But to her, It's wrong. She finally agreed to think about it though, so I have that going for me."

"Look, man, if we men can date a nineteen-year-old when we are in our sixties, which by the way, I fully intend on doing, then so can women," Mark snickered, then stopped. A dark look crossed his face. "Wait, she isn't a gold digger, is she? It's really easy to tell."

Ben started chuckling and shook his head. "No man—"

Mark held up his hand cutting Ben off. "No... no, let me explain. Does she wear sexy clothes and flounce around when you're together, or does she come on to you, like at all, even subtlety?"

Ben just stood there laughing at him.

"What's wrong with you man? I'm serious," Mark hissed.

"Right, I know you are, and no, she is none of those things," Ben denied. "She actually avoided me at first," he smiled, remembering.

"You need to be sure Ben. Hell, she could take every penny you ever made. Be reasonable."

A knock on the door had them both looking at it.

"Is that her?" Mark whispered, turning to look at Ben.

"Yeah, that will be her," he nodded, pushing away from the counter to go answer the door.

He figured he'd better set the record straight with Mark before letting her in. Stopping in his tracks to do just that, Mark bumped into him.

Looking at him, Ben asked suspiciously, "Can I help you?!"

"I want to see!!" Mark exclaimed excitedly.

Ben rolled his eyes. "Of course, you do."

He pointed to the chair Mark had just vacated from at the island. "Look, do it from over there. And before I let her in," he said to Mark's retreating back. "I'll answer your question. There is nothing wrong with me and she's not a gold digger. She probably has more money than I do, possibly the both of us," Ben stated, turning towards the door.

"*What?* Wait!" Mark pleaded, coming to a half stand. "How can she?"

Turning back, Ben replied, "She's an author, none other than Abbi Stevens," Ben smiled.

Mark rapidly blinked, "So?"

Ben stood there with one hand on his waist and the other wiping down his face. "You know the movie we are filming, The Jasper Killings?"

"Of course, with the filming budget you know it's going to be a blockbuster." Mark shrugged. "What does that have to do with anything?"

"She wrote the book."

"Oh..." Mark trailed off sitting down in thought.

"Yeah, just what I thought you'd say," Ben laughed with a satisfied nod.

Chapter 10

Abbi stood on the porch looking at her watch for the tenth time. He had fallen asleep, was her first thought, or maybe he had run to the store. But why wouldn't he take his car knowing she would be there soon?

She glanced down. Both dogs were sitting right in front of the door. Their heads tilted from side to side every so often as if they heard something coming from inside. Perhaps he was in the shower. Raising her hand to knock once more, the door abruptly opened.

"Oh, my goodness!" she jumped, laughing. "I just about knocked on your face."

Leaning one hand on the door frame, Ben smiled, gazing into her eyes. "Hi again, to you too." His eyes drank in the sight of her, as he placed an arm around her waist, and pulled her close. Leaning towards her, he laid a soft kiss on her lips. "I missed you," he murmured against her mouth, dipping for one more.

"Me too. Missed you... that is," she stammered.

A cough came from inside the house. At her questioning look, Ben sighed. "I have a guest."

"Oh? I didn't know you knew anyone from around here." She jerked a thumb in the direction of home. "I can leave..."

"I don't. And no. If anyone is leaving it will be him."

The dogs decided it was their turn for some attention from Ben. Brutus stood on his hind legs and wrapped his front paws around his waist.

Abbi cried in alarm and tugged on his collar, "I'm so sorry! He's never done that to anyone before. Brutus! Get the hell down!" She was no match for the beast.

"It's all good, Abbi," he said, smiling giving the big brute some love. He glanced down to see Lucy pawing the air for his attention as well. He scooped her up and was promptly awarded with kisses.

"I'm sorry for bringing them, I just hated to leave them behind again after such a long day," she explained.

Setting Lucy down, he replied, "It's fine, Abbi. I wouldn't expect you to," he told her and gave her another quick kiss.

The door swung open wider, revealing an attractive, tall man with dark brown hair. He promptly stuck his hand out, giving her a charming smile. "Nice to meet you, Abbi. I've heard so much about you. The name's Mark Donovan. Ben and I are coworkers."

Smiling, she shook his hand and said, "Nice to meet you." She glanced at Ben with a surprised look.

"Mark thought I was cleaning up for him, I told him all about you," Ben explained as he stepped aside for her and the dogs to enter.

By Mark's standards she was averagely pretty. Curvy in the right places but not the customary supermodel thin women that he dated. She had a pretty face, nice eyes, and lips, he noted. He thought she could use a bit more makeup than she was currently sporting though. She was certainly not the sort of woman that usually clamored around them for attention. Maybe that was what attracted Ben to her? It didn't matter, she was a member of the opposite sex and that was what appealed to Mark the most. He couldn't resist eyeballing her as she passed by.

"Yes, but he didn't mention how beautiful you are."

Ben shot him a disbelieving look. *"Don't even start man,"* he silently conveyed to his friend.

Looking at Ben, Mark put his hand up to block his mouth from Abbi's view. He mouthed the words, 'she's hot', as he pointed towards Abbi's back. Ben gave him a warning look. Mark's response was a thumbs up followed by a huge grin.

Shaking his head in disbelief, Ben walked over to the fridge, and took out a package of steaks. The sooner he cooked the food the sooner Mark would leave. He hoped. Ripping the package open, he placed them on a plate and added some seasonings.

"So, Abbi. Ben here told me you're an author?"

"Well, I've written one book," she nodded.

"And what a book it is." Mark leaned forward. "You're the newest hottest author."

"I wouldn't really call myself that," she replied, taking a stool at the island.

"Beautiful and modest," Mark said, tipping his beer bottle in salute to Ben.

Ben noticed the immediate blush come to Abbi's cheeks. Protectiveness came over him as he took a deep exasperated breath. Without a doubt, this was going to be a hell of a night.

Not wanting her embarrassed any further, Ben said, "Ah, Abbi. Would you like a glass of wine?" His gaze softened when he looked at her.

Nodding, she replied in a quiet voice, "Please, that would be nice."

He turned away to get a glass out of the cupboard.

Clearing her throat, she said, "Ben, I can get it," as she got up and went around to him. She whispered, "Please, let me do this."

He looked at her, with concern in his eyes.

"Go." She gave him a gentle push, but not before he gave her hand a reassuring squeeze. Abbi walked over to the cupboard Ben had been reaching for.

The guys were in deep conversation, thank God. She didn't want to answer questions from Mark or make small talk. She had nothing against the guy. She just wasn't impressed by how he tried to...flirt? Was that it? She snickered. Whatever it was, it wasn't happening.

Not bothering to look for a wine glass, she grabbed the closest glass object. All she cared about was that it held liquid. Searching under the counter for a bottle of wine, she came up dry. She looked in the cupboards and found a bottle. Excitement bubbled up inside her at finding it until she read the label. *Oh... Cooking Sherry, hmm, it might just do.*

Unscrewing the top, she took a whiff, wrinkling her nose she jerked back. She risked a glance at the guys. Shrugging, she tilted the bottle back, and took a swig.

Oh God, this is disgusting! Rushing to the sink she spit it out.

Ben was watching her with an amused grin. "It's in the fridge, Abbi," he supplied.

"Thanks," she gasped as she rinsed the sink with one hand while wiping her mouth with the back of the other.

She replaced the Sherry in the cupboard and headed towards the fridge.

Opening the door, she grabbed the bottle... red, her favorite, and chilled, too. Just the way she liked it. But it wasn't a twist-off. She didn't want to interrupt them, so she pulled out a drawer in search of a corkscrew.

"In the utensil holder," Ben said.

She nodded. "Right!"

She hated corks, all the bits falling into the wine after she struggled with the damned things. While she fought with the offending kitchen gadget, she decided she hated corkscrews, too. Struggling for what felt like an eternity, she froze in a moment of panic when two strong arms came around her; until she looked down and realized she knew those arms.

"Need a hand?" he murmured next to her ear.

Sweet heavens, he does crazy things to me with that voice!

She stumbled back against the wall of his chest as his lips brushed the side of her neck. She could feel his sharp intake of air against her back as he breathed in her scent.

"Did I mention how sexy you look in sweats?" he asked huskily, as his hips moved seductively against her backside.

She let out a soft, whimpering moan until she heard a door bang in the other room. *Mark!* Horrified, she looked up at Ben.

"Relax," he said, dropping a kiss on her nose. "He's outside starting the BBQ." Dropping his arms, he took the corkscrew and bottle and skillfully opened it. He took the cup she had waiting on the counter and filled it.

"You know." He smiled at what he held in his hand. "I do have wineglasses in the cupboard. Here," he said, handing her the measuring cup she'd sat on the counter. "I'll take this out to him." Ben grabbed the plate of steaks. His brow wrinkled as he turned away. He was losing all self control around her, and it was driving him crazy.

Heading towards the door to join Mark on the porch, he felt the need to reassure her. He stopped in midstride. "Abbi," he said, turning to look at her. "I shouldn't have done that. So you know for future, what we just shared will always be just for our eyes only. That is when you're ready, and the time is right." He could feel the desire rising again at the mere thought of it. He hurried on, "If you want me. I would never say or do anything in front of anyone that would make you uncomfortable or cause you to lose your trust in me, okay?" He needed to hear her response. "I'm sorry, I should have told you straight away that Mark was outside."

He watched her gulp down her wine as she came towards him.

Setting the empty cup on the counter, Abbi took the plate from him. She walked to the door and called out, "Mark, Ben just had to go to the washroom. He'll be right out." Handing the steaks over, she closed the door with a soft click and walked straight over to Ben.

Great, she's going to rip me a new one. He watched as she stopped before him.

Resting one hand on his chest, the other reaching up to touch the side of his face, Abbi gazed deeply into his eyes.

"That's the nicest thing anyone has ever said to me."

She reached around to caress his neck and felt goosebumps rise on his skin. With renewed confidence, she closed her eyes and placed a soft kiss on his lips. She felt his strong arms reach around her. *God, I love those arms...* She sighed in content as he gathered her closer.

Opening her mouth, she allowed him to deepen the kiss with his searching tongue. This time when he brought his hips forward, she met him with a boldness she hadn't known she had.

He groaned in restrained pleasure, his hands spanning her bottom as he hiked her closer to him. She could feel his arousal, rock hard against her. Even though Abbi was aroused, she was in control this time. She felt like a wanton wench and for once, she didn't care.

"Hey Ben! Uh, we've got a bit of a fire going on here," Mark yelled from outside, his voice raising with urgency.

They broke away from each other as if both were burned by an invisible flame. It took Abbi a bit of a moment to process what Mark had just yelled.

Ben sprang into action when they saw the orange glow from the fire. Moving quickly, he threw a door open near the stove, grabbed a fire extinguisher, and ran outside with Abbi right behind him.

The area around the BBQ was licking high with flames as Ben pulled the pin, directed it at it, and pulled the trigger. Finally, the fire died down enough that it allowed him to slam the barbeque lid shut.

They stood, surveying the damage. The floor and railings would need to be painted or replaced in that area. Luckily, it had only scorched the ceiling of the porch.

"Sorry man. I was playing fetch with the dogs and by the time I noticed, it was shooting flames," Mark said apologetically.

"It's all good! I'm just relieved it didn't spread further."

"So, who's up for pizza and wings?" Abbi inquired.

Mark held up his hand. "Me, I'm starving, but I'm buying, it's the least I can do."

She looked at Ben. "How about you, Ben? Are you hungry?" she asked, taking out her cellphone to call in the order.

"I'm famished," he winked, smiling at her.

Catching the innuendo, Abbi blushed and made a sound in her throat. "All right than! I'll order it right now and get it delivered," she said, stepping away to place the order.

FORTY MINUTES LATER, they were all sitting around the glass patio table in comfortable oversized chairs. They had just finished eating and were drinking some beer as the sun made its way to set on another day.

The loons called out over the still lake as Ben got up to light some torches around the patio. Abbi stood and started collecting the paper plates and takeout boxes to toss them in the recycling bin.

"Does anybody want anything else?" she asked, looking up from her task.

"I'm good," Mark answered.

"No thanks Abbi." Ben swept his hand at the mess. "You don't need to clean this up though, I can do it in the morning."

Mark pointed his beer bottle at him. "Ah no you don't want to do that. You'll have all sorts of critters making camp if you do," he warned.

"Mark's right. It's fine, I don't mind," she smiled and headed towards the house.

Mark leaned his arms on the table and looked at Ben. "Tell me. Why did I sell this place to you again?" he asked, taking a swig from his bottle.

"Good question. I'm glad you did. It's honestly the best decision I have ever made in my life," he said as he watched Abbi through the kitchen window. She was standing at the sink, talking to herself. He smiled at the sight of her. She did that often when she thought no one was looking.

Mark glanced to where Ben was staring. "Yeah, I'll say. How long has she lived here?"

"Four years."

"To think, I could have been with her all this time. Good thing you got to her before me," Mark said, laughing, seeing now what Ben saw in her.

Ben gave him a deadpanned look and raised a brow in question.

"What makes you think she'd be interested in you?"

"Come on," Mark said, holding his hands wide. "Who wouldn't want a piece of this." He gestured with his hands as if he were highlighting a prize on a game show.

Ben busted his gut laughing and nodded towards the house. "She wouldn't, I can guarantee it."

"Given the chance, I bet she would... if you weren't together," Mark said seriously. "Wanna bet? I'll even put money on it." He reached for his wallet than laid a hundred-dollar bill on the table.

After some thought, Ben hesitantly reached for his own wallet. Matching Mark's bet, he said, "All right. But." He pointed a finger at Mark, as he stuffed his wallet in his back pocket, "There are some conditions." Ben leaned back in his chair and crossed his arms in front of his chest.

Mark raised his brows. "You're *actually* letting *me* make *my* moves on *your* girl?"

Ben gave him a stony look. "First off, she isn't my girl... at least not yet. And no... You can't make your moves. And yes, that's the first condition and don't forget it!"

"Come on, man!" Mark held out a hand. "How is that a condition? You're not even in a relationship with her." He threw his hands up, almost ready to accept defeat... almost.

Ignoring his outburst, Ben continued, "Second. You lay a finger on her... at all, it's a guarantee that I'll shove my fist down your throat."

The idea of winning had Mark shouting out a triumphant, "*Hell yeah!*" as he fist-pumped the air.

What the hell did I just agree to?

What would he do if she did fall for Mark? Ben didn't want to pressure Abbi into being with him. But his gut, his mind, and more importantly, his heart was telling him everything was right with her.

He remembered the spark he felt the first time he met her, shaking her hand. The first night, lying on her kitchen floor, that first kiss they had shared, had him wanting more.

Earlier... in his car, and that moment hours ago in his kitchen had burned him to his soul. Whenever he was with her, he felt that spark. If those moments were the last, he ever shared with her, he would forever cherish them... forever long for them, but he would let her go if it made her happy.

"Um... one more thing." Ben took a deep breath as he met Abbi's gaze, through the window. He had to look away. "You have twenty-four hours."

Mark spit out a mouthful of beer. "*What?!*"

"One. Day," Ben clarified.

Raising his head, he saw Abbi close the patio door. Her eyes were seeking him out, a smile for him on her lips. He sent a sad smile her way. Maybe it would help her decide what she wanted. He could only hope it was him.

Chapter 11

Abbi was trying to stay busy in the house. The dogs were laying under the table in the dining room. Glancing at her watch, she saw that only fifteen minutes had passed.

Staring out the window above the sink she noticed the guys in deep discussion and saw a look of sadness on Ben's face. She walked to the patio doors and gave a sharp whistle calling the dogs. It was time they went out and she needed to wipe that look off his face.

Determined, she closed the door and headed straight for Ben.

Mark spoke first, "Abbi, sweetheart! So glad you decided to join us," he said dragging her chair towards him. "Why don't you sit your lovely self, right here..." He patted the seat.

He gave her what she could only describe as a leering grin. A creepy feeling tingled across her scalp and down her back.

What the hell did I miss?

As she looked to Ben, he turned his head away, leaned back in his chair, and let out a sigh.

She swung her gaze back and arched a brow at Mark. "No. I'm good, thanks. I think I'll just head back home now." She saw Ben tense at her response. She wanted nothing more than to bend down and make him look her in the eyes.

"*No!* ... I mean, don't do that, don't leave yet," Mark pleaded then chuckled to mask the desperation in his voice.

"Oh-kay than." She grabbed the back of the chair Mark had pulled over to his side. "I'll just move over here," she said, tugging on it.

She met resistance. Looking down, she saw Mark staring up at her, a smile on his face as he held onto the arm of the chair. Determined, she tugged on it harder to no avail.

She took a quick glance in Ben's direction. He didn't say a word. In fact, he seemed uninterested in the ensuing tug of war.

Giving a defeated huff, Abbi looked around for another chair. There were only three.

Well, I'll fix them both.

"You can have that chair, Mark." She scooped Lucy up and sat her upon it and smiled at him. "Lucy will keep you company."

She glided over to Ben; he glanced at her, deep in thought.

"Scooch your chair back."

Ben pushed back away from the table. He started to rise to give her his seat, but she put a staying hand on his shoulder. Abbi shook her head. "No, you're good. Do you mind if I sit?" she asked, innocently pointing to his lap.

Ben shot Mark a surprised look before locking eyes with Abbi. She saw the immediate change come over him. His eyes lit up at her request while his lips curved into a soft smile. Shimmying back, he patted his thighs.

"Course not love."

Guiding her onto his lap, he placed a hand on her hip and held her there. Abbi sat down with a satisfied sigh as felt his warm body pressed up against her backside. He made her feel safe, wanted, and loved. Wait, not love. More so, an extraordinarily strong like. It was way too soon to tell if it would develop beyond that.

He reached out taking her hand in his and began to trace soft circles on her palm with his thumb. She was delightfully surprised when she felt him doing the same to her hip.

She could really get used to his loving touch. As wonderful as it felt, she had to stop him though. If she didn't, in no time she would be a squirming mass of liquid in his lap. Abbi reached for the hand at her hip and brought it to cross over her stomach, holding it there with hers.

"So, Mark, how did you meet Ben?" she asked, genuinely interested. Leaning back against his chest, she looked across at Mark.

Why is he scowling?

Mark gave her a quick smile. "Well, it was on a movie set, what... three years ago Ben?"

Ben leaned forward a bit, looked around Abbi and said, "Yeah, that's about right mate." He shot Mark a victorious smile as he leaned back in his chair.

Mark just rolled his eyes. "Yeah, thought so... mate."

"Nice! What movie was it?" she asked, wondering if she had ever seen it, as she felt Ben shift under her.

Great, I'm putting his legs to sleep.

She moved her bum over towards his other leg, trying to ease some of her weight.

What the heck is that poking me in the butt?

She moved again, trying to push it out of the way. It couldn't be his wallet, he carried that in his back pocket. It had to be his cellphone.

She was listening intently to Mark explain all about the movie when she heard a humming. She looked around for the culprit. Glancing down at the table, she saw that it was a cell phone lit up. Ben's cell phone. *How can that be... was he hiding one?*

Freeing her hand from his, she leaned forward, lifted her bum, and slipped her hand between them. Patting around for the protruding object, she could feel Ben shaking with laughter... Something Mark must have said had him laughing she supposed. She herself had long given up listening to his chatter.

Her fingers found what they were searching for. She squinted her eyes in concentrated thought. Touching it with just her fingertips, she ran them along the length.

She was trying to picture in her mind as she squeezed it with her fingertips as to what it was. It was long, nearly twice the length of her hand from wrist to the tip of her middle finger. Wait, she stood corrected. A hand and a half, and, felt like a sock...

That's not a frickin sock or cell phone! Her mind screamed in horror. As she snatched her hand away, she banged it on the underside of the table.

"*Sonofa*...Ouch! Good *Lord!*" she shrieked, mortified, as her eyes bugged out of her head. *I'm 45! How in all that is holy could I be so stupid?! I was playing with his penis!*

She must have scared the hell out of Mark, for his brown eyes darkened. Concern flashed on his brow.

MOONLIT NIGHT

Mark braced his hands on the table. "*Whoa!*" He leaned away and added, "Abbi, are you all right? It looked like your eyes were gonna pop out of your head. For a minute there I thought you were being possessed," he spat, leaning forward to emphasize his words.

Ben let out a bark of laughter.

Thinking quick on the spot was never one of Abbi's strong suits. Her eyes darted everywhere trying to avoid Mark's face. She was thankful the torches threw such little light.

"Sorry, I didn't mean to scare you! I, uh... a bug ran across my hand... I think...," she licked her suddenly dry lips and shrugged, "... maybe a spider... I think... and I um, hit it on the table when I jerked it up. Yeah, that's what happened," she nodded, happy with her excuse.

Ben was in tears at this point, but managed to say, "You think?" He peeled out a fresh bout of laughter, "That's your story and you're sticking to it, is that right Abbi?"

I'll get you back.

She moved her hips ever so slightly, just enough to make him squirm. Ben's laughter stopped at once. She could feel the heat of his body as he moved closer. Her eyes fluttered closed, masking the pleasure of his breath as it caressed the nape of her neck.

Try as he might, Ben lost all self-control when she started squirming in his lap. He was thankful it was dark enough, and he was behind her so Mark couldn't see the sweet torture she was putting him through.

Leaning forward, he inhaled the intoxicating scent of her. Breathing harder, he buried his face in her hair at the back of her neck, placing his lips there, a desperate need to touch her. She was pure madness... he growled softly in her ear, "I don't know how much more I can take."

Mark turned his head, looking at Ben out of the side of his eye, he raised his brow. "Uh, hey, buddy. Ben, you doing okay?"

Coming back to reality, Ben took a deep breath feigning a loud yawn. He stretched his arms, bringing them forward to encircle Abbi within. He lightly kissed the side of her neck. "Yeah, just tired, you know?" he responded, glancing towards Mark.

Knowing that was his cue to go, Mark threw his hands up in defeat and stood. "You're perfect for each other... you both are nuts," he said, with a laugh. "Well, I best be going."

Abbi got up as well, followed quickly by Ben. He grabbed a hold of her shoulders, using her to block Mark from seeing exactly what was wrong with him.

"That money there," Ben motioned with his head towards their bet on the table. "Take it, dinner is on me," he said.

"Nah, you keep it. Take your beautiful lady here out on a fancy date for me," he said. Smiling, he looked at her, "Abbi, it was a pleasure meeting you." He took her hand and bowed his head, planting a quick kiss on the back of it. He stood and looked her in the eyes. "Ben is one of the best guys I know. He will treat you right. But if you ever tire of him, look me up," he shot her a wink. With a salute to Ben, Mark set off in the direction of the cabins, whistling a tune that faded away into the darkened night.

Abbi just stood there. She dared not look at Ben. She had done the exact thing he'd promised he wouldn't do, make her feel uncomfortable in front of someone. She had to say something, to tell him how sorry she was.

Slowly she turned around. With eyes downcast, she took hold of his waist. Bending her head down, she leaned it against his chest and stared at the ground.

"Um, I wanted to—" She felt him lift her chin. She had no choice but to look into his eyes. "Ben I—"

The hungry urgency of his lips silenced her. His hand slid to caress her jawline as he held her to him, deepening the kiss. The growl emitting from his throat caused a liquid fire to shoot through to her soul.

He was like a drug, one that she was quickly becoming addicted to. Placing her hands on his arms, she pushed down as she tore her mouth away. Looking into his eyes, clouded with desire had her craving another taste... almost. She held her hands together, preventing them from touching him. "Ben, I have to tell you how sorry I am for doing that with Mark being here," she whispered.

"Abbi," he said, "there is no need to apologize."

"Oh, but there is. Please, let me finish. I did the unthinkable, something just a couple of hours ago that you said you would never do to me."

Ben took a step towards her, reaching out. She knew he'd hug her, something she just couldn't handle right now.

"No. Stay there." At his wounded look, she explained, "Every time we touch, I lose my mind. I'm not used to these feelings you stir in me. It's been an awfully long time, if ever, that I've felt this way."

Hearing those words come from her lips had him feeling elated. There was hope. He knew then he had to take things slow; otherwise, she'd back off. She would close herself off and he'd lose any chance he had with her.

"If I promise to keep myself under control, can I hug you?" he asked softly, raising his brows.

A slow smile formed on her lips. He opened his arms wide as she gave him a slight nod. Embracing her, he knew he had to tell her about the bet with Mark.

"Now I have something to confess," he sighed.

Looking up, Abbi stared into his eyes, waiting.

"You know that money Mark left on the table?" he asked, tucking a curl away that had fallen over her eye.

At her nod, he took a deep breath.

"He bet me he could get you... interested in him." He rushed on... "I told him there was no way you would consider it, but he insisted you would and so he bet me." He could feel her tense up.

"Why did you do that?" she asked sadly.

He saw the hurt in her eyes and hesitated for a second. "I did it because of how I feel for you Abbi. I know it bothers you that I'm younger. I don't want it to seem like I'm pressuring you... I thought maybe it would help you to decide what you want."

She wrapped her arms around him and gave him a tight squeeze. It wouldn't matter because he's not you she wanted to say but remained silent.

"Mark's a guy who will flirt... relationship or not, with anyone." He hugged her tighter. "So, I matched his bet with some conditions." He kissed her forehead. "I'm sorry I did that. I felt like I had lost any chance of being with you."

Now she knew why he looked so sad earlier, she laid her head on his shoulder. "What were the conditions?"

Ben looked up, gazing in thought. "He asked me if I would let him put the moves on you. I said no, he couldn't, and that was a condition he better remember. He objected, of course, but I ignored him." He could feel her slight chuckle at that.

"The second condition was that he wasn't to lay a finger on you at all, or he would be a hurting unit." He heard her sniffle and chuckle as her arms tightened around him. "... and the third condition... he had twenty-four hours."

"Twenty-four hours?" she asked, looking up at him in confusion.

Leaning back, he lifted her chin and searched her eyes. They were glistening with tears. "Yeah. It happened on a moonlit night... the day we met," he breathed.

He watched as a single teardrop slipped down her cheek. "I gave him the same time it took me to fall for you," he said, softly kissing her tears away.

Still holding her, he leaned back not wanting things to get out of hand again. He gathered her close and dropped an innocent kiss on her hair as he felt a prickle on the back of his neck. It had nothing to do with the woman he held in his arms. And everything to do with something or someone watching them...

Chapter 12

"Oh for Pete's sake!" Abbi pushed back from her keyboard. The insistent cock-a-doodle-doo of her ring tone was getting to her. "I really ought to change that to something less distracting... like silent mode. Hello?" she snapped.

"Hey, Mom! What's wrong with you?" It was one of her sons.

"Lane! Nothing, uh, why do you ask?" she questioned suspiciously. Had he found out about her and Ben?

"No reason, it's just you sounded a little perturbed."

"Oh, sorry," she giggled, with relief. "I've just been writing for days because my agent has been after me to get it done. How many times did you call me?"

"Well, that explains it. Just once. Why?"

"There were a few calls, so I just wondered. I'll check to see who they were when we are through. So, what's up?"

"Oh, okay. Anyway, I'm calling about our plans for the long weekend. Luke and Ava will ride with me. And maybe Cassie, I don't know yet though. We should be up there Thursday afternoon."

She rubbed the back of her neck trying to smooth the tension away. "Cassie? Who is Cassie?"

"She's Luke's new girlfriend. They've been dating for like a week... kind of a floozy if you ask me. I told him that too, but you know how Luke is."

She frowned. "Now Lane, that isn't a nice thing to say." Abbi was now concerned how he would react to Ben.

He snickered. "It's true, Mom! He always gets with someone out of his league or after his money."

Lane had a point. Now she was worried. "Ah, well, you know, it's his life, he's an adult. He can decide that for himself."

"Where is this coming from? That doesn't sound like you at all?"

"People change, Lane," she said with a soft sigh. "Wait, did you say this coming Thursday... or next?"

"This."

Impossible, it couldn't have gone by that fast.

She grabbed the calendar off her desk and looked at the date on her laptop. Had she been so consumed with writing lately that she didn't even know what day it was? It *was* this Thursday! It meant she hadn't talked to Ben for five days.

She thought back to that last night they had been together. The night she had met Mark. Ben had been true to his word and kept his feelings and his hands in check. They ended it with a kiss on her front porch with neither of them wanting it to end.

After she had gone in the house with the dogs, little did he know, she stood watching him through a crack in the curtains from the front window. He sat on her porch step for a while before leaving. After fifteen minutes or so, he stood, paused on the top step, and glanced back at the door. It took every ounce of her willpower to resist flinging it open and dragging him into the house.

"Mom! Hey, are you there? Can you hear me?"

She shook her head to clear her thoughts. "Yes, I can hear you. Sorry, my mind drifted off."

"Well, you might want to do something about that than," he laughed into the phone.

"Oh, I will." She knew exactly what she'd do about that. No more wasting time. "Um, by the way, I will have a friend come by this weekend if he wants to."

"A friend? Oh, you mean, Mack?"

"Well, Mack is always invited out here, but no... his name is Ben," she mumbled, clearing her throat. "He moved to the house on the point about a month ago."

There was a moment of silence before he responded "Ah, what kind of friend?"

She got up from the desk and moved to the window. *The kind that you fall for without a care in the world... one who is too young for you, one that most woman would give their eye teeth for. That kind of friend, Lane!*

She heard muffled talking on his end, thankfully it stalled her from responding.

"Hey Mom, I have to run. My meeting is just about to start, so I'll see you on Thursday, okay?"

"Sure thing, honey. You have a safe trip up here. I'll see you then. Love you." She hit the end button before he changed his mind and asked more about Ben. Looking at her notifications, she saw that she had three missed calls from an unknown caller. Maybe Ben put her number in his phone without her knowledge. She'd have to mention it to him the next time she saw him. She rolled her shoulders trying to ease the tension.

Void entered the room and jumped on her desk then sat in the middle of her keyboard. "Are you trying to tell me something?" she asked, scratching his chin. She hadn't left the house since starting, only stepping away from the computer long enough to sleep and take care of hers and the animals needs.

Glancing out the window, she noticed a dark blue car parked along the road. "They are probably checking out the lake," she said to the cat, dismissively.

Her gaze drifted to the other window and Ben's house. She felt like it had been forever since they had seen each other and decided she'd go visit him. She headed out of the room and down the hall. Before she went anywhere, she needed to take a shower.

BEN WAS TRYING TO FIGURE out an excuse to go see Abbi. He wanted to give her space, but it was driving him crazy. The last time he saw her was magical. Kissing her in the moonlight would have been magical, if only he hadn't had that feeling they weren't alone.

As far as he could tell there was no one. The dogs hadn't seemed bothered; neither of them made a fuss. But he felt something was out of place. He stayed there for a bit longer after she had gone in, trying to hear in the darkness as to what it could be.

Whatever it was, it had moved on. He wanted nothing more than to take her back to his house for the night but knew she wouldn't have it. It had been five days of not seeing her, five days of fighting with himself. He needed to see how she was doing, even if she turned him away.

Going into the utility room, he snapped open a toolbox. Checking the contents, he closed the lid and carried it out to the dining room table. He would go over to her house and fix her step. Grabbing his jacket, he slipped it on and took an apple from the bowl on the table. Biting it, he held it there in his teeth as he retrieved the toolbox and snatched his keys from the side table. He opened the door and frowned.

What the hell is that? It looked like dried blood.

Setting the toolbox on the porch, he bent closer to get a better look at it. There were several drops of blood on each step, a fair amount had pooled at the door, then dripped back down the steps again... towards Abbi's house.

At once, Ben felt the panic rise in his throat. Tossing his apple into the yard, he slammed the door shut and sailed down the steps. Crashing through the trees straight for Abbi's house, he made it there in less than a minute. He bounded up the stairs and he started pounding on her door.

Why can't that woman ever answer her bloody door?

"Aargh!" he yelled, as he shoved his fingers through his hair in frustration. He rushed to the window, cupping his hands around his eyes to look inside. The dogs weren't there. That was good. Calming down at that discovery he saw her car in the laneway. Maybe they walked to the store. Ben cast his eyes to the road. Shielding them from the brightness of the sun, he looked to see if she was walking down it. All he saw was a dark blue car pulled off to the shoulder. He stalked back to the door. *One more round of pounding wasn't going to hurt,* he thought as he thumped with both fists, shouting her name.

Abbi was standing in the shower. She rolled her neck as the steamy water rained over her tired tight muscles. It was working, the tension was slowly easing up. As much as she hated the thought of getting out, she had to, she was running out of hot water.

Lucy and Brutus were waiting for her to step out of the shower, their tongues at the ready to lap the water droplets off her legs. She turned off the tap and jumped as Brutus gave a sharp bark. "Crap Brutus! What's the matter with you?"

Stepping out, she grabbed a towel off the rack and wrapped it around her head. Lucy trailed after her, licking her legs as she walked over to the door. Taking her robe off the hook she stuck her arm in and froze.

Abbi heard something. Standing still to get a better listen, she waited. Nothing. She slipped on her robe the rest of the way. There it was again. Someone was pounding extremely hard... By the sounds of it, on her front door. She slid the bathroom door open, and the dogs shoved past her, running to the front door barking their heads off.

She ran into her bedroom and hurriedly donned a sweatshirt and jeans. She quickly went to answer the door before whoever it was, broke it down.

BEN STOPPED POUNDING when he heard the dogs barking on the other side. Something had to be wrong with her. Why else did it take them so long to come running? "That's it. I'm breaking it down." Backing up as far as the porch edge would allow, he took a deep breath then hissed it out, steeling himself for the impact. He knew he'd have to put his shoulder into it, and knew it was going to hurt like hell.

"Here goes nothing." Taking another deep breath, he took a run at it, turning to put his shoulder into it. For good measure, he let out a yell that would match the call of any war cry in history.

"Who in the world is yelling like that?" Abbi flung open the door. "Sweet baby Jesus!" she shrieked, jumping back just in time from being plowed by... "Ben?!"

Ben just kept going... and yelling. The dogs gave chase as he landed with an "Oomph," smashing his shoulder on the floor.

Well, at least it wasn't the door, he thought lying in pain. He didn't move.

"What the...?" Abbi slammed the door shut and rushed to him. "Are you okay?"

He pulled himself to a sitting position and looked up at her. "Yeah. Where were you?" he asked, annoyance etched on his face as he held his arm.

"What do you mean, where was I? I was here, taking a shower." She pointed to the towel on her head.

"Oh," he said, feeling like a fool. "Right... sorry," he mumbled.

"You're hurt. Come on, get up." She reached around his waist, helping him to his feet, she ushered him to the table.

She pulled out a chair. "Here, sit down. Take your jacket and shirt off."

He raised his brows in surprise.

"I want to look at your shoulder, silly," she smiled.

"Oh, sure." He sat down and said, "Bloody hell, you have a hard floor." He winced while slipping his jacket off, struggling to move his arm. "Um... Abbi, can you help with my shirt? I can't seem to lift my arm."

She mentally braced herself; she remembered what he looked like without a shirt on.

"Um. Yep, I can do that," she answered, lifting the hem of his shirt.

God, how I've missed her, he thought, breathing in her scent. He closed his eyes, hiding the heat from her, that he knew was there. Her fingers accidentally grazed his stomach. He gasped at her touch, a touch that caused a shiver to run through him.

"Sorry! I'm trying not to hurt you any more than you already are."

"It's okay, I don't mind. I don't think it's too bad," he muffled into his shirt as she slipped it over his head.

She gently pulled it down his injured arm, sucking in a breath at the sight of it as she did so. She lightly laid a hand on his skin, shocked to see it was already turning an angry purple. "Oh lord that doesn't look good. How bad does it hurt?"

"Ah, not too bad, I suppose," he lied. He was no stranger to pain; he'd had his share of sprains and pulled muscles doing many of his own stunts. But if he was honest, on a pain scale of one to ten, it was a solid fifteen.

Rushing to the fridge, Abbi pulled out the freezer drawer, searching for an ice pack. Coming up empty, she grabbed a bag of frozen peas, took a clean towel out of a drawer and wrapped the bag in it. Snatching a bottle of water from the fridge and some ibuprofen from the window ledge, Abbi went back to him.

"Here, take these." She handed him a couple of pills and opened the water bottle before passing it to him. She took the wrapped peas and gently placed them on his shoulder. "Do you think you can move it at all?"

He did a bit, grimacing when he felt a burning sensation shoot to his hand. "I think it will be fine, just need a few days of rest," he said, looking up at her. "I'm sure it will be good as new, then."

"Were you planning on breaking my door down?" she asked, chuckling at the image of him charging into her house, as it played in her mind.

"Actually, yes I was," he nodded. "I came over to fix your step before someone breaks their neck on it. But when I came out of my house, there was a trail of blood leading up the steps and back down again towards here." He studied her face for a reaction.

That sobered her up. "You thought it was me?"

"I thought something might have been wrong, yes. Something might have happened to you. I panicked and now I feel like a fool."

She watched the expressions play over his features. It touched Abbi, not only from what he said but what his face showed.

"Oh, before I forget, take my phone. It's in my jacket pocket there. Please put your number in for me," he said, reaching up with his good hand to hold the bag of peas in place.

She glanced at him as she did what he asked.

"What is it?" he asked, noticing the look of confusion that crossed her lovely face.

She shrugged. "It's nothing. I just had three missed unknown calls earlier. I was thinking it might have been you."

Ben sat, lost in thought.

"As I said, it's nothing... happens all the time." She placed his cell on the table. "Now, let me take another look."

He looked up at her as he removed the bag and noticed the concern on her brow.

She laid her hand over his shoulder. It felt warm but not hot, but then again, he did just have ice on it. She leaned over and brushed her lips ever so lightly over his skin.

"Um, sorry. I wasn't thinking." She stood and took a step back when she saw the desire leap in his eyes.

She realized she couldn't keep doing this to him. The problem was she couldn't help herself. She knew what she wanted, and that was him; she just didn't want her kids finding out. Which was going to be a little hard with them coming up in a few days. There was no way she could stay away from Ben, nor did she want to. It was time. They needed to talk and the sooner the better.

"I think the pills are kicking in," he said, flexing his hand.

Thinking what her life would be like without him in it brought a sting to her eyes. It was a thought that she wasn't going to entertain any longer. Turning to him, she asked quietly, "Can you stay for a bit, Ben? We need to talk."

He saw the sadness in her eyes. In all honesty, what he saw in them made him want to fly back to England this second. "Yeah... sure Abbi. I can stay," he replied, disheartened.

Chapter 13

BEN SAT IN THE SAME chair on the porch that he had the first night of meeting her, waiting for her to join him. It was cruel in a way to have him come out there. Since the minute he saw the look on her face, he knew she was going to tell him it was over, and it scared the hell out of him. He could already feel the knife piercing his heart. It amazed him at how quickly the thought of losing her was turning him into a nervous wreck.

He honestly didn't know if he could handle it. When his ex and he had split, he had made a vow never to get involved with another woman unless he was sure she wanted the same thing. And he hadn't... until Abbi. She was different. But if that was what she wanted, then he just had to accept it. He wouldn't resort to begging, despite wanting to.

He tensed as he felt the breeze from her passing by, as she headed to the other chair.

"Here you go," she said. Setting a cup down beside him on the table, she took her seat. "I made us some tea." When he didn't say anything, she glanced at him and took a double take.

He was sitting, looking straight ahead, as if he was carved from stone.

His shoulder must be in agony....

Absently, she reached out to touch his thigh. "Ben are you okay?" she asked worriedly, studying his face. His gaze dropped to where her hand rested on his leg.

Abbi watched him lick his lips as confusion flashed across his handsome face.

He cleared his throat as he turned towards her, his eyes darted to her face. He was going to tell her to just get it over with, but he lost the nerve to do so.

Picturing the worst-case scenarios of what could be wrong with his arm in her mind, in a hurried panic she said, "Ben, we need to go now to the clinic."

All Ben heard was 'need to go now'. With a jerk of his head, he readied himself to stand. "Right, I won't bother you ever again."

She put out a hand to hold him in place. "*Wait*. What are you *talking* about?" Her concern exploded. "Did you hit your head when you fell?" she asked, laying a cool hand on his forehead. "My God Ben, you're so clammy!"

He reached up to grab her wrist; her touch scorching him. "Abbi, I'm fine. I have to go." He dropped her arm and started pushing himself up with his good hand to stand.

She was faster. She planted herself in front of him, blocking him from moving. "Like hell you do, mister. The only place you're going to is the clinic or my couch, you decide." She stood, tapping her foot impatiently.

He looked up at her, giving her a laugh of derision. "What do you want from me, Abbi? Tell me now!" His eyes pleaded with her. "Because I would really like to know."

He tore his gaze away, refusing to look at her.

Startled, she wondered where this was coming from and what had happened from the time, he left the kitchen until now. "What I want from you is to know what the hell is bothering you," she responded softly, kneeling in front of him.

He looked like someone had just punched him in the gut.

"How can you even ask me that? You said we needed to talk." He looked at her then. "The look on your face said it all. I know you want me to leave you alone, so please, step aside so I can do that."

Abbi was wracking her brain trying to figure out what she had been thinking when she had said that. She remembered now. Yes, they needed to talk, talk about this weekend coming up and how stressed she was for her kids to meet him.

Why was he giving up so easily?

Did everything they share mean so little to him? She had to know. She couldn't just let him walk away without ever knowing.

"Will you look me in the eyes? Please?"

When he didn't move a muscle, she reached up to caress his cheek. He closed his eyes in response.

Why did she have to do that? And why am I still sitting here enduring this torture?

"Ben, what do you want?" he heard her asking.

He turned his face towards her hand on his cheek. His mouth finding the center of her palm, he kissed her softly one last time before he backed off forever.

"Abbi, what I want doesn't matter."

Dropping her hand, she said firmly. "Yes, it does!"

Anger flashed in his eyes. "You're really something, aren't you? What do you want to hear, Abbi... hmm? Do you want to hear how the mere sight of you drives me insane?" Frustrated beyond belief he shoved his hands through his hair, groaned at the pain it caused. Ignoring it, he continued, "Or how the scent of you makes my heart feel like it's going to jump out of my chest?"

He decided to hell with it. He'd pour his soul out to her. "How about when you touch me? It feels like a thousand bolts of lightning coursing through my veins, or when you kiss me. Soft as a feather brushing against my lips, then crashing into a crescendo of waves, drowning me..." He threw a hand in her direction, accusingly "And *you!* ... You're my only lifeline," he mumbled miserably. Finally, he stopped, and stared into her eyes... eyes, he saw swimming with tears.

Taking a calming breath, he continued, "You want to know what else drives me insane?" he asked, softly, not waiting for a response. "The way you talk to yourself when you think no one is around and the way you make me laugh when you're not even trying."

He cupped her face with his hand and whispered softly, "The way your eyes change from soft to smoldering with one blink, or the way your tears rip my soul apart like they are doing right now."

That did it. The dam broke. Her tears were overflowing in streams down her face now. She didn't care that she was on the verge of an ugly cry, damn it. She. Did. Not. Care. Knowing he thought she wanted nothing to do with him, crushed her. Then, to hear her described through his eyes was more than she could handle. She couldn't respond, for the life of her.

"I never wanted to tell you any of this Abbi. I never wanted to make you feel pressured into being with me."

Ben wanted to rub his hands down her arms, to touch her back and hug her fiercely to take her pain away, but he dared not. He knew if he did, he could never let her go.

"What I'm trying to say, Abbi." He lifted her chin, looking deeply into her eyes. "What I want is you, no one else but you. If that's something you want right now, not tomorrow... not next week, but today..." He paused, and sighed, "...then please, don't make me wait anymore. Tell me what you want because I can't keep doing this. I can't keep living, not knowing from day to day what I am to you... what I mean to you."

He fell silent, waiting for her to tell him to get out.

The ugly crying was happening, and it was raw. She placed her hands on his knees, clawing her way up onto his lap. She straddled his legs and wrapped her arms around his neck and laid her head on his shoulder and sobbed.

She felt his good arm come around her, followed slowly by the other. This man was not going anywhere she decided as her tears subsided. She kissed the side of his neck then leaned back. Placing her hands on either side of his face, she searched his eyes.

"I'm sorry, I wet your shirt," she hiccupped stroking his face.

"It's fine," he smiled softly.

"No, it's not!" Her voice broke. Her face was going to do it again! She could feel it scrunching up despite her trying unsuccessfully to stop it. The damn thing had a mind of its own.

She pulled his face towards hers. Running her fingers through his hair, softly touching his lips with her own. She held on for dear life as she deepened the kiss. Ben was the first to break it off, searching her eyes, her face captivating him.

"You have never been more beautiful to me than you are at this very moment," he murmured, his eyes dropping to her lips, then back up to her red rimmed eyes. He softly kissed each one as he whispered, "Does this mean no more waiting, no more guessing?"

She sat back on his thighs and planted her feet on either side of his legs. "Ahh," she exhaled a long breath as she wiped her eyes on her sleeves. She stopped to look at him. "How's your shoulder?"

"Abbi, it's fine, still sore but getting better." He lied again.

"Good, good. Um I don't know how to tell you this. But the reason I said we needed to talk was that my kids are coming up this weekend, should be here Thursday." She paused and analyzed his face. She thought for sure she'd see remorse there of his admission. When there wasn't she continued. "And I wanted to see if you would come here to celebrate with us." She covered her mouth with her hand, waiting for his response.

"I'll come. But just so you know," he said as he took her hand away and held it, "everything I said to you, it came from my soul. I regret nothing."

He brought her hand to his lips, kissing the back of it as he looked into her eyes, "Are you going to answer me now?"

Abbi cleared her throat. "Just so you know, everything you said, how you feel about me, it's like you were reading my thoughts... about you. I would be crazy to let that go... let you go... without seeing how things might be."

Ben had waited for what seemed like an eternity to hear those words from her sweet lips. He laid his hand against the side of her neck, guiding her to him and lightly brushed her mouth with his. Passion rose sharp and swift for both, as they clung to one another, their kiss intensifying.

Brutus came barreling out the door, startling them apart. He headed straight to the water's edge, and began growling, and pacing back and forth.

Abbi got up from Ben's lap and stood. Looking out over the water, all she could see was a boat roughly 100 feet from her shore. Ben now saw it too.

"Do you know them?" he asked as he stood with a frown, remembering the night he felt something was off.

"It's hard to make out the person, but the boat is a rental from down the road, must be someone on vacation." She shrugged it off. "Are you hungry?" she looked over her shoulder, as she took a step into the house. "Those pills must be wearing off by now."

"Ah, yeah, a bit of both," he replied absently, turning to follow her in. He stopped and glanced back towards the water. The boat was still there. God only knew how long it had been there before the dog had spied it.

That uneasy feeling from a few nights ago was back. Ben gave a sharp whistle, calling Brutus back to the house. Waiting for the beast to bound up the steps, his eyes never left the boat. He didn't see a glint off a zoom lens, so he felt confident it wasn't the paparazzi. Ben followed Brutus as he sailed through the door and made sure he closed it tightly and locked the handle and deadbolt. If it wasn't the paparazzi, then who was it?

Chapter 14

Abbi was standing at the counter chopping vegetables for the stir-fry she was making for dinner. She had put the animals' dishes down and Brutus was already devouring his.

She wondered what was taking Ben so long. She could have sworn he was right behind her when she came into the house. Just as she was going to call out to him, he came around the corner talking on his cell. And from the sounds of it, he was getting frustrated.

"Mum, no... I'm... No. I'm good." Pausing, he moved the phone away, rolled his eyes, and returned it to his ear.

Smirking, Abbi continued to listen to the one-sided conversation as she dumped the veggies in a pan.

"Yeah, Mum. Yes, I'm eating!" With another pause, he exclaimed, "No! Don't do that! You stay there! Put Dad on, will you? Yes, I love you, too. ... Dad! Thank God! Will you..." Moving the phone away from his mouth, he groaned in frustration listening to his dad. He inhaled deeply, raised his brows, and licked his lips. He looked as if he was mentally counting to ten. Impatience was etched on his face, no doubt about it, but, yet he held his tongue. At that moment, Abbi thought he was beautiful.

Can a man be considered beautiful? She decided this man could.

She heard a sizzling... the telltale sound of the pan beginning to scorch. She whipped around to the stove just in time and peered at their dinner.

Meh, a little scorched food never hurt anyone.

"I'm good Dad, more than good. That's why I need you to keep Mum there just a bit longer, you know?" He paused, listening. "I know she misses me. I miss both of you. But... I've met someone, Dad. Someone..."

Abbi turned back around as she heard Ben's father yelling through the phone, clear across the room. A grin broke out on Ben's face as he held the phone at arm's length.

Returning it to his ear once the shouting simmered down, she heard him say, "Her name is Abbi, and she's gorgeous." He smiled at her and shot her a smoking hot look that made her melt on the spot.

"Yeah... right, right... Yes, exactly! Thank you, Dad. I promise to let you know as soon as I can, alright? No, I don't want to talk to mum again, just tell her I'll call soon.... Love you, too. Bye."

Ben disconnected the call and walked directly over to Abbi. He brought his arm around her, his hand splayed across her belly, drawing her to him. Leaning down, he kissed the side of her neck just below her ear. A thrilling shiver raced along her spine as goosebumps played over her skin.

Breathlessly, she said, "Dinner is ready," as she looked over her shoulder to meet his lips.

He turned her towards him, never breaking contact with her mouth. Deepening the kiss, he brought her up tight against his arousal. She had a fleeting thought of how foolish she'd been mistaking *that* for a sock! She moaned in response. For better leverage, she grabbed hold of his shoulders, causing him to gasp in pain.

Oh, my goodness, his shoulder...!

"This will have to wait." She backed away looking up at him, with worry in her eyes. "Let's eat, shall we? I'll get you more pain pills."

Pushing him towards the table, she grabbed the bottle from the window ledge and stuffed it in her pocket. She took two plates down from the cupboard, utensils from the drawer, grabbed a potholder, stuck a ladle in the pan, and headed to the table.

"I'm sorry. I don't do fancy around here." Setting the plates on the table, she tossed the potholder down and set the frying pan on it. "Can you help yourself, or do you want—"

"I'm fine Abbi, sit down."

"Oh wait, before I forget... here." She opened the pill bottle and shook out two tablets. Setting them on the table beside his fork she turned to get them each a drink.

"Abbi, sit. You don't have to wait on me hand and foot," he said, with a happy grin.

"Relax! I'm just grabbing us a drink. Believe you me, enjoy it while you can," she laughed, returning with two glasses of iced tea. "Besides, you only have one good hand at the moment, I don't mind." She took her seat, her eyes grew large as she looked down at her plate, noticing he had filled it... the whole plate. She smiled her thanks as she picked up her fork.

With the first bite, Ben groaned in pure delight. "My God, Abbi this is delicious," he said, smacking his lips.

"Thanks," she laughed, watching him eat the burnt food with gusto. "What have you been eating exactly since you moved here?"

"Oh, you know," he shrugged. "Apples, eggs, and crisps," he grinned.

She shook her head. "No wonder you like this so much," she said. Glancing at her plate she stabbed a broccoli floret with her fork. "So how are your parents doing?" she raised her eyes to him.

Grabbing a napkin from the holder in the middle of the table, Ben wiped his mouth. "Good." He chuckled. "My mum has been trying to convince my dad to fly over since the day I left, apparently."

"Really? That's sweet. I give her credit for her restraint. Honestly, if it were one of my kids that moved across the world, I would have left an hour after them. Well, maybe."

"Huh... I never really thought of it from her perspective before," Ben said. "She drives me crazy at times, honestly, but she is my mum. It's her right, I suppose."

"Absolutely it is," she laughed. She'd had enough of the food; the burnt taste wasn't doing it for her. Getting up to dump her food in the garbage, Ben put a hand on her arm, stopping her. "Wait, what are you doing with that?" he asked looking at the plate in her hand.

She paused. She seriously believed he was only being nice when he said it was delicious. She raised a brow, "Do you want it?"

"Sure!" he said, taking it from her.

She sat back down and watched him for a minute before she spoke. "So, when you're done eating, I want to take another look at your shoulder."

He noticed the worry was back on her face. "It's fine Abbi, really it is."

If he was being honest, it felt like he broke something. He just didn't want to alarm her.

She shook her head. "I don't care. I'm looking at it. If it's worse, we are going to the clinic... and then you can stay here tonight when we get back."

With the last bit of food on his fork, his hand froze midway to his mouth as his eyes darted to hers. His face lit up. "Really?" His brows rose as a smile broke on his lips.

Nodding she replied, "Yes." Without missing a beat, she added, "In the spare room."

His face fell, recovering quickly with a stern look, he gave a curt nod. "Oh... Yeah, right." He shrugged. "I knew that."

She laughed at him as she took the dirty dishes to the sink. "One day, perhaps... possibly soon," she whispered under her breath.

Noticing that he looked like a kid on Christmas morning she realized he'd heard her mutterings. Blushing terribly, she walked to him and laid her hand on his back. "Time to let me see what's going on with your shoulder."

"You just enjoy seeing me with my shirt off," he teased, lifting the hem of his t-shirt.

"Guilty," she chuckled, turning beet red. She did enjoy seeing him with his shirt off. Any women with a set of eyes in her head would, she wasn't going to deny it. Sighing softly, she was in a daze of a memory. She loved watching his muscles ripple under his skin. Skin so soft to the...

Abbi get a grip and help the man!!

Once he freed his good arm, she helped him lift it over his head and down the other to expose his shoulder area.

Oh no. No, no, that can't be good...

His shoulder was swollen. She laid her hand gently on his skin, trying to feel around for something out of place. She did feel something but wasn't entirely sure what. She wished Kim her sister was here. Being a nurse, she would know what to do.

The bruising had spread from the shoulder down his arm and up towards his neck. She stepped back and saw that it was noticeably lower.

"Does your neck hurt?" she asked.

He rotated it. "Hmm, a bit, nothing out of the ordinary, though."

"Try to look down," she suggested.

He did and said with surprise, "Huh... my chest is bruised."

Abbi jerked her eyes to his chest, her eyes darting everywhere but at the bruising. "Oh my," she sighed, breathlessly. "I just said that out loud, didn't I." *Damn it, and that too!*

She swallowed hard as Ben looked into her eyes, "What do you suppose it is?" he asked, completely ignoring the fact she spoke her thoughts out loud.

"Um... it's your chest." She pointed to the bruising that she just now saw, felt her face go red again as her heart raced.

Laughing, Ben grabbed her hand, laying it over his heart. "You do the same thing to me Abbi. See?" he murmured, holding her hand there.

She could feel the beat of it racing faster with just the touch of her hand.

Leaning down, she placed her free hand on his thigh and looked him straight in the eyes. "As much as I would love to sit here all night feeling each others heartbeats, we need to get you to the clinic... now," she said, planting a quick kiss on his lips. She took his shirt and helped him put it back on. "I'm just going to grab a sweater," she told him, disappearing down a hallway.

He moved to get up, walking to the door he waited for her to join him.

"I'm ready. Let's go," she said, shoving her arms into the sleeves of a downy soft sweater.

Ben opened the door to let her pass by. "Hey, aren't you going to set the alarm?" he questioned, surprised when she didn't.

"Nah, it'll be fine, the clinic is like two seconds from Mack's," she responded lightly, grabbing her keys and purse.

"Abbi set the alarm. Please," he said, a pressing tone in his voice.

She searched his face. "Okay, if it means that much to you," she punched in the code.

"It does," he quietly said. Something was going on; he had been playing this game far too long to be blind from what was happening. Someone was snooping around. He just wasn't sure who it was yet.

"SO, IT LOOKS LIKE YOU have a dislocated shoulder," Doc Spence said as he breezed into the examination room. He pulled up the x-rays on the computer screen and turned it for Ben and Abbi to see.

"Hell, no wonder it hurts like a bugger," Ben muttered, as he looked at the monitor.

"Yup. So, what we need to do now is pop it back into place and put a brace on it, which you will need to wear for a few weeks until the swelling and pain subside."

Doc Spence moved to a cabinet along the wall. Taking a syringe out of a tray, he tore the packaging off and stuck it into a small glass vial.

Abbi watched as the clear liquid filled the plastic tube. She hated needles and when Doc turned to Ben, she felt the colour drain from her face and could no longer watch. Instead, she jerked her eyes to the ceiling and started counting the holes in the tiles.

Doc wiped an alcohol-soaked cotton ball over his shoulder. He picked up the syringe and said, "Now, this will sting a bit, but only for a moment."

He poked the needle in Ben's shoulder, pushing the plunger down. "It should only take a few minutes for the freezing to kick in. Be right back," he said as he headed out the door.

Abbi was sitting on a chair while Ben sat on the exam table. She reached over to rub his thigh. "You should have told me how bad it was hurting."

"Meh," he shrugged his good shoulder. "It's not a big deal, and we needed to hash out more important things," he said, taking her hand in his. "And you should have told me how much you hate needles," he grinned, rubbing his thumb across the back of her hand.

Just then the doctor returned. "How's it feeling?" he asked, taking out a tool to test the freezing.

"Good, I can't feel much of anything now."

"Great! I'll get you to lie down, flat on your back," Doc said, taking Ben's arm as he did so.

"Abbi, I'll get you to go on the other side of Ben here, and grip that sheet that's under him. Hang on tight... we don't want him slipping off the table."

Abbi balked at helping, but she jumped up and went around to the other side, gripping the sheet with both hands. "Now what?" she asked, licking her suddenly dry lips.

"Now lean back, he's pretty solid," Doc instructed.

You don't know the half of it, Doc...

"Okay, slowly throw your weight against it," he told her as he did the same, gently he tugged on Ben's arm, slowly rotating it as he did.

Abbi's heart went out to Ben as she watched a sheen of sweat break out on his skin, a grimace of pain etched on his handsome face.

"Yup, that's it," Doc said, "just... a... bit... more."

Abbi heard a pop, followed by immediate relief on Ben's face.

"There you go!" Doc said, moving Ben's arm at different angles. "There is still a bit of freezing, but how does that feel?"

"Much better, thank you."

Doc made his way to the door. "Awesome, once the freezing comes out, it will hurt like a bitch, so I'll write up a script for some pain meds. Only take them as needed after the first day," Doc looked at him sternly.

At Ben's nod, he smacked the side of the door frame and tossed over his shoulder as he headed out the door, "Good, be right back."

Ben sat up on the edge of the bed and patted the spot beside him for Abbi to sit down. He put an arm around her, bringing her close.

"Thanks, luv." He planted a kiss on her forehead.

She looked up at him. "For what?"

"For making me come here. For holding onto the sheet, when I could see that you clearly didn't want to," he snickered.

"I didn't want to cause you any more pain. Honestly, I wanted to yell at him to stop, but, thought better of it," she smiled. "I mean he is the doctor."

Doc returned with a brace in one hand and a script in the other, that he handed to Abbi. She got up and moved out of the way so he could put the brace on Ben.

"Okay, so, keep this on for the first forty-eight hours at least. You can take it off to shower but immediately put it back on and make sure you keep it on while you sleep. I'll put this sling on you too, it will help to keep it immobilized. That script I gave Abbi you can fill it at the pharmacy next door. I checked and they have it in stock. Also, do you have someone at home with you?" He looked at Ben, as he tied the sling around his neck.

"No I don't, it's just me."

Doc turned to Abbi. "He can't be left alone... not while on those pills."

She nodded her understanding. "He will stay with me," she said, darting a glance at Ben.

Turning back to Ben, Doc said, "I gave you enough for five days. Come back if it doesn't start feeling better by then. And I repeat... only take them as prescribed, starting when you get home." Before stepping away, Doc added, "Oh, before I forget, can you sign this?"

Doc Spence handed him his prescription pad. At Ben's questioning look he chuckled, "I'm a huge fan, seen all your movies."

Ben let out a bark of laughter at the doctor's admission. "Right, sure," he said, smiling, he took the proffered pen. He scribbled on the pad and handed it back.

"Thanks Doc," he said, holding out his good hand to shake.

"You're welcome. Abbi, you got a minute?" Doc asked, jerking his head towards the waiting area.

"Um, yeah," she said, getting up to follow him.

He's going to ask me what's going on, I just know it...

Her and Doc Spence had known each other since she moved to Pearl Lake. They had gone to Mack's a few times for coffee, but that's as far as it went.

"What's up?" she asked when she was out of Ben's earshot.

He took his glasses off. "Those pills I gave him... if he acts out of sorts at all, call me at once. They are highly addictive."

"Can't you give him something else? What about an over-the-counter pain med?"

He shook his head. "Wouldn't even touch the pain he will be feeling in the next 48 hours. I called the pharmacy to see what they had in stock before I even mentioned it, knowing he'd need something. That's all they have."

"What if something was shipped in? Just give him a couple of days' worth. Would that be okay?" she asked, concerned. "I mean, he is an adult so I can't decide for him, but..."

"We will leave it as it is for now. He's only to get one every 12 hours. I'll call in the morning to Springbank and see if I can get something brought in. If I can, I'll just put the order in and get it sent out to your house?"

She nodded. "Yeah, that's fine."

"Another thing. What's going on between you two?"

Leaning against the secretary's desk, he looked at her with a smile, then folded his arms across his chest, waiting for her response.

"Whatever do you mean Doc?" she looked at him innocently.

"Come on Abbi," he motioned with his hand. "A blind man could see the way you two look at each other."

Blushing to the tips of her roots, she cleared her throat. "Um, well... whatever you think is going on between us," she gave a quick nod as she continued, "is going on."

Here it comes, he's going to tell me I'm robbing the damn cradle.

She braced for the impact of those words.

"That's... awesome!" he said, his face breaking out into a huge grin. "Honestly, Abbi, I think that's great!"

He grabbed her in a bear hug just as Ben stepped out of the exam room. Seeing Abbi in the arms of the doctor brought an immediate sense of jealousy to Ben. He never felt like that before.

Man, get a grip, they're friends...

He cleared his throat to make his arrival known.

"Hey Ben." The doctor dropped his arms and took a step towards him, holding his arms out wide. "I have to congratulate the man that captured our Abbi's heart here... didn't think that would ever happen," he said with a chuckle, putting his arms around Ben to hug him but stopped when he remembered why there were there. "Whoops watch that arm," Doc laughed, smacking him on the back instead.

Ben felt like a fool, jumping to the worst-case scenario for nothing. He'd been doing a lot of that lately. "Thanks." Glancing at Abbi, Ben said, "She gave me a run for my money, and I'd do it all over again, every day of my life if I had to," he spoke only to her, forgetting that the doctor was there.

Abbi held out her hand and wiggled her fingers. "Come on. Let's go home. See you later, Doc." They waved their goodbyes as they walked out to her waiting car.

ABBI WAS ABOUT TO PULL away from the curb when she remembered the medication. "Damn, I forgot your prescription." She threw the gearshift into park and reached to take her seat belt off when she felt his hand stopping her.

"Abbi just go home. I'll just take what you were giving me."

"But Doc said..."

She was cut off by his lips on hers. He moved so quickly he made her head spin.

Good Lord, I'm melting...

He pulled away just far enough to mumble against her mouth. "Go home, now, please." Quickly he touched her mouth once more before sitting back in his seat.

She sucked in a deep breath to settle her racing heart. "Okay, I can do that," she nodded with determination.

Just before pulling onto the road, she had a giddy thought. She didn't know if she should be happy or running in the other direction. Her mind was in overdrive.

I'm in for one hell of a ride, aren't I? Too late Abbi girl, you're head over heels for him...

With a stupid grin on her face, she glanced over her shoulder before pulling onto the road.

REACHING OVER, A GLOVED hand, lovingly stroked the blood-red roses that were lying on the seat next to them.

Hmm, interesting. She's hanging around Ben Everett a little too much... What does she see in HIM when she can have ME? It's time I finally get noticed; I think. Yes, most definitely. He's sniffing around my Abbi just a little too much lately.

The hand crushed the flowers, destroying them, thorns, and all. Blood dripped from the leather clad hand.

Oh well, what's a little more bloodshed. You would have thought the gift I left on Benny boy's step would have backed him off. Some are harder to convince than others, I suppose...

They threw their head back and laughed. Their cackle echoing along the empty road as they drove the familiar route to Abbi's house.

Chapter 15

It was almost dark as Abbi drove towards home. It was that time of night when headlights were not all that effective in lighting the way.

Ben was awfully quiet. Just past the bend that would take them straight to their homes, she took her eyes off the road for a second to look at him. Finding him asleep, she turned her attention back to the road. Instinctively, she quickly shot her arm out in front of him as she slammed on the brakes. Ben jerked awake looking around rapidly, not focusing on anything.

"What the bloody hell?" he asked, confused. He looked down at his chest where Abbi's hand laid. Taking hold of it, he wondered what she was doing.

He looked over at her to find her staring out the windshield, shaking like a leaf. "Abbi, what is wrong?" he asked, adrenaline racing through his veins. He looked to where she was staring. There, where the trees grew on both sides, sat a medium-sized bear in the middle of the road.

"Is that the same bear we saw the other day?" he asked.

She looked at him as if he were insane.

"What? If that were the bear, how would I know? They all look the same. That's a dog Ben, a shaggy, dirty black dog…. and I almost hit him." Taking her seat belt off, she reached into the back seat, producing a pair of gloves. Putting them on, she opened her door and slowly got out.

"Wait for me!" Ben said hurriedly, struggling with his seat belt.

She paused, never taking her eyes off the mutt. Finally, he joined her in front of the car.

"Do you think he'll come to us?" Ben asked.

"I don't know. Let's find out." Cautiously she walked towards the dog, cooing to it, "It's okay boy. We won't hurt you."

The dog responded by standing on all fours, it's body tense, ready to bolt.

"I think he's going to dart Abbi," Ben muttered. "Let me try."

He went down on his knees, edging closer and closer to it. The dog took a step forward, slowly stretching out its nose to Ben's extended hand.

Abbi froze, she dared not make a move, fearing the dog would attack Ben. She held her breath, watching as it tucked its tail between its legs. Abbi found it strange that its fur shimmered in the beam of the headlights as if it were coated with oil. Being a black dog, it was hard to tell exactly what it was.

"Be careful, it might lunge at you," she warned.

"It's okay. I'm not going to hurt you." Ben crooned softly. Even the dog couldn't resist that tone of voice. Stretching its neck as far as possible, the mutt sniffed the air, then it's tongue darted out to lick his hand. "That's right, we're here to help," he said, slowly getting to his feet. Just as slowly, he backed towards the car.

The dog took tentative steps towards him, only to stop and glance around. As it got closer, Abbi saw its fur was covered in blood.

Alarmed, she cried out, "It's bleeding!"

Ben turned to look at her, his brow creased. "Are you certain?" At her nod, he told her, "I'll walk to your place. Hopefully, he will follow."

"With what you've just been through? No. It's fine. If you can get him into the car, it will be faster anyway." She got in behind the steering wheel, softly closed her door.

Ben shook his head and looked at her through his open window. "I don't want him bleeding all over your seats Abbi."

"Really, it's fine. The seats will wash and by the looks of this guy, he needs some medical attention now. And besides, you're exhausted."

He couldn't argue with that.

Ben opened the back passenger door. "Come on boy," he softly called, patting the seat in hopes the dog would take the hint. He was relieved when it took one leap into the car, turned itself around and laid down. He slammed the door shut before getting in the front.

"Where will we find a vet this late at night?" he asked, glancing in the back when the dog let out a huge sigh.

"Well, this pooch is in luck. Mack is a retired Veterinarian." Turning the car around to head back to the store, she glanced at him, "Hopefully, he's chipped so we can get him back to his owner."

"Hmm." Deep in thought, Ben asked, "What will happen to him if there is no owner found?"

"It's hard to say, really. The closest shelter is in Springbank," she glanced at him. "Why... what do you have in mind?"

"Oh, I'm just thinking if he has no home, I can take him in... I would need to figure out what I would do with him when I have to leave for filming."

"I could watch him over at my place. If he gets along with Brutus and Lucy, I don't mind."

"That would be great. Unless, of course, he has a home to go to."

"That too," she said, pulling up beside Mack's store. "Let's find out." Abbi opened her door and ducked her head down to look at him. "You stay here. I'll just get Mack to come out for a minute." She turned and jogged into the store.

THE DARK BLUE CAR STOPPED on the side of the road. It was almost dark, so it would be easy to see Abbi flitting from room to room in her house.

Silly girl, she should really close her curtains at night.

'But if she did that there would be no way for you to see her you fool!'

That is true. Hmm, the house is in darkness, which is odd. No car either... where did they go off to now?

'You should have been quicker at following them!' the voice screamed.

Panic struck them with the thought of Abbi at Ben's house.

I know. I'll just drive by there... I will say I'm lost if they ask. Yes, that will work. I had better get a move on. I still need to make that special delivery, but only when she's home.

They stroked the broken roses, as they headed towards Ben's house.

BEN GOT OUT AND OPENED the back door. "Come on, let's get you looked at," he murmured, to the sad eyes looking up at him.

Glancing up over the roof of the car, he saw Abbi coming around the front of the vehicle with Mack in tow.

"Hey Mack."

"Hi Ben, how are you doing?" Mack inquired, leaning in the open door to get a look at the dog. "Where did you find him?"

"Just past the bend on our road, he was sitting in the middle of it," Abbi said.

"Okay. Can he walk?" Mack looked to them for an answer.

"Yeah, he can," Ben responded as he called the dog out of the car.

"Let's get him into the back of my store."

Mack led the way to a rear door of the building. Taking out his keys, he unlocked it, pushing it open for them to enter.

"Abbi, will you watch the store front for me for a bit, please? See that door there? Just go through it, and it will take you out by the washrooms," he said, jerking his head towards the door in question.

"Sure thing, Mack," she answered, making her way to it.

"Just leave it open in case we need a hand here. I'll yell for you if we do," Mack said as he got out his medical bag. "Okay. Let's see what we have here. Can you give me a hand lifting him, Ben?"

"Yeah sure, I'll grab the rear if you can get the head," Ben replied, showing him his arm.

"No problem. What did you do to it?" Mack asked, as they settled the dog on the table. "Abbi fall on you or something?" he laughed, as he started checking the dog over.

Ben chuckled. "Nah, nothing like that. It was my own stupidity. I ran to her place after I noticed some blood on my porch, thinking she might have had some trouble."

He scratched his head at the memory. He felt like an ass now, the way he'd reacted.

"Is that so?" Mack shot him a look of concern.

"She didn't answer at first, so I got the idea to bust her door down. I was going full tilt when she opened it." He laughed, as the event replayed in his mind. "I crashed to her floor, and this happened." He lifted his arm in reference. Wishing he hadn't when the pain shot to his wrist. "Dislocated my shoulder. We were just heading back from the clinic when this guy appeared on the road."

"Well, he's lucky you guys came along when you did."

"How is he, Mack? Will he be, okay?"

"Well, I'll give her some shots. Get her caught up on her vaccines, which, by the looks of it, she's sadly lacking," Mack told him, as he readied the needles.

"He's, a she?" Ben looked the dog in the eyes.

"Yep, she is," Mack smiled. "She doesn't have a chip, so not sure where she's from. But that wound there on her side, that's a clean slice. If I'm not mistaken, it looks like they used a scalpel on her," Mack said, with a worried look.

"A scalpel?" Ben asked, shocked. "Who in the hell would do that to an innocent animal?"

"A sick one," Mack replied, adding, "I'm not a hundred percent sure, but I wouldn't discount it either. It's relatively fresh, I would say today, maybe yesterday was the very earliest that it happened."

Mack moved to a counter and removed some medical supplies, he continued, "Luckily, she could reach it and cleaned it herself. But I'll wash the wound and put some glue on it. It should be good as new in a few days." Mack got to work. "Hold her tight Ben. This is going to hurt her."

Ben talked softly to the dog, resting his head on hers. Trying to keep her calm, he could feel her muscles tensing up as if she were planning to bolt from the table.

THE STORE WAS EMPTY and long past closing time. Abbi had tidied up before turning the sign and locking the door. She made her way back to the examination room to see how things were going. Leaning against the door frame, she dared not speak a word for fear of scaring the dog as Mack bent over it and gently cleaned the wound.

Abbi's brow knitted with concern; her heart went out to the hound as it whimpered. She shifted her eyes to Ben, standing head-to-head with the dog.

He's such a remarkable man...

At that moment, Abbi realized how lucky she was to have met him. Not too many men would have bothered with the dog in the first place, let alone rest their head next to an animal so neglected.

Abbi jumped when the dog let out an ear-splitting yelp right next to Ben's head, yet he didn't flinch.

"That's all I can do for her," Mack said, straightening up. "I'll run into the house and get her some antibiotics, just in case," he said, washing his hands.

Grabbing some paper towels, he noticed Abbi standing there. "Hiya Abbi, anyone come in?" he asked, drying his hands off.

"Nope. I turned the sign around to closed, and locked the door for you," she said, slipping her hands into her jean's pockets.

"Good, good. I'm just going to run to the house. Be right back," he stated, leaving the room.

"A girl is she?" Abbi smiled as she came into the room. At Ben's worried nod, she asked, "How's she doing? Is she going to be okay?"

"Yeah. Mack gave her some shots to get her up to date. He checked for a chip and there isn't one." He smiled at that, but it was at once replaced with a look of concern. "Ah, however, her wound... Mack thinks, it's fresh from this morning or yesterday, he can't be certain."

"Is it a bite?" Abbi asked.

"No." Frowning, he shook his head. "Mack's not sure, but he thinks it looks like someone cut her with a scalpel."

"Oh my God, that's terrible!" Abbi cried out. "Who would do such a thing?" she asked in a horrified whisper.

"My sentiments exactly," he nodded in agreement, scratching the dog's chin. "Abbi, there's something I have to tell you—"

Ben was cut off by Mack's return.

"Here you go, guys. I wrote the instructions on the envelope. Just keep her quiet for a few days. I know she's dirty but don't let her get wet, at least not for a day or two preferably," he said, handing the medication over to Ben. "I'll put some feelers out there, see if anyone is missing a dog."

"Thanks Mack, if she doesn't have a home, I think she will in no time," Abbi told him as she rubbed the dog's head. "Yes, you do, you sweet thing you," she crooned planting a kiss on the dogs' wet nose. She wrapped her arms around its chest while Ben took the rear and together, they set her on the floor.

"Come on. You two need a good night's sleep," she said to both man and dog.

"Thanks Mack," Ben called out tiredly, as he followed Abbi and the dog back to the car.

"No problem." Mack waved from the doorstep. "Glad I could help."

All three got settled in the car. "At least now we can relax knowing she'll be fine," Abbi said. Starting the engine, she threw in into gear and headed towards home.

"That is true. I guess banging up my shoulder was meant to be," Ben snickered. "But man, I can't believe how knackered I am," he yawned, wiping his eyes.

"Huh?" Abbi looked at him and giggled. She couldn't help but wonder what the heck he meant by knackered.

"Exhausted Abbi, I'm utterly spent."

"Yeah? Well. That makes sense. It's been quite a day," she murmured in agreement as she pulled into her laneway. Shutting the car off, she looked at him. "What was it you were meaning to tell me back at Mack's?"

"Oh. Right. Um, just something I wanted to run by you. It can wait until we get in the house," he yawned loudly.

She laughed at him. "I think it can wait until tomorrow. What do you think?"

He looked her deeply in the eyes. He didn't want to put any fear into those beautiful orbs tonight. Nodding in agreement, he said, "Yeah, tomorrow will be soon enough."

They got out of the vehicle and together managed to get the dog set on all fours on the ground. As they were walking up the path to her house, Ben said lightly, "So, I was thinking, how's Molly sound for a name?"

She giggled. He just couldn't help himself. "I think Molly is a perfect name for her," she smiled, unlocking the door. "Maybe just stay here with her for a bit and I'll get her some food and bring Brutus. We'll introduce them out here before letting her in the house."

"Right, good idea," he agreed, sitting down heavily on the top step as she went inside. He could hear Brutus scratching at the door, eager to get out. Minutes later, they appeared from the house. Brutus in a harness with a muzzle covering his mouth.

Ben was stunned.

Would he attack Molly?

God, he hoped not, he didn't have the strength to fend him off if the need arose. Abbi held out a bowl of dog food to Ben. He took it from her, holding it until Brutus settled down.

"Just in case," Abbi explained, reading the expression on Ben's face. "I never know how he will react most times." He nodded his understanding.

The big dog playfully lunged at Molly, his tail whipping back and forth with excitement. He seemed to decide that she was friend and not foe with the first sniff of her rear end. He quietly sat down next to her while she dug into the food.

"What about Lucy? How do you think she will react?" Ben asked, stroking both dogs.

She waved his concern away. "Lucy is laid back. She loves any animal that I've brought into the house, she'll be fine. Do you want anything to eat or drink?" She looked at him. "I never thought, did you need anything from your place?"

"Now that you mention it, yeah, I should have grabbed a change of clothes," he said, standing. "Care to go for a moonlit walk with me?" he asked, running his hand through his hair.

"Certainly," she smiled. "Just let me get Lucy. She could use the walk, too."

Ben was waiting in the yard, holding Brutus' leash, when Abbi came out with Lucy in tow.

"Do you think Molly will stay or should I grab a leash for her as well?" she asked, her hand on the doorknob.

He made a face. "I don't think she needs one, she's stayed with us since we found her."

Nodding, she closed the door and bounded down the steps. "Okay, I'll keep Brutus leashed for now, at least. On the way back, I'll let him run. Maybe, depends on how well he behaves," she said, joining him in the yard.

She took his offered hand, tingling at the warmth of his touch as they headed towards his house. She had concerns about the next few days ahead of them. Her kids would arrive in three days, and she felt the need to warn him.

She cleared her throat. "I know we touched on the topic about my kids..." She stopped, wondering how to tell him.

"Go on," he encouraged her.

"Well, there's Luke, Lane and Ava."

"Yeah? You've told me before, Abbi," he smiled at her.

"I know, but I have to warn you, Luke will be fine with us... likely will encourage it," she smiled, knowing exactly what Luke would say. The smile fell from her face when she continued, "As for Lane and Ava... frankly, I'm worried about what they will say..." She wrinkled her brow. "... to you..."

They reached his yard, the motion light caught their movement, washing them in its glow.

Ben stopped. Letting go of her hand, he put his arm around her and gazed into her eyes. "Do you care what they say or what they think?"

"No! Not really. It's just neither of them has a filter. Know what I mean?" She sighed. "They don't care what they say to anyone. It doesn't matter who it is."

He stroked her back, trying to smooth the tension away and said, "Abbi don't worry about it. I'm man enough to handle whatever it is they can dish out."

"I know you are. I just wanted to give you a heads-up, so you're not shocked, is all."

The thought saddened her. She could see them demanding that she stop seeing Ben. If they did, things would get ugly quick. There was no way she'd give up her happiness for her grown, adult children who lived hundreds of miles away. No, it wasn't going to happen!

"What are you thinking about?" he murmured.

"Nothing."

He grinned. "I can tell when the gears are moving Abbi, just by looking in your eyes."

"Nothing!" she laughed, kissing him quickly on the lips. She ran away and up the steps as her laughter turned to giggles, that abruptly stopped.

"Right," he said, shaking his head, smiling as he followed her up the steps.

"Ben, what the hell is that?" she stood transfixed, pointing to the floor.

'That' was the pool of dried blood. Molly was lying next to it while Brutus and Lucy curled up against her on either side. Now that he wasn't in a panic, he noticed how large it was. Looking at Molly and again at the stain; his anger rose swift and sharp.

"Son of a bitch," he swore.

"You... you don't think that was from her, do you?" Abbi stammered, horrified at the thought.

"It sure looks to be, considering she was bleeding when we found her and it's about the same size as her." Crouching down, he looked at Molly's fur splayed out around her. Looking at the stain, he noticed how the same pattern was feathering out from it.

He threw his hand towards the house in frustration. "To think, she was out here bleeding, when I was in there sleeping. If I find the bastard who did this to her, I'll wring his bloody neck." Riddled with guilt, he shoved his hand through his hair.

Abbi put her hand on his chest. "Ben, you can't think like that. You had no idea she was even around here," she reasoned with him. "Maybe Mack was mistaken, and she was cut by a wire."

He took her hand and brought it to his mouth, not kissing it, but just holding it there. He looked at Abbi's face. Every emotion possible was displayed on her soft features. He let out a sigh and said, "You're right. It could have been anything."

In his heart, he knew differently. Yes, he had jumped to conclusions today, more than once. But his gut was telling him that this wasn't the case. Did someone do this to Molly, just to drop her off on his property as a warning or was it just a coincidence?

He turned away to unlock the door, his eyes falling on the chair beside it. There, sat perfectly in the middle of it, was a shiny red apple. He knew it was the one he'd tossed in the yard earlier before striking out to Abbi's. His teeth marks were still visible, browning around the edges. That wasn't a coincidence.

Whatever was going on, he dared not tell Abbi tonight. Tomorrow was soon enough.

Chapter 16

His mind raced as he took his keys out of his pocket and unlocked the door, pushing it wide for Abbi to enter. *Act cool Ben, otherwise, she'll know something is up,* he told himself.

"Come on guys," he called to the dogs, closing the door behind them. "Do you think I could chance a quick shower?" he asked her, tossing his keys on the island. Looking down at his clothes, he noticed that Molly's blood was smeared on his jeans.

"I guess you could try, but you'll need to take that brace off," she answered, looking out the window. She could see the lights through the trees of her house. "Why don't you gather what you need and just take one at my place?" Turning she looked at him. "That way, we can get the dogs settled and I can help you, if need be," she suggested quietly.

"Sure, I'll just grab a few things and we can leave," he said, going into his bedroom.

"Hey! Did you ever get those curtains hung?" she called out to him.

"Um... well, sort of," he chuckled. "Come have a look."

She walked into the hall that would lead to his bedroom. Standing at the door, she leaned against the frame gazing at the black covered windows.

"Wow!" she laughed, walking to it. "How creative," she remarked, smiling as she fingered the garbage bags taped to the window frame.

"Yeah, I thought so, too," he laughed, shutting the dresser drawer.

He stuffed a change of clothes and good grief, pajama bottoms in a backpack. Normally he slept in the raw but not tonight. He didn't think Abbi would approve.

"I'll be right back," he tossed over his shoulder as he walked out of the room.

She turned to mumble, "Mhm..." her eyes caught the bed in the center of the room, the covers laid where he'd tossed them. She could picture in her mind, him lying there. The slow rise and fall of his chest with every breath he took. He'd look like an angel... no... a God...

In the bathroom, Ben collected his toothbrush, deodorant, and body wash and sauntered back to his room. He noticed Abbi was off in a trance.

Staring at my bed, is she? He grinned, shaking his head.

"Abbi are you ready to go?" he asked, zipping up the bag. "Abbi!" A smile played on his lips.

She about jumped out of her skin. "What?" she said, matching his tone.

"I'm ready to go, are you?" he asked, slinging the pack on his shoulder.

"Yes, yes, of course!" She hurried to the door and down the hallway.

Ben followed her through to the kitchen. He rather enjoyed following her; she gave off such a nice view.

Abbi looked over her shoulder and caught him eyeing her, a warm sensation flowed through her body to her very core.

"Do you have everything?" She squeaked out.

At his nod, she called the dogs and opened the door to let them outside. She snagged a hold of Brutus' leash before he bounded out the door, unsnapping the catch, she gave him a gentle push and told him to go.

"Yeah, I think so," he replied, grabbing his keys. He locked and closed the door firmly behind him.

He took the apple off the chair and sent it flying into the bushes.

Abbi glanced at him. "What will you do about that stain on the porch?"

"Ah, I haven't really thought about it honestly. Hopefully, a couple of coats of paint will cover it. Which it needs anyway since the BBQ caught fire."

"True. I can give you a hand if you like," she offered. "There's a power washer in my shed." She laughed. "Buried under something, I'm sure."

Putting his arm around her shoulders, he said softly, "I'll tell you what. You help me with my porch, and I'll help you clean out your shed."

"Deal," she replied. "I would shake on it, but your hands are busy," she chuckled as they stepped into her yard.

"I'll do one better." He moved his hand to the back of her head. Bending towards her, he searched out her lips with his own. He gently kissed her, feeling her arms go around his waist, he deepened the kiss. On any other night, he could have stayed right there kissing her, but this wasn't any normal night.

Breaking for air, he whispered, "As much as I would love to stand here kissing your sweet lips till dawn Abbi, I'm exhausted." He yawned loudly. "Let's get in the house before I curl up here in the bushes and pass out."

"You started it," she accused.

Nodding he smiled. "Right, I did. And just so you know, I plan on finishing it," he told her, as they climbed the steps. "Just not tonight." He sent her a wink.

She unlocked the door, blushing profusely as Brutus shoved it wide with his nose for all to enter.

"Do you still want that shower?" she looked at him, locking the door.

He glanced at her as he set his bag on the table. "If you don't mind giving me a hand, I would."

"Um, sure." Remembering what Doc had said about the pain, she asked, "Are you needing any meds yet?"

"Please. The freezing is long gone. Makes me regret stopping you from getting the prescription," he said with a tight smile.

"If you want to head to the bathroom, I'll bring them to you. I'm just going to put on the kettle. Do you want a cup of hot chocolate?"

Ben noticed she was rambling on; she was nervous. "Sure, that will be great," he answered, heading to the bathroom.

YOU CAN DO THIS ABBI!... She tried to reassure herself. *Sure, I can! I just haven't seen a man naked for... Oh... five years. No big deal.*

Oh, but it was. It was a huge deal.

She took the kettle, filling it with water, she sat it on the stove and switched it on. Leaning back against the counter she folded her arms across her chest, waiting for the kettle to scream that it was ready. Big mistake, her mind began to wander...

Ben isn't any ordinary man; he's all muscle. He makes me melt with just a look. And his skin! Lordy! So soft... like satin.

Which brought her thoughts to his chest, she sucked in a breath and held it as the image of that, played in her mind. *Well defined, a light scattering of hair trailing over his stomach... Sweet baby Jesus. I'm going to hell.*

Abbi gulped, when the image of his stomach teased her mind...

One glorious ripple after another. And that soft dusting of hair around his belly button, dropping below his waistband.

Her eyes, yet to see where it ended. Not even realizing she still held her breath, it whooshed past her lips and had her gasping for air.

Girl, what is wrong with you?!

She absently poured the boiling water into the awaiting mugs when she heard a noise from the bathroom. Good grief she forgot all about him waiting!

Why did you just have to think about him now, when you have to go in there and help him!

"Abbi are you coming?" he called out.

"Close to it!" She clamped her mouth shut and cringed. Taking the bottle of pain meds from the windowsill she called out louder, "Ah. Yeah, be right there!"

She took a deep steadying breath, grabbed his bag off the table, carefully snatched up the mugs off the counter and walked on shaky legs to the bathroom.

Stopping just outside the open door, she peeked through the gap between the door and the frame. There he was, sitting on the closed lid of the toilet. His head in his hand, fully clothed. Her heart went out to him. He looked utterly spent.

She moved so she could peek around the edge of the door. In response, the floor creaked at that very moment, causing him to jerk his head in her direction. He caught her standing there with only one eye looking at him and two steaming mugs in her hands.

A bubble of laughter rose in his chest. "What exactly are you doing?"

"I... ahh... nothing," she said. Walking into the bathroom, she sat the hot chocolates on the vanity. "I'll just start the shower for you."

She had to compose herself. She purposely avoided looking at him and made a beeline to the shower where she busied herself adjusting the temperature.

When she had control over her racing heart, she turned back to face him and saw that he was standing, swaying in place.

Abbi rushed to his side before he face-planted on the floor. "Here, let me get this sling off for you." Going around his back she untied it and slipped it off.

Ben slowly rotated his head, trying to ease the stiffness in his neck. "God, that's a relief."

Not fully trusting herself to not say something stupid, she stayed behind him, holding his shirt as he pulled his arm out. She tugged it over his head and tossed it to the floor.

Worriedly, she looked at the brace, "Are you sure about this Ben? I don't know if I'll be able to figure out how to take it off, let alone put it back on."

"There's a strap there, just pull on it, the one that goes around my chest, and another one on my arm, just below my shoulder. Do you see it?"

She answered by pulling on the strap under his arm and heard a tearing sound as she did. She did the same with the strap on his shoulder, allowing it to slip off easily. His back was just as well defined as the front of him, which brought her gaze to the waist of his pants.

"Um, I'll just reach around you here and undo your jeans for you, okay?"

"Yeah, that will be fine," he smirked, knowing things were about to get extremely interesting.

She unbuttoned his pants and pulled on the zipper. Everything was great until the damn thing got caught. She tugged and tugged but it wouldn't budge.

Groaning in frustration of having no choice, she moved around to the front of him, and tried again.

"What is it?" he asked nonchalantly. He had to bite his lip; otherwise, he'd laugh in her face.

She gritted her teeth. "The zipper... is... stuck," she said as she tugged to no avail. She shoved her hair out of her face. "Hang on, I'll just grab a bar of soap." She took the bar from the shower and rubbed it on the zipper and gave it a whirl. "Got it! Now, sit down on the toilet so I can take your pants off," she shooed him away before grabbing some towels from the shelf.

As tired as he was, a mischievous glint lit his eyes. He couldn't help teasing her. "Take my pants off... I rather like the sound of that."

She sat the towels on the counter giving him a sidelong glance. "Hmm, I bet you do. Lift your butt please."

Bracing himself against the wall, he did as he was told. She slipped his pants past his hips and noticed the effort it took him to resettle himself on the toilet. Tugging on one pant leg she slipped it off, followed by the other, then his socks. Standing with her hands on her hips, all that was left were his briefs.

How the heck is this going to work? ... She gnawed at her bottom lip.

He stood and saw the look in her eyes. That look when she was lost in thought and the look of panic.

"Why don't you just put a towel around my waist until I get in?"

She pointed a finger at him. "Good idea!" She grabbed a towel and wrapped it around him.

With that done, Abbi pulled her shirt from her skin, back and forth rapidly. *"My God, it's getting hot in here!"* she said, trying to get some air flowing. It wasn't working.

"Hang on. Don't do anything," she warned. Throwing her hair up into a messy bun, she went to the shelf and grabbed a clip, securing it in place.

Ben watched in surprise when she took the hem of her shirt and pulled it off in one fluid motion. He was disappointed when a tank top was revealed but had to chuckle when she whipped it to the corner in exasperation.

"Oh-kay. I'm ready, now what?" she asked, puffing a stray hair out of her eyes.

He covered the laugh with a quick cough. "Um, now I guess I'll just shimmy out of my, uh... shorts."

Puzzled, she looked at him. "How are you going to do that with a towel wrapped around you and one good hand?"

She was right. She also had him captivated.

She was beautiful standing there looking at him, a frown on her face. Her hair softly curling, now up, showed the graceful curve of her neck. He wanted to plant a kiss there but stopped himself.

"I'll hold another towel up while you do that," she suggested, grabbing another one.

She shook it out and held it like a matador holding his cape. "Okay, I'm ready..." Her eyes grew huge when she saw that the towel around his waist was now larger. She stumbled back against the counter. Recovering quickly, she said, "Ah. Hurry up, we need to get you to bed!"

She made a grimace and bit her tongue.

Her words snapped him out of his trance. "Right. I'll do that," he nodded.

Damn, I have no self-control when I'm around her.

He dropped the towel and managed to take off his briefs one handed. Moving the shower curtain aside, he climbed in under the steaming water.

"You good?" She wasn't waiting for his response. "Good. Okay, I'll go make the hot chocolate. Oops sorry! Almost forgot." Taking the bottle of pills out of her pocket, she shook two in her hand.

"Um, Abbi. You already made the hot chocolate. You set the cups on the vanity, remember?"

She froze. A nervous giggle bubbled past her lips. "Ah...Right, how silly of me." She stuck her hand behind the curtain. "Here are the pills. I'll just go and do... something."

"Thanks. Just drop them luv."

He opened his mouth under her hand, added some water from the shower and swallowed as he heard her make a hasty retreat. He laughed at her antics, then about cried from the pain it caused.

Hoping the pills kicked in fast, he stood there for a solid ten minutes he guessed; just turning slowly in circles under the steamy water. It felt wonderful on his sore muscles.

He pumped the shampoo bottle one-handed and slapped it on his head, just as he heard Abbi returning.

"Are you doing good in there?" she called out.

"Not too bad, just scrubbing my hair right now."

"Nice, I have your bag here. Do you need anything out of it?"

"Yeah, could you get me my body wash, please?" he asked.

She stuck her hand in the shower holding the bottle out to him, "Grab that puff thing there and I'll squirt some on it for you."

"The what?" he asked with amusement in his voice.

"The pink thing hanging there on the hook, you know, a puff?"

"Never heard of it by that name before," he said, holding it out for the body wash. "Usually, I just dump it in my hand and rub it all over my body."

Thanks. I really needed that visual. All over your wet... glistening... hardness.

The sound of him hissing made her come back to the moment at hand.

"What's wrong?" she asked, a bit too anxiously as if he could read her thoughts.

"Nothing, just rubbed a little hard on my shoulder, is all."

"Okay, let me know when you're done, and I'll get the towel ready for you."

The water shut off the second the words were out of her mouth.

"Shit!! Wait a minute! I'm not ready!"

He could hear her scrambling as something crashed to the floor. Smiling to himself, he waited for her to give the all-clear.

Breathlessly she said, "Okay, go ahead."

He moved the curtain aside and stepped out of the shower and noticed her face was turned towards the door. He took one end of the towel, draping it behind him and around to his front where she held the other end.

She risked a glance at him to see if he was covered. Finding that he was, she wrapped her end around his front, and tucked the corner in at his waist.

"There. It's perfect. C'mon, I'll show you the spare bedroom, you can put your stuff in there and get dressed."

He followed her out and down the hall. Looking as she pointed to the left.

For some reason Abbi thought it was the perfect time to give him the grand tour. "That's my library, where I do all of my writing."

Moving along, she pointed to the left again. "The mongrels' room is that one."

Stopping, she flicked the light on to see the three dogs sound asleep. Brutus and Lucy were sleeping beside Molly as if they were giving her their strength and warmth. Both cats were curled up in the bay window snoring away, either oblivious to their new roommate or they just didn't care.

Turning the light off, she continued onward. She turned to the right where there was another short hallway with two doors across from each other. Abbi opened the first one on the left. "This one is mine," she said, flicking on the light switch.

Ben's brows shot up in surprise. A huge four-poster bed sat in the center, not against a wall, but in the center of the room; a person could lay in bed and see the water from it. A sheer, brown curtain from corner to corner draped across the top, dipping in the middle. The same material trailed down all four columns of the bed to the floor.

The mattress was covered by a quilt with wildflowers etched on it. Their stems and leaves, a soft green, entwined. Their colour perfectly matched the bedroom walls and plump pillows in the bay window that faced the lake. To the right of that, there was a foyer with a set of French doors overlooking the back porch. The whole room screamed, earthy, it screamed Abbi.

"I know. It's a little over the top, but it's my dream bedroom," she said shyly.

"No! Not at all. Abbi, it's you," he murmured, brushing her hair out of her eyes.

She wanted to kiss him for his understanding but remembered he only wore the towel.

She needed more clothes between them, more than a strip of cloth that could slip off at a moment's notice. She ducked her head and turned.

"And this here is the spare room," she said, taking the few steps away from her door.

Pushing the door open on the right, she walked into the room over to the bed and pulled the blankets back. Ben saw a queen-sized bed, the head, pushed up against the wall. A floral print quilt covered it, with plump pillows resting on the headboard. A lamp on the dresser cast a soft glow over the room.

Like her room, the low window gave a view to the lake from the bed. He could picture what it would look like come morning, watching it come alive with the first stream of sunrise hitting the lake.

Nodding towards a door, Abbi said, "There is a connecting bathroom there to my room."

Ben looked back into the hall for a door to the bathroom.

Knowing what he was looking for, she told him, "You only can access it from the bedrooms."

"Hmm, that's cool."

"Yeah, it was actually another bedroom, but I liked the idea of having a private bath back here," she said, sliding the pocket door open for him to step in.

"My room is through there," she motioned at the door directly across from where they were standing.

"Wow!" Ben was floored by what he saw. The wall that faced the lake was a solid pane of glass from floor to ceiling. One step took you up to an oval-shaped tub large enough for two people to lay back and relax comfortably.

He stood looking at that wall of glass, squinting.

"Ah..." he pointed to the bathtub, "... aren't you afraid of someone seeing you while you bathe?" he asked, tilting his head to look at her.

She laughed. "Everyone that's seen it asks the same thing. No, it's one-sided glass, like the cop's use."

"Good to know, otherwise, I thought it pretty brazen of you," he grinned, chuckling.

"Yeah, no." She laughed and turned around. "The shower is over there and the toilet and vanity through there," she pointed, showing him the doorway.

"This is gorgeous," he said, looking around in awe.

"Thanks! I designed it myself."

"Even more impressive," he nodded, a look of admiration in his eyes.

He made her smile at that. She walked back into his room.

"So, if you want to get... dressed, I'll go get your brace. Do you think you can handle it?" *Please say yes.*

"Yeah, I should be fine," he said, looking around.

"Crap, we forgot your bag. I'll get it too. Do you want your drink brought in here?" she asked.

"That would be great, thanks, Abbi." He wanted nothing more than to sit up all night talking to her, but reality was kicking him in the ass. *I need sleep, and I need it now,* he thought as he sat heavily on the edge of the bed.

Abbi took off down the hall to collect his bag, his brace and their drinks that were more than likely cold by now.

She picked up his clothes and quickly ran them into the laundry room, spraying the dried blood with a stain remover. She threw them in the washer and started it. Going into the bathroom, she grabbed up his bag, slung it over her shoulder, tucked his brace under her arm and picked up their mugs. She made a mental note, to tell him to remind her to get his pills at the pharmacy tomorrow as she headed back to him.

"So, hey.... *Oh!*" she said softly, her eyes instantly matching her tone.

He had fallen asleep. Flat on his back, his legs hanging over the edge of the bed. The towel had slipped, revealing smooth, perfect skin from hip to thigh.

"Sweet baby Jesus!" she muttered, sucking in a ragged breath than started gnawing her lower lip.

She had work to do. She couldn't leave him all night to sleep in a wet towel.

Chapter 17

Thankfully, that's all it had revealed. Abbi wasn't entirely sure if she could contain herself if it hadn't. *Of course, you could... stop acting like a sex-deprived fool!* She was sex deprived, but not enough to take advantage of him.

She tiptoed to the dresser and quietly sat the cups down along with the brace. She watched him as she eased his bag off her shoulder. Sitting it on the floor, she slowly unzipped it, pawing through it until she found his pajama pants. She'd forgo the underwear; the pants would be challenging enough. She approached the bed, hunched over, stealth like, holding onto them.

How am I going to do this without waking him up...? Her eyes ran over his body from head to toe...

She gulped. The towel had slipped open. At least the important part was covered. He really was a work of art. Satiny skin stretched across his hip to his thigh. She reached out a hand to touch it, knowing it would be soft as a baby's bum. She snapped her hand back and took a deep calming breath.

Enough Abbi! Get the man's pants on and let him sleep...

Bending to slip the waistband over one foot then the other, she slid them up to his knees without so much as a twitch from him. Now, all she had to do was shimmy the rest up to his waist.

She gripped the waistband so hard her knuckles turned white. Inch by excruciating inch they slid upwards under the towel. She took a quick glance at his face to see if he was awake and watching her.

Thankfully, he wasn't. She got as far as his thighs and hissed out the breath she was holding.

She inhaled sharply again, steeling herself for what was to come next. She carefully eased onto the bed, straddling his thighs with her knees, she dared not sit on him.

Getting a firm grip on the pants once again she leaned forward, careful not to brush up against him, she checked his face for a sign that he was awake.

She slowly resumed pulling them upwards, silently congratulating herself until she met with resistance. They got stuck on his butt and... other things, she noticed. She pushed down with the back of her hands into the mattress as she gripped the waist.

Just need to get them over this beautiful ass...

She grunted aloud. Stifling a giggle, she quickly looked at his face and saw that he was still fast asleep. Straightening up on her knees, she leaned back, putting her hands on her hips to study her work.

Just then, Ben opened his eyes. She froze, hoping he didn't see her and would fall back asleep. He did, thankfully.

She gently grabbed the waistband again and leaned forward as she eased them up past his— She looked down; her eyes fell on his... package. One that the towel still covered. She had a vivid image of face planting onto him.

A horrified look settled on her features. In one swift movement, she yanked the pants up to his waist and tugged on the towel. Heaven help her, the towel was stuck.

That would be because he is laying on it, you fool!

She stumbled to stand on the floor just as Ben bolted upright.

"Abbi, what... where...?" he stopped, clearly disoriented.

"Sorry about that," she motioned. "I didn't want to leave you laying in a wet towel all night."

She grabbed the edge of it and tugged. "Here, just ...let me get that for you," she grunted, yanking on it. It finally let loose, and she fell back against the wall, sliding to the floor. Where she decided she would rather stay than face him right now.

"Are you okay?" Ben peeked at her over the edge of the bed. When she didn't respond, he moved to push himself off the mattress, ready to spring to her aide.

She waved a hand at him. "No, no. You stay there. I'm good. Just resting a bit."

She couldn't help but blush at the memory of what she had just done. Slowly she came to her feet, ready to face him. "Um, now that you're awake, we really should put the brace back on." She hurriedly snatched it from the dresser.

"Sure, maybe it will help. I'm having some doubts about it working," he replied in pain.

She took a mug and handed it to him. "Here, it's still warm, drink up while I do this."

He took a sip while she slipped the brace over his hand and up to his shoulder. Reaching around his back, she fastened it, making sure it was snug.

MOONLIT NIGHT

"There, how does that feel?" she asked, tugging at it.

"Better, thanks." He gave her a sleepy smile, then sat his cup on the bedside table and crawled up to rest against the pillows. "Lay with me? I promise nothing will happen."

The look in his eyes made it impossible for her to say no. Nodding her head, she crept up beside him and laid facing him.

"What time is it?" He yawned.

"Good question." Pulling her cell out of her back pocket she said, "Um, it's 11:30." She noticed five missed calls. She swiped the screen to see the call log, thinking it was one of her kids, she frowned.

Ben was watching her. "What is it?"

"Oh, nothing. Just a few missed calls," she said, turning away to set her phone on the table. She turned back towards him. "What?" she asked when she noticed him staring at her intently.

He had propped his arm under his head and was mesmerized by her every move. "Nothing," he mumbled. He loved watching her.

The light from the glow of the lamp played over her features. A sense of protectiveness for her came over him. He worried about what was going on. He was on the verge of telling her, but now wasn't the time. Not here, not now.

Abbi was watching him, too. Watched his brow wrinkle in thought.

What is he thinking about? She reached a hand to smooth out the lines on his forehead.

"You look so tired," she softly murmured, her hand slipping into his hair. She ran her fingers through it, marveling at how soft it felt to the touch. Everything on him was soft. She trailed her hand down the side of his face to his cheek.

"I am," he murmured, turning his face to kiss her palm.

She felt a little fire spark from his lips to her hand, down her arm that flared throughout her body.

He turned his head and looked into her eyes. She moved her head closer, planting a soft kiss on his lips.

She leaned back against the pillows, opened her arms, and whispered, "Come here."

That was all Ben needed to hear. He slipped his good arm under her as she guided his head to her chest, the other in the brace resting across her stomach. She breathed in his masculine scent. Her lips grazed his forehead as she stroked his back.

Ben felt his eyes drifting shut, felt her fingers trailing softly over his bare skin, her lips touching his forehead. Despite his exhaustion, his body reacted to her touch. Sadly, he was too tired to reciprocate. The beat of her heart was lulling him to sleep. He heard her softly say, 'go to sleep darling' as his eyes drifted closed in exhaustion.

SOMETHING WAS CRAWLING on Ben. He opened his eyes to see Abbi's neck before him. Her hair was covering her face, tickling his nose. He leaned forward and brushed a kiss against her soft skin.

He could feel her pulse beating steadily beneath his lips, his tongue darting out to taste her sweetness. She moaned softly in her sleep, gathering him closer to her. His reaction was instant. He wanted nothing more than to take her in his arms and make love to her while slowly watching her body awaken with desire.

Instead, he gently eased away, watching her as he did so. Untangling himself from her embrace, he touched his lips to hers before slipping out of the bed. He would let the dogs out and make her breakfast, he decided, heading to the bathroom.

ABBI WOKE SLOWLY, REACHING out to seek Ben, only to find the bed empty. Feeling disappointed, she thought about last night. She had lain awake for a bit after he had fallen asleep, just holding him in her arms. She loved the weight of him on her. His soft breathing with every rise and fall of his chest.

Reaching for her cell, she looked to see the time... 8:30 am... she groaned. Getting up, she stumbled into the bathroom, did her business, and jumped in to take a quick shower.

Turning the taps off, she could hear the dogs barking outside and hurried to get dressed in her room. Throwing on sweatpants and a tank top, she tugged on a zip-up hoodie with 'Canada' emblazoned across her chest. As she slipped her bare feet into some fuzzy slippers, she made her way into the hall, following the scent of bacon frying coming from the kitchen. She found Ben standing at the stove, bare-chested in his pajama pants.

"Morning. I've fed the gang; the dogs are outside just now." He smiled at her. "I hope you don't mind me cooking?" he asked, pouring her a cup of coffee.

She took it from him, smiling her thanks. She glanced at the table to see that he had set it too. An impressive feat considering he only had the use of one hand.

"Not at all. I could get used to this you know," she motioned at the table with her cup, tossing him a grin. "How's your shoulder feeling?" she asked, setting her coffee down on the counter. She walked over to him, making sure the brace was still snug.

He turned towards her. "Better, I think. I needed that sleep," he said, slipping his arm around her waist, he pulled her close. "Thank you, Abbi for taking care of me." He glanced at her lips before bending his head to kiss her. Cradling her head in his hand, he tilted her chin back as he laid quick kisses along her jawline before dropping a soft one on her mouth. The toaster popped just then.

She slid her hands down his bare chest, trailing her nails against his skin, watching in awe as goosebumps sprung to the surface. "Are you cold?" she asked, buttering the toast.

"No, Abbi. I'm not cold; it's just what you do to me. You really have no idea, do you?"

She glanced at him over her shoulder. "Um, a little. Maybe. I still have my doubts about... you. Us."

"Seriously.... How could you think that? Do you take me for the type of man to go around kissing just anyone?" Annoyed, he walked to the table, setting the plate of bacon on it. Pulling out a chair he sat, brooding. "Why don't you believe me?"

"Look, Ben," she began. "It's not that I don't think you have feelings for me or that I don't believe you. I know that you do. It's just..."

"It's just what, Abbi?"

She brought the plate of toast to the table along with a jug of orange juice. Sitting down, she turned her chair towards him, and looked him in the eyes. "It's just..." *Stop worrying about it and tell him....* "It's just," she cleared her throat. "I'm ashamed... of my body." She cast her eyes around the room before settling them on a spot on the floor. She dared not look him in the eyes right then.

Well, that shocked the hell out of him. He was sure she'd say she was too old again. For the life of him, he couldn't think why she'd be ashamed.

She risked a quick glance at him and could see the puzzlement play over his face.

"Of what?" dumbfounded, he shook his head.

Chapter 18

"Ben, I had three kids... two being twins." She waited for him to clue in. His brows shot up. Tilting his head, his eyes round, he spat out, "So?"

She closed her eyes and rubbed her forehead. "I have stretch marks and scars, OK? I was huge when I was pregnant with the boys, going under the knife was the only way to get them out... sixteen years old and my body has been ruined ever since."

She opened her eyes, needing to see his reaction. "Ava was also born by C-section, so not only was I cut once... but twice."

She watched his face soften with understanding.

"Abbi... luv." He took her hand in his, bringing it to his lips, "Your body doesn't define who you are." Squinting in disbelief, he asked, "Do you honestly think I would judge you for it?"

"Well... No..." She shrugged. "I guess not. It's just you meet gorgeous women every day." She dashed away a tear that sprang to her eye. Standing, she began pacing the floor. "I can't compete with someone with smooth uncut, wrinkle-free skin, Ben."

"You don't have to compete with anyone Abbi. You have my heart... Please, don't ever for a second forget it," he said earnestly. Catching her hand, he dragged her onto his lap.

Turning her face towards him, he kissed her, convincing her his words were true.

Ben pulled away from her and tilted his head. "What the hell is that?"

"Huh? What do you mean?" she asked, breathlessly.

He motioned with his hand towards the hall. "That... it sounds like a rooster. Do you have one of those I've yet to meet?" He laughed at the thought.

"Oh! It's my phone!!" Jumping up, she took off down the hall to the spare bedroom. Grabbing it from the bedside table, she answered it with a breathless, "Hello?" and headed back to the kitchen.

Ben was making a bacon sandwich, squirting ketchup on it, as she came into the room. He glanced up when he heard her saying, "Hello... I can't hear you... is anyone there?" Shrugging her shoulders, she hit the end button.

"Who was it?" he probed, biting into his sandwich.

She shook her head, putting the phone on the table. "I'm not sure. It was unknown caller again." Sitting down, she snatched a piece of bacon. Thoughtfully she said, "Someone was there, I could hear them breathing."

Ben's suspicions were back.

"Right," he nodded, chewing. Setting his sandwich on the plate, he dusted the crumbs from his hands. "Okay. I was so tired last night. I can't remember if I mentioned this to you or not." He took a sip of his juice. "I think something is going on here, Abbi."

She darted a look at him. "Going on? What makes you say that?" she asked, biting the bacon in half.

Taking a deep breath, he said, "At first I thought maybe the paparazzi had found out I was living here."

"Hmm. I'm listening."

"You remember the night Mark was over at my place, after he left?" At her nod, he continued. "And when we kissed on your porch... both times I had the feeling we weren't alone."

"How so?" she frowned, licking the grease from her fingers. "The dogs would have sensed someone out there," she pointed out smacking her lips.

"That's what I thought. But the feeling was there all the same. I sat for a spell outside, thinking I might hear or see something."

Her brows shot up.

So that's why he stayed so long...

Now she felt foolish, thinking he was pining away for her. She chuckled at the memory of it.

"I'm serious..."

She put her hand up. "I know, I know. I'm laughing at something else." She waved her hand, dismissing it. "The trees around here can make you think you see something when it's not really there." She gathered the dishes and walked to the counter. "Plus, the lake carries sound, causing an echo off them."

She pointed a dirty fork in his direction. "Take for instance, the day I was cleaning my windows. I heard your music playing loud and clear over here... and then when I tripped on the last step and fell flat on my face? I heard you laughing at me." She smiled as she loaded the dishwasher. "Which wasn't very nice of you, I might add."

My God, it isn't the paparazzi at all. It's her they are after...

"Abbi." He sat there, drumming the table with his fingers.

Glancing at him, she said, "Yeah?" She saw his face had lost all colour. He looked suddenly sick. "What is it?"

"I haven't played music, nor did I laugh at you. The only time that I've seen you trip was the day I caught you in Mack's store."

She stood there shaking her head in denial. "No, no, no, that... that just can't be."

He got up and walked over to her, taking her by the arms. "Abbi listen to me. The phone calls..." He threw his hand towards the lake. "The boat no less than a hundred feet from your shore... the laughing and music... I promise you that wasn't me."

He licked his lips. "What if what happened to Molly was done on purpose..."

She started to squawk.

He held up a finger. "No, hear me out. Mack said it looked like she was cut with a scalpel, not a knife or a piece of wire, but a scalpel... He's a retired Veterinarian. I'm confident he'd know the difference."

God, I hate doing this to her.

She shook her head. "But why would someone hurt her if they were after me? It just doesn't make any sense."

Deep down she had a feeling he was right, about everything except Molly. What kind of person could do such a thing to a defenseless animal?

Ben sighed. "A warning for me."

She jerked her head up, looking deeply into his eyes.

"To stay away from you…" he answered quietly. "That's not all. Remember me whipping that apple last night into the bushes? The one sitting on the chair?"

At her nod he continued. "Right. Well, I was going to eat that apple until I saw the blood on my porch. I threw it in the yard before heading over here."

Abbi went ghostly white.

"What happened to the guy that was stalking you? Did you go to the police about him?" he asked softly.

She nodded her head. "I did. And I had a restraining order put on him. After that, he left me alone." She suddenly felt a cold shiver run down her spine at the memory of it. "You don't think it's him, do you?"

Ben swore. Taking a step back, he shoved his hand through his hair. The look on her face said it all. She was terrified.

"I'm sorry Abbi. Come here." He put his arm around her, pulling her closer when she started to shiver uncontrollably. "I'm here. No one will get near you," he soothed quietly.

"Maybe it's all just a coincidence. I'm sure that's what it is," she said against his chest.

"Coincidence or not I'm calling the police." He rubbed her back. "Do you recall his name?" He hated to put her through this but had little choice.

"Ah, yeah. It was…" she rubbed her forehead. It was suddenly pounding. "Um, Jacob…?" For the life of her, she couldn't remember his last name.

She pulled herself out of the safety of his arms. "I need… I have to look on my computer for his last name," she said woodenly, walking to the library.

Ben watched her with unease. He'd follow her shortly, as soon as he called the dogs in and locked the door.

ABBI WAS SITTING AT her computer, staring blankly at the screen when Ben joined her.

"Hey, luv." No response. Taking a chair, he watched her face as he sat beside her.

She didn't say a word, just kept staring at the computer screen as he gazed at her profile.

"Abbi. Look at me," he murmured. Reaching for her chin he turned her gently to face him. Hoping she would look at him.

She did. And the look she gave him tore his heart out. Her once beautiful, sparkling eyes were despondent. He stood taking her hand in his; the call to the police could wait.

Tugging her away from the desk, he guided her to the couch. Sitting, he pulled her onto his lap and grabbed a throw blanket, spreading it over them. Ben wrapped his arm around her as she collapsed on his chest. He could feel her body wrack with sobs as he gently rubbed her back.

"It's okay sweet one. I'm here. Let it all out." He crooned in hushed tones, holding her tight. "No one will ever hurt you."

Slowly her body melted into his, her sobs turning into the odd sniffle.

He reached for a box of tissues from the table and held it while she took a handful. Mopping her face, she dabbed his chest too. With a shaky laugh, she said, "I always seem to be crying on you."

"That's okay... I don't mind."

She looked up at him and laid a soft hand on his face, locking her eyes with his.

"What did I ever do to deserve you?" Holding onto his face for dear life, she gently placed a kiss on his lips. She was so very grateful that this man was in her life.

He groaned when he felt her tongue dance with his.

God, she is pure torture...

His arousal was immediate when she turned to straddle his thighs. He could feel her hands running down his chest, down further to his stomach, causing him to tighten it at her touch.

Leaning his head back, he broke the kiss off, fully intending to stop. He felt her hot wet tongue trail down his neck, lapping and tasting at his throat, her teeth nipping him there.

Hissing out a breath, he grabbed her hands that were fast approaching the waistband of his pajama pants.

Holding onto them, he looked into her desire filled eyes, seeing the same raw emotion he knew that was in his own.

Softly he asked, "Are you sure this is what you want Abbi?"

She leaned forward gazing intently into his eyes. Coming closer inch by inch until their noses touched. She murmured against his lips, "I have never been surer of anything in my life Ben."

He hiked her closer. Using his good hand to cradle her bottom as their lips clung to each other. There was no question in either of their minds where this was leading them.

He stood, lifting her as he did. She wrapped her legs around his waist as he carried her to her bedroom. Devouring her with his mouth, he gently laid her on the bed.

Pulling the clip from her hair, he ran his fingers through the softness of it as he covered her body with his. His mouth trailing hot kisses just below her ear.

A soft whimper escaped past her parted lips as she felt him unzip her sweater, tugging it off one arm, then the other, his lips never leaving her skin.

His mouth left a blazing trail as he brushed the tops of her breasts above her tank top. She needed to touch him, or she'd go insane. She trailed her hands across his back, through his hair, as she felt his wonderful mouth taste her skin.

"Abbi. Take this off me." Ben said, lifting his arm in the brace.

"You can't!" she cried, shaking her head.

"It's fine, I'll be fine," he reassured her.

"I don't know about this." Reaching up, she pulled on the straps releasing his arm.

The second it was off Ben moved between her legs. The fact she still had her pants on, didn't stop him. His lips blazed a fiery trail along her inner thighs, up to the flatness of her stomach. He moved his mouth to her hipbone, nipping it as he reached for the hem of her shirt, slowly pushing it upwards.

Abbi was spinning out of control. Until she felt his hands touch her tank top. A horrified image of him running away entered her head.

Oh no, there's no way he can see my stomach...

He felt Abbi's hands grab his, stopping him from going further. Ben looked at her, seeing the slight shake of her head he slid up the length of her to look her in the eyes.

His gaze dropped to her lips, softly he murmured, "Abbi, my sweet one." He nibbled on her bottom lip, "When we make love..." he paused slipping his tongue in to plunder her mouth. Pulling slowly away he looked into her eyes again, "I'll make love to every inch of your beautiful body," he growled, dipping his head to suck on her earlobe.

She moaned, nodding her head. This time when he reached for the hem of her shirt, she didn't stop him. For the life of her, she couldn't stop him even if she wanted to.

He gently pulled it up, stopping at her bra where he laid a soft kiss just below the band that rested against her ribcage.

Straddling her legs, he peeled it off the rest of the way. "Am I too heavy for you, luv?" he asked, concern in his eyes.

She couldn't respond. Instead, she vigorously shook her head no.

He bent down to kiss her mouth once more before he made his descent down her body.

Hooking a finger into her bra strap, he dragged it down as he trailed his mouth onto new territory. He reached behind her back and in one deft motion he was tugging off her bra.

Abbi closed her eyes, her hands clenching the blanket beneath her when she felt his mouth tugging and suckling. A heavy fiery wetness overcame her, exploding to her most private core.

She ran her hands through his hair, holding him fast to her, feeling his mouth dip down her ribcage to her belly, just above the waistband of her pants.

Okay ... this is it. One look at my stretch marks and he will hightail it out of here... Sure, they were long faded, but they were still there.

Ben gripped the waistband of her pants. With one hand he tugged them down as he glided the other over her bare skin. Pulling them off, he touched his tongue to her knee, tasting her skin.

He caressed each leg with his hands as his mouth made the same blazing trail once again along her thighs to her panty clad hip bone, biting it softly. Only this time, he gently touched his lips to the lines that would forever mar her body. He didn't care. They could cover her from head to toe and he'd still want her as much as he did at this very moment.

She tensed. Any second, he would jump up and run for home. She clenched her eyes closed... waiting for the heat of his body to leave her.

Yep, there he goes...

She felt the cool air on her skin where the warmth of his body had been just a few moments ago. She slowly opened one eye. There he was, sitting as still as a statue, gazing down at her.

She lifted her head to see what he was looking at. Nothing but her stretch marks and scars as far as she could see. Despite feeling the heat of his gaze as his eyes travelled over her, she started to squirm, like a bug under a microscope.

He mumbled something, bounded off the bed and left the room.

She knew it. There was no way he'd be back. She pulled the corner of the quilt and covered herself from head to toe.

She needed to wallow in self-pity before she had to face him again, if ever.

Hearing a rustling sound, she ignored it and laid as still as she could.

"I'm back.... Abbi? Where did you go?"

Glancing at the bed he saw that she was gone. He looked in the bathroom only to find it empty. It took him seconds to cross the hall to search in his bag for a condom. She couldn't have gone far. He looked at the bed again when he noticed her hair peeking out from above the quilt.

He walked over and sat down, pulling the corner of the cover back as he did so.

He chuckled. "What are you doing?"

She opened her eyes, looking at him with sadness. "I know the sight of me turned you off," she mumbled.

He let out a bark of laughter, one brow raised in question. "Are you, insane woman?"

"Well, why else would you leave after staring at me?" She put a self-conscious hand on her blanket covered stomach.

His eyes darkened with passion. "I was staring at you because I'm in awe of you. You're stunning Abbi," he breathed. "And... I left to get this." He held up a package, shaking it. His head tilted to the side, a sexy smile on his glorious lips.

Her eyes grew large. "Oh!" She felt like such a fool.

"Yeah," he said. Removing the hand at her stomach he laced his fingers with hers. Still holding it firmly, he laid her arm above her head while he leaned over to kiss her.

The heaviness returned to her at the touch of his lips. Wrapping her free hand behind his neck, she pulled him down to her.

His other hand found her breast, his thumb softly flicking the tight bud that had formed there. At the sound of her whimper, he groaned deep in his throat.

If I don't stop this sweet torture soon, I'll be of no use to her...

Still sitting on the bed beside her, he pulled away, turning, so she was looking at his back. Ben bent towards her waist, tugging her panties down all the way to her ankles. Abbi helped by rapidly kicking them off.

Slowly, he ran his hands back up her calves, trailing kisses on her knees and thighs.

His hands followed his lips. Only stopping to slip one finger inside her, he found her dripping as he nipped her hip bone.

She bucked and moaned under his touch. *Lord have mercy, that was just his finger.* She cried out reaching for him, blindly grabbing his arm as she tugged him to her.

He crawled up beside her, laying his head next to hers. He kissed her then, so passionately; she thought she'd pass out from lack of air. Reaching out, she ran her hand down his stomach past his waistband, seeking his arousal, her fingers lightly stroked its softness. She needed to feel him... feel him inside her before she lost all control.

Ben pulled back, grabbing her hand. "Careful my love," he whispered hotly against her lips.

"I can't... I... Ben, I can't wait any longer... please," she begged on a whimper as she tugged at his pajamas, pulling them down.

"Where did the condom go?" he asked, searching for it.

She rapidly shook her head, "It doesn't matter, I can't get pregnant," she panted, as she pulled his pants off.

I about fainted last night trying to put them on him, now I'm acting like a harlot to get them off.

"Are you sure?" he asked, surprised.

"Yes, damnit!" She shouted in frustration, pushing him back onto the pillows.

Ben laughed at her eagerness as she moved to straddle him. At once his laughter was replaced with a low growl as liquid fire spread through his loins.

She rose and fell twice before he grabbed her by the waist and turned her around to lay her on her back. She instinctively wrapped her legs around his hips, trying desperately to draw him closer.

Holding her thighs, he slowly withdrew. Just the tip still inside her warmth... waiting.

She clenched her legs, bringing her hips up to meet his as he slowly pushed forward, stroking inside her.

He withdrew again. Teasing her, marveling at the sounds coming from her throat. Sounds that were for him and him only. Until finally, he could no longer control himself.

When she arched up to meet him this time, he grabbed her hips, thrusting deep inside. He felt her insides clench around him, knew that she was on the verge of climaxing from the sweet sounds coming from her throat, the shuddering pleasure coursing through her body.

With one last thrust, he brought them both over the edge of pure ecstasy. They soared together among the stars before coming down in quivering waves of spent pleasure.

He collapsed on top of Abbi. Rolling over onto his back, Ben brought her with him. She lay there, softly nestled on his chest.

Abbi could hear his heartbeat slowly return to normal, as did her own. She was in awe at what they had just shared. She was utterly spent. Never in her life had she ever felt so alive, so loved, so respected, so like... jello.

Sighing in contentment, she curled up against Ben's warmth. She started shivering; she didn't want to move just yet. She didn't want this moment to ever end.

Ben titled his head, looking down at her. She was breathing softly. The gentle rise and fall of her chest told him she was sleeping. He slowly took the quilt, covering them both with it. Pulling her tighter to him, he kissed her forehead. His shoulder hurt something fierce, but it was worth it. He closed his eyes, relishing in the feel of her soft body next to his.

Later, when they woke, he'd see about getting that prescription that Doc had given him and call the police. *With everything that is going on, I need it to heal like yesterday...* he thought, falling off in a light slumber.

THE PERSON STUMBLED on a limb that had fallen from one of the trees that graced Abbi's property. They cursed as they fell along the shore of her backyard, splashing into the water. The focus had been on her house and not where they were walking. They needed to see what the couple inside were doing at that very moment.

Do I dare go closer to the house?

It was known that Ben had stayed the night. The thought of him and Abbi spending any time together was enough to make them want to gouge Ben's eyes out. To stay the night was more than could be tolerated. They wanted to maim him... The dogs barking from within, told them they needed to get out of there, and fast.

'*Uh, uh, uh... Patience is a virtue, all good things come to those who wait.*'

They felt like saying to that voice to shut the hell up, but knew it was right.

Ben and Abbi need to be separated like the need for my next breath.

But how?

'*Create a diversion! One that removes Ben for good*'.... The voice echoed in their mind as they scurried away.

Chapter 19
Book 2 (Moonlit Stalker)

ABBI SAT STRAIGHT UP in bed; something had awakened her. Feeling a cool breeze, she looked down at her chest and noticed her lack of clothing. With a jerk, she yanked the blankets up to her shoulders and sat in a daze.

Good Lord, I've never slept naked in my life.

For a second, she was confused until she felt the bed moving. Then it hit her like a ton of bricks... she and Ben taking a tumble between the sheets. She had been, for lack of a better word, reckless. She hadn't known she could even be that word, but she had. And it had felt awesome. Abbi giggled as she laid against the pillows and nestled into the blankets.

She turned her head and watched him while he slept.

He's a gorgeous human being. Kind, sweet, attentive, sexy as hell. And he wants me.

Sighing softly, she leaned over and kissed him on the cheek.

The dogs started freaking out the second her lips touched his skin, not their usual way of communicating, but full-blown 'someone is about to break into your house' freaking out. She turned to her bedside table and sat up. Opening the drawer, she removed the laptop from within. Turning it on, she waited for it to boot up.

"Hey," Ben murmured, rubbing her back.

Abbi looked over her shoulder at him. "Hey handsome." She smiled. "Did you sleep well?"

Ben moved closer to her, smiling. "I did, as a matter of fact," he said, softly brushing a kiss along her ribcage.

A thrill went through her as the laptop came alive with a beep, catching both of their attention. The screen filled with a live feed from the cameras, inside and out of the house.

"That's impressive," Ben said, leaning on his arm behind her.

"Ah... yeah," she replied distractedly, her brows knitted together as she scanned the different views. "The dogs are going berserk."

Ben sat up; eyes fixed on the screen. Frowning, he pointed to the view of her driveway where a car was parked and tapped the screen.

"Who is that?"

Abbi turned her head to get a better look. "Hmm... I don't know."

Ben edged closer. His brows pulled together in concentration.

"Someone is walking around the car."

Abbi clicked on the screen to enlarge it. She didn't recognize the vehicle, so she zoomed in to get a better look at the person... persons she corrected herself. They watched as the unknown people turned to watch another car pull into her driveway.

Both leaned forward, staring intently at the screen. The people from the second car got out and headed towards the first couple.

At the same time, Abbi, and Ben, had a horrified realization.

She tossed the laptop on the bed. Turning towards each other, Ben grabbed Abbi by her shoulders as she grabbed his arms and in unison they said, "Bloody hell my parents are here!" "Oh no! My kids are here!"

They moved as one, scattering in opposite directions.

"Your brace! Come here, I'll put it on you." She snatched it from the floor and made quick work of the task. Turning away from him, she grabbed up her pants. Abbi glanced at him as she pulled on her sweats.

"You cannot put your pajama pants back on!!!" she hissed.

With one leg in, Ben paused a moment in thought. "Yeah... you're right!!" He turned and ran out of the room.

Abbi shoved her arms into her tank top, tugging it over her head. Pulling her sweater on, she noticed her pants were on backward.

"Aargh!" she uttered in frustration. Whipping them down, she spun them the right way.

She wondered where Ben had gone off to as she took a glance in the mirror and groaned. The memory of his hands in her hair made her blush terribly. Grabbing a ball cap, she gathered it into a ponytail and stuffed it through the hole in the back. Darting her gaze to the monitor she saw Ava walking up the sidewalk to the porch.

"Ben!!! Where are you?" she called walking into the hall.

"Right here luv." He appeared behind her, zipping up his jeans.

"Hey." He caught her hand and pulled her around to face him. "Before we need to deal with this, know that every second that they are here, I'm thinking of you." He cupped her neck, his thumb trailed along her jawline as he closed the gap between them and brushed his lips softly against hers.

She kissed him back, clinging to him, desperate to remember the taste of him, the feel of his mouth against her own. It would be agony not to touch him for a week.

The ringing of her doorbell broke them apart. The dogs beat a trail once again to the door, in a frenzy of barks. There was no way they could prolong the meeting any longer.

Ben gave her one last longing look before she turned away, taking his hand in hers, she led the way to the kitchen.

"Ready?" she asked. Taking a deep breath, she walked to the door.

"Yeah," he gave a quick nod. Smiling to reassure her that all would be fine, he added, "As I'll ever be."

Abbi gripped the handle and opened the door wide. The dogs flew out, clamoring for attention from anyone who would give it.

"Ava, honey." Abbi held out her arms.

"Mom!! It's good to see you. I've missed you so much," she said, rubbing her back, she spied Ben standing there. "And who is this?"

"The name's Ben," he smiled, offering his hand. "Your mom has told me all about you."

"Funny, she didn't tell me a thing about you!" Ava smiled, shaking it.

Abbi gulped and sent her daughter the look. "That's because you never called me, Ava."

"Yeah. Well, I think I just met your parents." She glanced out the door, motioning to the gathered group. "The rest are just talking to them now."

He nodded. "Yeah, that would be them. Excuse me. Nice to meet you, Ava."

Ben turned to Abbi, his hand settling at her waist, he softly said, "I'll be right back. I'll just greet my parents."

Abbi stepped out onto the porch, watching him approach the group. She watched as his mom turned around. A look of pure heaven crossed her lovely features. She took his face in her hands, kissing him on the cheek. She then glanced at his arm in the brace, covering her mouth when she saw it. She wrapped her arms around him and cried happy tears at the sight of her son. Ben's dad continued to talk to Luke, Lane, and a beautiful girl.... *Cassie, was it?* She couldn't remember.

Her sister, Kim, had broken off from the group and was walking towards the house, stopping here and there to admire the plants in Abbi's gardens. Ava stepped up beside her mom, putting an arm around her waist. Abbi did the same, pulling her close to her side.

"So... Mom..."

"Yes, sweetie?"

Ava glanced towards her giving her a sidelong stare. Abbi raised her brows in question. "About that Ben. He's ah...fine-looking, isn't he?" she grinned.

"I have noticed, yes." Abbi smiled as she watched Ben's dad give him a bear hug. His mother dabbed her eyes as she talked to Cassie.

"His parents are nice too, really informative," Ava said, nodding her head.

Abbi furrowed her brows. "Hmm. Nice. I haven't met them yet."

What is Ava getting at...

She tried to remember what Ben said to his father on the phone the other day...

Wait, that was just yesterday? Oh my God! He told his dad about us...

"Yeah. They said they just had to come from England to meet the woman who captured their son's heart. Hmm... imagine that." Ava stroked her chin looking at the sky in thought.

Abbi swallowed hard. A golf ball-sized lump in her throat refused to go down. "Really?" she squeaked.

"Mhm... They went to his house after getting directions from Mack. He told them if Ben wasn't at home, he might be here." She moved her arm from Abbi's waist to rest it on her shoulders.

"Nice people they are. I think their English accents are just the cutest thing." Ava grinned. "Especially when they said how nice it was that Ben found a woman who lived right beside him. His girlfriend if I'm not mistaken. Any new houses being built since the last time we were all together, Mom?" she queried, chuckling as she looked around.

"You are a horrible daughter." Abbi laughed, hugging her.

Ava grinned. "A-ha! I'm sorry! I just couldn't help myself."

The smile fell from her daughters' beautiful face, worry replacing it. "Is he the real deal though, Mom? Or is he after your money?"

Noting Abbi's stern look, Ava backed away, holding out her hands defensively. "Correct me if I'm wrong. I just worry about you... up here all by yourself."

Abbi took her daughter's face in her hands, her eyes softening. "Yes honey, he's the real deal. At least it feels like he is." She kissed the tip of Ava's nose. "And he has his own money too, so please don't worry about that."

If Ava didn't know that he was an actor, it wasn't Abbi's place to tell her. She watched Ben shake hands with Luke then Lane, as his father introduced them. All smiling and happy... for now.

"You're not like... having sex, are you?" Ava asked, searching her mother's face. "Oh... My... God! You are!!!" she said, her voice rising with every word.

"Shh!! Keep it down. I don't want the entire world to know for goodness' sake!" Pointing her finger at her daughter she chided, "And don't you dare breathe a word about this to anyone. We are keeping our relationship quiet for now."

"Your secret is safe with me." Ava grinned. "But everyone here already knows that you and he are a couple. It doesn't take Einstein to see. Besides, Ben's parents already spilled the beans."

"Great... just great," Abbi said, dryly. "I wanted to tell Lane. Luke won't care, but you and Lane..." Abbi trailed off shaking her head. Scrunching her forehead, she looked at Ava.

"Why are you guys here anyway? Lane said Thursday, today is Tuesday."

Abbi could feel the tension seeping in her shoulders. "And Aunt Kim? Lane never mentioned bringing her along." Abbi wondered where everyone would sleep.

Ava gripped her mom's shoulders, massaging the tightness that she knew was there. "We all got off a few days early and wanted to surprise you. Aunt Kim got herself into trouble at work and just wanted to tag along," she explained, working on a stubborn knot.

"I'm sorry, honey." Abbi was. She had no cause to snap at Ava like that. "I've just been under a tremendous amount of stress lately," she said, watching Cassie who now joined Kim over by the plants. Abbi followed Cassie's line of sight.

How sweet. She's watching Luke... Nope, that's not who she's looking at.

Ava at once felt the tension she had just been working to relieve, suddenly return. Something was bothering her mother; she could feel it under her hands. Looking over her mom's shoulder, she saw exactly what the cause of it was.

Cassie... watching Ben with hunger in her eyes. Ava rested her chin on Abbi's shoulder. "Ah, yeah, Mom... you might want to nip that in the bud," she mumbled.

Chapter 20

Ben overheard his mom telling Abbi's sons, that his dad and she had traveled straight from England the minute they had hung up the phone with him yesterday. He didn't doubt it.

"Hey, Mum."

He waited for the onslaught from his mother at the sound of his voice. She stopped in mid-sentence. Turning around, she let out a delighted squeal. Taking hold of his face, she kissed him on the cheek as she rocked them to and fro. Nancy backed away as she heard a groan coming from her son, her gaze fell to his arm.

Nancy gasped. "Oh, my goodness, Benjamin!" she cried. "What happened to you? Did you get attacked by a bear?"

"No mum." Ben chuckled. "I ah, took a tumble is all. It's good to see you." He meant it; he just wished they had waited a tad longer, or at least given a heads up.

"I've missed you so," she said. She took him in her arms, rocking side to side.

Ben glanced over at his father. "Dad, so good to see you."

His mother still hung on tight.

His dad laughed, "Nancy, let him go for God's sake."

She reluctantly took a step back, dropping her arms as she did.

"You will drive him up a wall and he'll have us on the first flight back to England." Stepping forward, he gave his son a hug. "Ben, it's good to see you," Greg said.

Lowering his voice so only Ben could hear he added, "Sorry about all this, she just wouldn't wait and threatened to come by herself."

Ben's eyes lit with amusement; he could picture it. He gave a quick nod and smiled. "It's fine, Dad. I figured as much."

Stepping back, Greg turned to the group gathered.

"Have you met Abbi's sons? Luke and Lane, and is it Luke's girlfriend, Cassie?" he said looking at them for affirmation.

Ben took Luke's hand in a firm grip. It was hard to tell apart the two men standing before him; they were a mirror image of each other. "Hey, how's it going?"

"Good man, nice to meet you and I'm Luke."

Ben turned to the other man. "Lane, I take it?" he asked with a grin, shaking his hand.

"Indeed, it is. How's the good old Canadian north treating you?" Lane asked him.

"Good. No complaints so far."

"Nice!" Luke nodded. "Oh, this here is Cassie," he said draping an arm around her shoulders.

Ben squinted as if the sun was streaming in his eyes. It wasn't. He just recognized the look that Cassie was tossing his way. "Pleased to meet you," Ben nodded, not bothering to extend his hand. She murmured a greeting and walked away.

"So, Ben, what is it you do for a living?" Lane asked. "You know, seeing how you're dating our—"

Luke smacked Lane on the arm, cutting him off from finishing what he was saying.

"Duuude. You just met the guy. *Really?* You gotta ask that now?" Luke changed the subject. "Let's go say hi to mom, I'm sure she'd just love the break from Ava's interrogation."

Lane looked at Ben apologetically, "Sorry, he's right. Mr. and Mrs. Quinn, I'm sure you would like to meet her as well?"

"Oh, of course! It would be a delight," Nancy said, striding along with them, as she tugged on Greg's hand.

Ben stood there for a second, watching the four of them make their way to the front porch. He glanced towards Cassie and a lady he had yet to meet. Cassie was staring at him intently with a come-hither look. He ignored her as he followed the rest to the house.

Abbi's eyes flashed with disappointment when she saw Cassie giving Ben a smoldering look. Abbi had to deal with a full house for a week, but she also had to deal with Cassie undressing Ben with her eyes. She honestly didn't know if she could handle it without hitting her.

"Mom, you're ravishing as usual," Luke said, hugging her.

"And you're still a sweet talker I see," she laughed, wrapping her arms around him.

Lane came up behind Luke reaching out. He, too, gave her a hug and a kiss on the cheek. "Hey mom, how's it going?" he asked, a look of concern on his face.

"Good, Honey, it's going well," she said, reaching out to give his hand a reassuring squeeze.

Abbi heard Ben's mom whisper to his dad. "Oh my, she is a darling."

Ben stepped forward taking Abbi's hand in his, he searched her face. He wanted to drop a quick kiss on her lips, but not in front of both their families. Instead, he gave her a slight questioning nod. She returned it with one of her own. He took a deep breath.

"Mum, Dad. I'd like you to meet Abbi Peterson. Abbi, my parents, Nancy, and Greg Quinn." He inclined his head towards them.

"Nice to meet you both," Abbi said, holding out her hand.

Neither of them took it; both just stood there staring at her. She quickly risked a glance at Ben's face, he seemed to be holding his breath. Abbi saw her kids were too.

Awesome! They hate me...

She was ready to go jump in the lake when his mother let out a squeal and threw her arms out for a hug. "Oh, my goodness you sweet, sweet, girl you!!" She grabbed Abbi into the folds of her embrace and started jumping in place.

Abbi was shocked. *Girl?*

"Nancy. For God's sake! You will give the girl a headache, let her go!" Greg laughed. "Come here young lady, and let me look at you," Greg said, taking her by the shoulders.

Girl... young lady? His parents are lovely, but their eyesight is questionable...

"Please, excuse Nancy. I fear the jet lag is getting to her a bit. That and we never thought Ben would ever find another woman. Not after what that slag did to him while he was off—" Nancy jabbed him in the ribs.

Luke, Ava, and Lane's brows shot up at the mention of the word slag. None of them had a clue what it was, but it couldn't be a good thing.

"Dad..." Ben uttered the one word, giving him a 'seriously, shut the hell up' look. Which was enough for Greg to understand it was a warning not to continue. "Abbi already knows what happened, and I would prefer it wasn't talked about anymore," he said, looking at them both. He smiled to soften his words.

Greg nodded with understanding.

Ava clapped her hands, "So, who wants a drink? Ben? Mr. and Mrs. Quinn? Would you like one?" she asked, nodding her head. Not waiting for a response, she turned on her heel and walked into the house.

"Please, call us Nancy and Greg, dear. And that sounds divine," Nancy replied, eagerly tugging Greg's hand as she followed Lane and Ava into the house.

"Luke, can you grab Aunt Kim," Ava yelled. She scrunched up her nose. "And... what's her name again?"

"Cassie, for the tenth time, Ava." Luke said, shaking his head. "After a six-hour drive, you'd think you'd know by now," he mumbled as he turned to fetch them.

"Yeah, that's right. Grab her too," she called.

Ben and Abbi were standing there staring at one another when they heard, "Well... hellooo, stranger."

It was Kim.

Abbi turned to see her sister climbing the steps, with Luke and Cassie, hot on her heels.

"Well, hello to you too stranger," Ben grinned.

"Ben, this is my sister, Kim," Abbi said, glancing at Cassie.

She needn't feel jealous. But she did. There was this beautiful young woman, openly showing an interest in Ben, looking like she was about to pounce on him at any minute. The kicker... Luke was standing right next to her.

Kim opened her arms in a way of greeting him. "Get over here big boy!" she chuckled.

Ben let out a bark of laughter. "Ah..." he looked to Abbi for help. "What should I do?" His eyes pleaded with her to give him the knowledge.

Kim spoke first, "You should give me a hug that's what. Careful though, I might just take a nibble!" she hooted.

Ben looked at her with a mix between horror and fascination. Kim could no longer stand it.

"I'm just kidding with you. I love getting peoples feathers riled up. Besides, I can tell, you're a one-woman man, aren't you stud?" she asked, giving him a wink.

Ben nodded without saying a word.

"Good. Nothing but the best for my baby sister." Kim turned her head around and locked eyes with Cassie.

"You two, take a lesson from this man. Now, let's go and get our drink on."

Kim stepped aside to let the young couple pass. Looking pointedly at Ben she muttered out the side of her mouth, as she pointed to Cassie's back. "Keep an eye on that one," she warned him before sauntering in after the two.

Ben reached in and closed the door, shutting them off from the others inside.

"Your sister is something else, isn't she?" Ben chuckled as he took Abbi's hand and led her a few feet away from it.

"That she is," Abbi nodded, a grin on her face.

"Do you think if we left and went to my house, they would notice us gone?" he asked, taking her into his arms.

Abbi looked up at him. "Hmm, we can try." She smiled, "That didn't go so bad, I think."

Pursing his lips, he nodded. "Yeah, not too bad. My parents like you a lot."

"The feeling is mutual," she grinned. "The kids hit it off with you okay?"

"Seemed to. I've missed you," he murmured against her lips. Pressing the small of her back, he drew her towards him and showed her exactly how true that was. Her eyes flashed with desire, causing him to groan with frustration.

Wrapped up in one another, neither of them heard the door open. Ava poked her head out. "Hey, you two. Aren't you guys coming... *Whoa!* Good God! *Get* a room, will you?" she said, slamming it closed.

Her reaction mortified Abbi. She pulled herself out of Ben's arms, "We shouldn't have done that."

Ben didn't reach for her this time. "Abbi, she's an adult. I'm sure she doesn't expect her mother to be single for the rest of her life, does she?" he reasoned.

"No. I don't think she does." Motioning with her hand, she said, "She knows about us... You know... US!"

He squinted his eyes in thought. "You mean she knows that we've made love, is that what you mean?"

Just above a whisper, she replied, "Yeah." Abbi laid a hand on his chest. "I didn't tell her. She just guessed it."

He took her hand in his, kissing it. "Good. Sweetheart, I will shout it to the world if you want me to." He grinned.

"Noo!" Punching him playfully on his good arm, she said, "You wouldn't dare."

"Try me." He winked at her.

Laughing, she rushed over to the door. Her hand stilled on the doorknob, and she looked at him. "Ready?"

"Do we have to?"

"We don't have to do anything we don't want to. But I think we should."

"Fine." He walked up behind her and nuzzled her neck. "But the second we are alone I'm going to ravish every inch of your body," he growled in her ear.

Chapter 21

After supper, everyone pitched in clearing the mess away and were sitting down by the lake around the firepit. A bonfire within, cast its warmth and kept the darkness at bay. Ben sat on one side of Abbi, Ava on the other.

A coziness settled in Abbi's bones as she glanced across the fire at Ben's parents. They were sitting, hand in hand, heads bent towards each other, talking in hushed tones. Abbi marvelled at how sweet they were to each other. She watched as Nancy leaned forward to kiss Greg. He looked swiftly around to see if anyone noticed. Abbi smiled.

Ben doesn't get his forwardness from his dad...

"Mom, how is the book coming along?" Luke asked, poking the fire with a stick.

"Oh, good!" she nodded. "I hit a wall for a bit there, just needed some inspiration was all." She looked at Ben. He was her inspiration.

Nancy leaned forward, smiling. "You're a writer? How exciting! Do you write romance novels by any chance? I do so love a good romance."

Abbi winced and glanced at Ben for help. He was sitting there with his elbow resting on the back of her chair, his head in his hand. "Um... not exactly," she said. "I write—"

"She writes about murder mum," Ben supplied. Looking at Abbi, he shot her a wink and a soft smile.

Abbi gawked at him, her eyes growing large. *You could have been a tad more tactful!* She silently conveyed.

"Ha! Right up my alley," Greg interjected.

Nancy looked as if she just ate a frog or sucked on a lemon. Abbi wasn't entirely sure which, but the poor woman looked disappointed and repulsed at the same time.

"What's the name of your book, dear?" Greg asked, genuinely interested.

Abbi smiled. "The Jasper Killings."

"The Jasper Killings?" Greg looked around in thought. "Where have I heard that name before? I haven't read it, but the title is very familiar," he said, tapping his chin with a finger.

Ben had a moment of panic. He didn't care if the others knew about him being an actor. But he didn't want Cassie to know. She had her phone in her hand most of the night, which was perfectly fine by him. At least when she was looking at it, she wasn't trying to catch his attention. But every time he glanced over to talk to Luke, she was staring at him. He'd bet money on it the second she found out he was in movies; it would hit the social media sites. Something that he didn't want.

"Say, Dad," Ben said, standing up. He jerked a thumb towards the garden shed, his brows raised. "Can you come and have a look at Abbi's power washer with me for a minute? We can't seem to get it running."

"Sure thing! Would love to tinker with it." Greg jumped up, coming to stand beside Ben.

Abbi glanced around at him.

What the hell is he talking about?

Ben put his hand on her shoulder, giving her a gentle squeeze. "Love, can you get the keys?" he asked, nodding at her.

"Aww, how sweet? He called you love, Mom," Ava hiccupped, looking down into her empty glass.

Abbi got up and headed to the house. Her kids' happy banter trailing her as she went.

"Have a little one too many, there Ava?" Lane burst out laughing, with Luke joining in.

Abbi was halfway to the house when Ben caught up to her, steering her away to the bushes where no one could see them.

She giggled, "What are you doing?"

"This." He planted his lips on hers hungrily.

She tore her mouth from his. "Where is your dad?" she asked breathlessly.

He jerked his head back, biting his lip as his eyes twinkled at her. "Standing at the shed waiting for us."

"You're terrible." She laughed, shaking her head.

"Come on. I'll walk with you." He linked his fingers with hers as they headed towards the house.

Once inside he ran to the bathroom while she rummaged in the junk drawer in the kitchen for the keys.

"Aha!" she held them up triumphantly as Ben walked into the kitchen. She noted a flash of pain cross his face as he stretched his arm.

"How's your shoulder doing?" she asked as she gathered the makings for s'mores. Just in case, she grabbed a bag of chips and a box of cookies as well.

"The pain is a mild ache now. Earlier, I could have ripped someone's head off. But the beer seems to have dulled it," he said, leaning against the counter.

"Remind me and I'll call Doc Spence tomorrow. He told me he'd try to get some other medication for you brought in from Springbank."

At the mention of the doctor, Ben's thoughts turned to everything that had happened in the past few days. Sure, both of their families were here, so the likelihood of something else happening was slim. But he still hadn't called the police about it. He needed to get a hold of Mark; he'd know who to contact. If Ben remembered correctly, his brother was a cop. He was itching to call him this second.

"You ready to go open the shed now for your dad? He must be sick of waiting." Abbi looked at him, noticing he was deep in thought.

She put the items on the counter. "Hey. What's wrong?" she asked as she turned him around. She felt his neck and shoulder and new he was in more pain than he was willing to admit. Rubbing her hands across his skin, she massaged the tightness away.

He relaxed under her touch, her hands like a soothing balm to his soul. "Nothing," he mumbled. Turning around to look at her, he dropped a quick kiss on the tip of her nose. "Thank you love."

She knew something was up, but clearly, he didn't want to talk about it. Nor did she press him. "Are you coming?" Her brows rose with the question as she gathered the food off the counter.

"Yeah. Uh..." he scratched his head, not meeting her eyes. "I'll be right there in a bit; you go on ahead," he gestured towards the lake. Ben saw the flash of concern on her beautiful face. He wanted to tell her what he was up to but doing so would only make her worry. Something he didn't want her to do. She gave a quick nod. "Try not to be too long, okay," she said as she walked into the living room and out the door.

He let out a heavy sigh, watching her as she approached his dad. She must have said something funny because his dad was roaring with laughter. Ben grabbed his cell from his back pocket. Looking at his caller's list, he connected to Mark's number.

"Mark buddy! It's Ben. I got a favor to ask you." He laughed. "No, Abbi isn't free to date you. No this is serious; you got a minute...?"

"HI, GREG! HERE ARE the keys," Abbi said, handing them over. "Um, I'm not sure which one it is. I just keep trying until I get the right one. Funny how it's always the last one," she shrugged.

Greg looked at the ring she handed him. There had to be at least thirty keys on it. He threw his head back, barking like a seal.

Abbi joined in; she couldn't help herself; his laughter was so infectious.

Grinning, she said, "I'll be right back, just going to take this stuff to fire."

She set off towards the fire at a quick jaunt.

"Here Lane," she tossed him the bag of marshmallows and sat the rest on a chair.

"Right on." He got up collecting branches off a nearby tree.

"Nancy, do you need anything?" Abbi asked her.

"No thank you, dear. I'm just sitting here all toasty and warm," she said, dreamily staring at the flames.

The loons were out on the lake now, calling to each other. Nancy turned in her chair and looked at the lake. "What in the world is that glorious sound?" she asked.

"That's just the loons," Lane answered, offering a fist full of sticks to everyone. As he explained exactly what loons were to Nancy, Abbi glanced around.

Ava was just about passed out in her chair. Luke was on his phone. Kim and Cassie were nowhere to be seen. Maybe they went for a walk…She turned around and headed back to Greg.

As she approached, she heard him talking to someone, expecting it to be Ben. Abbi was mildly shocked when she saw Kim bent over, looking at the power washer. "Hey, you two, where is Cassie?"

"Ah, I saw her go up to the house a few minutes ago," Kim said, untangling the power cord.

Abbi glanced at the house… Ben was in there… alone. She took off at a fast walk, jogging the rest of the way to the house. She suddenly stopped just at the top of the steps.

Do I want to see what's going on in there? …

She trusted Ben, thinking back to the time when they went shopping and how he acted around those girls.

That's just it, Abbi... acted, he is an actor...

She wanted to tell her mind to shut up, but sadly, she knew it was right. With her mind made up, she took a step forward. There was no stopping her from going into her own home. She'd sneak quietly into the living room. Sticking close to the wall, she'd slip in and easily slip right back out, none the wiser.

BEN WAS EXPLAINING to Mark exactly everything that had happened since he had last seen him.

"Right. So, all he'd need is the last name to go with the first and he could trace him?"

He could hear someone walking around the house. Thinking it was Abbi coming in from her bedroom entrance, he needed to change the subject fast, he didn't want her knowing what he was talking to Mark about.

"So, yeah." He cleared his throat. "When are you coming back this way?"

He could hear the footsteps coming into the kitchen, stopping just behind him.

"Really, that's great! Look, I need to get back outside, but why don't you pop over on the weekend then? Abbi's family is here and so are my parents and I know they would love to see you again."

A smile broke out on his face as he felt her hand running along his spine. It felt wonderful...

Wait... no it doesn't!

Whipping around he saw Cassie standing there, a smile on her painted lips.

"Bloody hell!" he yelled. "No Mark, I'm not yelling at you! Just come over on the weekend. Right? I'll see you then."

He stuck his phone in his back pocket as he glared at Cassie, anger flashed from his eyes. "Just what the hell do you think you're doing?"

ABBI COULD HEAR BEN on the phone with Mark. She was about to leave when she heard him bringing the call to a close. Then he yelled 'bloody hell'. Thinking he'd caught her in the act, she let out a little squeal and turned to hightail in out of there. Until she heard him ask what the hell someone thought they were doing. She stopped in her tracks. It could only be Cassie.

Abbi had heard enough, she had to get Luke. Damn it she was torn; the lake was so far. She was bound to miss something.

Turning on her heel, she snuck towards the porch. Luckily, she didn't have far to go. Luke was coming up the back steps. She motioned for him to stop and placed a finger to her lips as she grabbed his arm, together they snuck in along the wall and waited.

"I SAW YOU LOOKING AT me all night," Cassie said, advancing towards Ben like a lion stalking its prey.

Ben backed away. "Uh, no you didn't," he snickered, moving so the counter separated them. Clearly, the woman was delusional. He needed to get out of there and fast.

"Yes, I did. I've been watching you from the moment we arrived. I know you want me," she said, seductively. She lunged for him over the counter and wrapped her arms around his neck. Pulling him close, she aimed her mouth at his.

Ben turned his head to avoid contact with her lips. His glance fell on the box of cookies that Abbi had left behind. Snatching it up he promptly put it in front of his face then heard Cassie sputtering as her mouth met the cardboard.

LOOKING AT LUKE, ABBI'S brows shot up when they heard a rustling sound. Shortly, followed by what sounded like Cassie spitting out a mouthful of dirt.

"I love a man who plays hard to get," they heard Cassie growl.

"Look, Cassie. Believe me when I tell you, I have no inclination whatsoever to play hard to get with you."

Ben removed her hands from around his neck and stepped away from her, inching slowly back towards the living room.

"First off. You must be blind not to notice I'm with Abbi, something I take very seriously." He stepped back another inch. He'd dealt with women like this before and knew at any second it could get ugly.

"Blinded by your sexiness," she crooned, tossing her hair.

Ben ignored her comment. "Second, you're not my type and thirdly you're with Luke."

He had thought he had finally gotten through to her until a lecherous grin spread on her thin lips. "So, you mean I still have a chance?"

Abbi heard enough. She stood up ready to fend the witch off, but Luke caught hold of her waist. Shaking his head, he motioned for her to stay. Her eyes flashing fire, she gave him a pointed look as she headed back towards the porch.

Cassie's lips reminded Ben of earthworms, skinny earthworms. He physically gagged at that thought. "Are you daft, woman?"

Luke couldn't have chosen a better word himself. He stepped out from behind the wall. "Hey Ben. Need some help?" Luke tossed Cassie a disgusted look.

Ben turned, relief flooding his face. He nodded and said, "Thanks man," as he headed through the living room and outside to search for Abbi.

Chapter 22

He didn't need to go far. Abbi was leaning up against the porch railing, her hands folded across her chest. From the look of her stance, he knew she had heard what happened in there.

"Hey sweet one," he softly said. Reaching out, he smoothed her hair away from her face.

She glanced at him, catching his hand in hers. "Walk with me?"

"Always," he murmured, dropping a soft kiss on her lips.

Neither of them said a word as they headed to the shed, and neither were expecting to see his dad and Kim still working on the power washer. Ben looked down at it, guiltily. "Hey, dad...ah, yeah... that's not broken."

Greg frowned. "Well... It is now. We will have another go at it tomorrow when it's daylight."

Ben glanced between his dad and Kim. "I'm sorry about that. I just needed an excuse to get you away from there."

"Why ever would you say that it was broke?" Kim asked, the wrench she was holding clanged to the cement floor. "Couldn't you have just said, 'Hey dad come look at Abbi's piece of shit power washer?'... No offense," she replied, looking at Abbi.

Abbi laughed at her sister. "None taken." Oh, how she loved that woman's forwardness.

"I didn't want my dad to let it slip," Ben shoved a hand through his hair.

Kim scrunched up her face, clearly trying to figure out what the hell Ben was going on about. "Does he always talk in circles?"

Abbi shook her head and smiled. "Hmm... No."

Greg nodded, chuckled, "Yes. Most of the time, he makes a habit of it."

Ben rubbed the tension from the back of his neck. He looked at Kim. "I didn't want my dad to slip where he heard about Abbi's book."

Greg looked as confused as Kim did, Abbi thought, amusement shining in her eyes.

Draping his arm around Abbi's shoulders, Ben said, "The Jasper Killings rings a bell to you because it's the movie I'm filming Dad."

"What! You... *You're* an actor?" Kim stammered.

Beaming with pride, Greg piped up, "He is. And a damn fine one too!"

"Wait... So that means. You're in Abbi's book—"

"Technically speaking, no," Ben interrupted. It didn't matter; Kim was on a roll.

"Holy crap!" Kim hooted with laughter, nudging her sister with her elbow. "You bagged a hottie here, didn't you Abbi?"

Abbi was thankful that the darkness of night was taking over. If Kim saw the three shades of red, she just turned she would have cackled about that too.

Kim took a step and said, "I gotta tell the kids!"

"No Kim!" Ben snagged her by the wrist. "Please don't do that. I don't want Cassie finding out."

Ben told them the reason for the secrecy. "And dad, that's why I asked you to look at this." He motioned to the power washer.

"Got you loud and clear," Kim nodded. Out of the corner of her mouth, she said, "Cassie is a bit of a hussy, if you ask me."

Abbi tugged on her shirt. "Kim, please don't say anything to her. I don't want to upset Luke more than he already is."

Kim looked at her. "Abbi, I won't. It's not my place to."

She might think differently if she knew what just happened in the house... Ben thought.

Greg offered his arm to Kim. "Shall we return to the fire and back to my lovely wife?"

"Why certainly dear chap," Kim mimicked his accent. Taking his proffered arm, she turned and said over her shoulder, "I need to find me a British man... Onward Gregory!" she pointed. Her cackle of laughter echoing across the lake as the two skipped merrily away.

"Your sister is quite something isn't she?" Ben looked down, smiling at Abbi as they walked.

She nodded in agreement. "She certainly is a hoot at times, I'll give her that," she said, as they joined the others at the fire.

Taking their seats, Lane reached out and handed the marshmallows to Ben along with a stick. He held up one for Abbi. "Mom?" he offered.

Shaking her head, she declined.

Ava's loud snoring had her looking down. The poor girl was lying on the ground sound asleep. Which led Abbi to wonder where everyone else would sleep. She wasn't expecting Cassie and Kim coming along too. She only had her bedroom and the spare. There were two couches as well, but they weren't very comfortable to sleep on.

Ben leaned over and whispered in her ear, "Love, I think I'll take my parents back to my house." He inclined his head towards his mom. "She's beat, but she'll never admit it."

"Why don't they just stay here. They can sleep in my room," Abbi offered.

He raised his brows in surprise. Touched at her offer. "You would really give up your bed for them?"

"Of course I would!" Standing, she bent down to brush her lips against his temple. "Just let me go change the bedding first."

A shiver ran along his spine at the mention of the bedding. "I'll be there in a minute to give you a hand. I'll just tell my parents and then come and help you."

She looked into his eyes. "You don't have to. It will take no time at all."

"No, I want to. Besides, we need to figure out where everyone else will be sleeping."

"Okay. I'll see you soon then," she smiled, turning away.

Ben watched her disappear into the darkness. He heard a sharp whistle... her call for the dogs to follow. He watched as all three bounded after her. Pulling himself out of his chair, he walked over to his parents and crouched down. His mother was dozing off at that point; gently he shook her arm. "Mom, wake up."

"I'm awake dear, just resting my eyes," she mumbled, snoring softly as she drifted back to sleep.

He turned his attention to Greg. "Dad, do you think you can wake her enough to get her in the house? Abbi is changing the bedding. You two can sleep in her room tonight."

"Sure thing," Greg nodded. "It may take a few minutes, but we will be there right shortly."

"Okay, I'm going to give Abbi a hand. When you come up, just hang a right on the porch to the double doors. They lead to Abbi's room."

Ben jogged up to the house, sailed up the steps and followed the porch to Abbi's room. He quietly entered through the French doors, soundlessly closing them behind him. Walking through the entryway, he stopped at the sight of her. She was standing with her back to him, hugging the sheets to her chest. A soft smile played on his lips.

What is she doing?

She inhaled deeply; her face buried in the sheets. Ben turned his head to the side, watching her. "What are you doing?"

Startled, Abbi whipped the sheets to the floor as if they were a snake and spun around. With a blush on her cheeks, she asked, "Must you sneak up on me like that?"

He walked to her, taking her in his arms. "Truly, I'm sorry." He arched a brow in question and chuckled, "But were you just sniffing the sheets?"

"No." She looked guiltily away, her eyes darting around the room.

"Yeah, you were," he teased. "I caught you."

She gave him a quick kiss. "Yep, you did. Now help me make the bed before your parents get in here."

Together they made short work of getting the bedroom ready for his parents. Abbi headed into the bathroom, while Ben fluffed the pillows. She wanted to make sure there were enough clean towels and soap for his parents and was just coming out as they knocked on the doors.

"Oh, my! What a lovely room. I do want to thank you, Abbi, for giving up your bed for us. It's very sweet of you," Nancy said, looking longingly towards it.

"You're welcome. Um, did you bring any luggage?" Abbi asked.

"Pfft, did we ever. It's out in the car," Greg said. "Ben, come give me a hand?"

Nodding, Ben followed his dad out in the hall.

"Nancy, the bathroom is just through that door," Abbi pointed. "Please, make yourself at home and have a bath if you like."

Nancy sat on the edge of the bed and patted the spot beside her. "Abbi, do you mind sitting with me for a minute, please?"

Oh, no...A feeling of dread came over Abbi at her request. She had a feeling his mother secretly disapproved of Ben and her. "Ah, sure. I can do that."

Taking a calming breath, she sat beside Nancy and tried to steady her nerves. If his mom hated her, now was the time she would say it.

"Dear, I don't know how to put this." Nancy paused. "So, I'll just say it. I've been watching you tonight with my son.

The way you two look at each other reminds me of how Greg and I were when we first met."

Abbi didn't dare say a word.

"I had my doubts of Ben ever finding a love like ours," Nancy sadly shook her head.

Now Abbi spoke. "Ah, with all due respect Nancy. I'm not sure what we have going on is love. I mean we only met, not even a month ago." Abbi stood. She could no longer sit still and so began to pace. "Honestly, I've had reservations about Ben and me," she stopped and looking at his mother said, "With you and Greg, I'm sure you had normal lives. Ben doesn't have a normal life. In fact, it's the polar opposite."

She started to pace again. "We've talked about it and yes, he was very reassuring. But I mean, come on! He meets glamourous women every single day." Abbi pointed at her chest, "I'm forty-five, with saggy boobs, stretch marks galore, three kids almost as old as him and a house full of animals, what the hell does he see in me?" Abbi clamped her mouth shut. Groaning she said, "I'm sorry. I shouldn't have ranted like that." She felt like a fool baring her heart out to his mother. Sighing, she sat heavily on the bed.

Nancy put a comforting arm around her shoulders. "Perhaps dear. But I know my son. He may not be in love with you right now, but he loves you. The girl he was with before. They never showed affection to one another at all, ever. I've never seen him this happy before, not even when he got the part for your book."

Abbi looked at her in surprise. "Oh, Greg must have told you."

Nancy smiled sweetly. "Not at all. I just looked on the internet when Ben told me he got the part. Of course, it led me right to you... I would say that it was fate that you two met, wouldn't you agree?"

"I never thought of that before." Abbi wasn't one to believe in fate, but she had to admit it seemed like the stars had certainly lined up for them to meet.

A bang at the doorway had them both turning as the two men arrived with the luggage.

"Mom, what the hell did you pack in here that weighs a ton?" Ben grunted, setting the suitcases down with a thud.

"The kitchen sink I do believe," Greg replied, rubbing his back.

Nancy rolled her eyes, "Hardly, you're just getting old Gregory."

"Possibly. But what is Ben's excuse?"

"Ah. Never mind that. We'll get out of the way so you guys can get some rest," Ben said, watching as Abbi came towards him, he had other ideas on what to do with the rest of the evening and it wasn't talking to his parents.

"Goodnight you two," Abbi called out as they headed into the hallway. She closed the door with a soft thud.

Abbi glanced at Ben. "Now, where is everyone else going to sleep?"

He jerked a thumb over his shoulder at the closed door, "Well, Kim dragged Ava into the spare room, they are sharing the bed, and Luke and Lane took the couches."

"Okay. So where is Cassie?"

Ben chuckled. Folding his arms across his chest, he leaned back against the wall. "Luke told me he called a cab, sent her to Springbank to catch a bus back home."

She covered her mouth with her hand. "*No!* He didn't?"

"So, you know what this means, don't you?" he asked, giving her a sly grin.

She raised her brows in question.

Taking her hand, Ben led her down the hall, through the kitchen, and out the front door, closing it quietly behind them. Putting an arm around her shoulders, he guided her down the steps. On the ground, he turned to look at her. The moon was shining on her face, lighting up her eyes. Eyes he fell in love with the very first time she laid them on him. With one finger, he tilted her chin upwards. "It means, sweetness, we have my house to ourselves."

He kissed her with a hunger that they both were feeling; a need to be closer, to be one. Pulling away, he whispered against her soft lips, "Let's head over to my place."

They started to run for his house when Abbi suddenly stopped. "Wait, shouldn't we leave a note?"

Bending down, Ben said, "Already taken care of. Get on."

"Huh... what? On what?"

"Get on my back. I'll give you a ride."

She laughed. "Are you crazy?"

"Only for you Abbi," he said, waiting for her to climb on.

"What about your shoulder?"

"It's just a short distance, it'll be fine," he answered, patiently waiting.

"But..."

"Woman! Would you just get on already?!" he laughed.

"Fine!"

She climbed on, feeling giddy like a schoolgirl. He jostled her into position as he walked.

"Oh my!" Her eyes grew large when she felt his hands cover her bottom. "You are a devil, aren't you?" she kissed his neck, running her fingers through his hair.

"This is nothing, just you wait."

She smiled at that as he set her down on the porch to unlock the door. Once inside, she stood in the middle of the kitchen, suddenly feeling sick in the pit of her stomach.

Ben turned to look at her, concern replaced the desire in his eyes. He slowly approached her; she had the look of a deer, caught in headlights.

He gently brushed her cheek with the back of his hand.

"What's the matter, Abbi?" he asked her softly, searching her face.

"I'm not sure, honestly." She felt anxious or was it just excitement? She wasn't sure; it had been so long since she felt pure joy like this. She was afraid of it all slipping from her fingers forever and never feeling this way again.

"Are you sure?" he asked, rubbing her arms. His eyes softened as he looked at her.

"No. I know what it is. I'm not sure I can talk about it just yet," she answered, looking at the floor.

Lifting her chin, he gazed into her eyes. "Is there anything I can do to help?"

She wanted to yell at him, to tell him to never leave her. But she dared not. She couldn't control him, nor did she want to.

"Just love me please."

He gazed deeply into her eyes as he took her into his arms. "Would you believe I've been thinking about this all day?"

She nodded mutely because she had too.

He pulled her closer, his hand went to the small of her back. "I've wanted to feel you..." he kissed the sensitive spot behind her ear as he grinded his hips against hers.

She gasped then moaned as his teeth grazed her skin in a path down her neck to her chest. Uncontrollable shivers started to pass through her body as he continued to seduce her with his words.

"To taste you..." his lips trailed to the swell of her breast.

He nipped her there, then flicked his tongue over the spot to soothe the sting away, only to repeat it on the other side.

Leaning back against his arm, she bared herself to his seeking mouth. Ben inhaled deeply and said, "To smell our mingled scent that only we create."

Dear God...

If anyone ever tried to take this man from me, I'd end up in a prison cell for the rest of my life.

Taking his face in her hands she brought his mouth to hers. She was going to hell; she knew it. What she felt for him was shameless... to some even sinful. But it was about time she felt like this. Some people never did, and if she was going to hell for it than she damn well was going to enjoy the ride there.

Ben clung to her lips. A low groan erupting from deep within his throat as he backed her up against the wall. Taking the hem of his shirt, she tugged it over his head, needing to feel his skin against her. She ran her hands down his chest, reveling at the muscles that played below the surface of his smooth skin.

He leaned his head against the wall, breathing heavily as he felt Abbi's mouth scorch down his body. He sucked in a ragged breath as her lips touched his stomach, causing it to tighten in response to her seeking mouth. Her hands reached to his jeans, pulling the button loose. As she tugged on the zipper, she could feel the heat coming off him.

He knew full well that if she followed with her mouth, he'd lose all control. As much as he hated to stop her, he had to. Grabbing her hands, he pulled her up to meet his mouth and guided her to his bedroom. Their lips clung to one another's with every step they took as he peeled off her sweater.

Abbi stopped him at the foot of the bed, shoving him so he sat down on the edge. She stood before him, slowly undressing. She saw the fire leap into his eyes as he wet his lips, leaning back.

He crooked a finger at her. "Come here," he murmured, his voice thick with desire.

Abbi crawled on top of him as he guided her head, bringing her mouth to his in a frenzy of passion. His other hand drew circles over her breast, teasing it to a peak, that she thought would surely burst. His mouth replaced his hand, biting and lapping. The fiery ache he caused, filled her to her core. Abbi felt like screaming as she held him fast to her chest. She needed to do something, anything to stop the sweet torture his mouth was doing to her.

Pushing herself up, she straddled his hips and shoved him back onto the bed. She met him there with her mouth, tasting the sheen on his body. Moving her bottom to his thighs, she pulled away from his lips and she moved her hands once again to his pants; this time he made no move to stop her. She shimmied her way down his legs, pulling his clothes along as she did. She laid down beside him, her eyes even with his hips, taking in the view before her.

With a feather touch, she took one finger and ran it down his chest, trailing over his stomach and further down. How she loved that trail of hair that dipped down below his bellybutton. She trailed wispy wet kisses there, her reward from him was a guttural groan of agony. Her lips continued their path, making her way to the base of his... she glanced at it. Penis was such an ugly word for such a beautiful thing that created such an intense pleasure in her; she'd decide on a better name for it later. For now, she tenderly placed her lips on that wonderful tip that he had so skillfully teased her with before. She opened her mouth taking him in, swirling her tongue around the edge.

Clenching his jaw, Ben growled out, "Abbi! For the love of God, you need to stop!"

She glanced up to meet his eyes and saw his veins standing out on his neck from restraining himself. "Are you sure?" she whispered; her breath hot against his already fevered skin.

"No! Yes! You're driving me bloody insane!"

With one last touch to it with her lips, she drew herself up. Straddling his hips, she gently seated herself over him. He groaned loudly as he felt her warm wetness encase him. Grabbing her hips, he held her to him, impaling her with his shaft.

She arched her back when she felt his hand glide to her breast. He sat up wrapping his arms around her while his mouth replaced his hand once again. She rode him as if the very hounds of hell were at her back. She could feel him shudder under her touch. She was in control this time, bringing them together to the edge of the universe in a blast of shimmering stars.

They collapsed together on the bed. Their ragged breathing slowly returned to normal. Abbi rested her chin on his chest, looked him in the eyes and inhaled deeply.

"I see now what you meant when you said about our mingled scent." She grinned at him.

"Yeah?" He kissed her on the forehead. Laying a hand on her hair, he guided her head to his chest.

"Go to sleep my love," he said as he pulled the blankets over them. Drawing her tightly in his arms, he knew he never wanted to be with anyone else for the rest of his life. His final thoughts before sleep claimed him was how was he going to convince her of that?

Chapter 23

Ben was standing in the middle of Abbi's kitchen. His parents sat at the table, sipping their tea while they played a game with Kim, Abbi, and her kids. He was watching her. She had woven a spell over him, around his heart. He was falling in love with her more as each day passed.

She was laughing and carrying on with them, sitting there in old sweats, her hair up in a messy bun, makeup-free, oblivious to her own beauty. She glanced at him then, a soft smile on her lips. Yeah, he was falling for her... hard. The need to protect her was maddening; four days had passed since their families arrived. Three days since he found the name of her stalker, Jacob Randal aka Jacob Smith, on her computer. A quick internet search brought up thousands, too many to glean any information to narrow it down. He had contacted Mark at once with the name and all the information in the file.

Ben took his cell out of his pocket. Checking to see if he missed a call, he inwardly groaned. As usual, there was nothing. Mark said the second he heard anything he'd call him; he was still waiting, he also said he'd stop by today. The waiting was driving Ben crazy. Soon, Abbi would sense something was up. He just didn't want to face her questions when it happened.

He checked his email, just in case, and saw that Tony had messaged him two days ago. Opening it, Ben frowned as he started reading:

'Hey Ben, hope all is well! As luck would have it, it looks like we will start up in a week. Will need you back here in two weeks if all is a go. Will be in touch, Tony.'

Great, he thought, just what we needed. He felt like telling Tony he couldn't make it in two weeks. But doing so would be in breach of his contract. He frowned.

What if we don't catch who is doing all this shit before I need to go back?

Sure, it could be this Jacob guy, but what if it wasn't? He had no idea how he would protect her then.

"Ha....!" Ava said, giving her teammates high fives. She looked to Abbi and her brothers, a triumphant gleam in her eyes. "We won! I told you we would."

"That's because it was four against three... how is that fair?" Lane laughed at her.

"Doesn't matter, losers feed the winners."

"Whiners, you mean?" Luke ducked, laughing, as Ava sent a smack his way. He then nodded. "Fine, we get to pick the menu, pizza and wings it is." He whipped out his cell.

Just then, all three dogs perked their ears up. Brutus raced towards the door and let out a woof as the doorbell rang.

Abbi hurried to answer it, grabbing hold of the dogs' collar as she did so. "Brutus back up."

"Abbi sweets!" Mark said as he crossed the threshold. "How're you doing, girl?" He took her in his arms and whirled her around to the counter.

"Mark! Good! Nice to see you again," she laughed, genuinely happy to see him.

He spun her out of his arms as Ben approached.

"Benny boy! My man! How's it going?" Mark asked, smacking Ben on the back. "I've got the intel," he muttered, giving Ben a serious look as he backed away.

Immediate relief washed over Ben. He leaned against the counter, pulling Abbi to him. She leaned back against his solid length and held onto his hands at her waist.

Mark turned and walked to the table, a smile on his face. "Hi there, Mrs. and Mr. Q... What are you guys doing on this side of the pond?" He took Nancy's hand in his and placed a quick kiss on the back of it.

"Oh Marcus, what are you going on about?" she giggled.

"You know you're the only woman for me," he smiled saucily, winking at her.

"Mark, how are you doing, son?" Greg stood up, folding Mark in a bear hug.

"Good Greg! Just got back from Cali. Needed some R and R, know what I'm saying?"

"That I do, that I do."

Mark glanced to the next person sitting at the table. "And who are you? Wait! Don't tell me, you must be Abbi's sister?" He held out a hand, bowing slightly.

Taking his proffered hand, Kim let out a cackle and studied his face. "That I am, you cheeky bastard. I'm Kim."

Luke leaned across the table, offering his hand. "I'm Luke, Abbi's oldest."

"I'm Lane... pleased to meet you." Lane nodded, a smile tugging his lips as he shook Mark's hand too.

Kim butted in. "Say, why do you look so familiar? Are you from around here?"

Mark turned to Ben; his brows raised in question. "I don't know. Why do I look so familiar Ben?"

They had an agreement. Whenever either of them met someone new in the presence of each other, they never gave away who they were unless the other was fine with it. Ben gave him a slight nod.

Mark looked back at Kim. "Ah... erm... no. Not really from around here, per se. I'm Canadian that is. I sold Ben my house, and we're co-workers you could say—"

He was about to tell her where they co-worked at, when a ravishing young lady stepped in the room.

Ava pointed at Mark, hopping from one foot to the other. "Oh my God!! You. You're... Mark Donovan!"

Kim wrinkled her forehead. "Who?"

"You know! The movie we saw last year together." Ava spun to look at Kim. "What was it called? You know...You said it was boring and fell asleep and the people in front of us were pissed because you were snoring so loud."

Ben snorted out a laugh. He knew exactly the movie she was trying to remember. "Delusion," he said, grinning.

Ava pointed and snapped her fingers at Ben. "That's it!"

"Huh..." Kim finally remembered the movie. No wonder she had fallen asleep.

Mark looked at Ava straight-faced. "Yes, that was one of my worst movies to date. Anyway, pleased to meet you. And you are?"

"Ava... my name is Ava... Abbi's daughter," she smiled sweetly... "Wait, so if you two are co-workers..." Ava looked between Ben and Mark. "What is it you do, Ben?"

There was no need in hiding his job now, with Cassie out of the picture.

"I'm an actor. The two of us are filming your mom's book, currently production is down." He sighed heavily, glancing down at Abbi. "But will be heading back in a couple of weeks."

She looked up at him. A look of sadness in her eyes.

"I got the email today," he told her quietly, tightening his arms around her.

She knew it was only a matter of time before he had to leave. She hated the thought of him going; she honestly didn't know what she'd do without him here.

"You have got to be joking." Ava hooted. "How..." She was at a loss for words.

Mark held up his hand, giving the universal hand signal. "We joke you not! Scout's honour. Wait... How can you know about me, but not Ben?" Mark wondered out loud. "He's a hell of a lot more famous than me."

Ava just shrugged her shoulders, not knowing the answer to his question.

The doorbell rang, announcing the pizza delivery. Luke got up to answer the door, pulling his wallet from his pocket as he flung the door open.

"Mark, will you stay for dinner?" Ava asked. She was starstruck. "I mean if you have no other plans..."

"I would be delighted to." Pulling out a chair at the table, he sat and smiled as Ava hurriedly planted her butt on the chair beside him, planting her chin onto her hand.

"Good. Can you tell me all about what it's like to be in the movies?"

Abbi knelt to get paper plates from under the counter, a frown working its way onto her forehead. She knew Ben had to leave soon. But she wished it wasn't this soon. Two feet appeared beside her had her slowly looking up, seeing an offered hand. It was Ben.

"Let me help."

He gave her hand a light squeeze before taking the plates from her to the table, setting the stack on its surface. He piled one with pizza and tossed a few wings on top, then walked to the fridge. Grabbing a pop, he tucked it under his arm and took Abbi by the hand. He led her through the living room to the back porch. Setting the food and drink on the table, he took her into his arms. "I don't want to leave yet," he murmured. "Not now, maybe never."

"It's okay Ben. I know you have a job to do. It's a couple of weeks away. Let's not think about it till then." She leaned back, looking into his eyes. "Who knows? Maybe it will be delayed again."

Ben saw her eyes glisten with unshed tears, and it nearly tore his heart out.

He sighed heavily and nodded despite knowing that wouldn't happen. "Right, you're right. Let's eat, shall we?"

They sat down, digging into the food, each lost in their thoughts.

If Mark didn't have any useful information for him, Ben decided he would find a way to stay here or bring Abbi along. Tony wouldn't like it, he found it distracting for the actors when friends and family were milling about. But Tony could hardly refuse the author from attending the set. Ben bit into a slice of pizza and decided that's exactly what he'd do.

"Say, Abbi, when was the last time you went on a holiday?"

"Hmm, let me think... Never," she said. She chuckled at the stunned look on his face.

"What! How could you not?"

"I don't like traveling."

He took a swig of the pop. "I see..." Well, he could understand that. He rather hated it himself.

"Why? Were you thinking of taking me with you?"

He brushed crumbs from his hands. "The thought crossed my mind."

"Maybe... For you I'll do it this one time." She gave him a weak smile.

"You would? For me?"

Abbi nodded.

"It's settled. When the time comes, you're coming with me." He leaned over, giving a quick kiss to her lips. "Deal?"

"Yes, it's a deal... wait. Filming is where, right now?" Abbi frowned.

Ben wiped his mouth. "Madrid, Spain." He glanced at her, noticing the frown. "Why?"

She sighed already feeling anxious. "Well, I best be drunk or drugged.... I don't do planes," she laughed apprehensively.

He raised his brows. "Seriously?"

"Yes. Seriously. Maybe I'll just stay here."

"No way, we sealed it with a kiss, remember?" he teased. He'd never make her do anything she didn't want to.

She remembered. She would never forget those lips. *Damn it! Fine, I'll go.* She held her hands up in defeat. "I know, I know! I'll go. But be forewarned. If I go a little crazy, don't blame me."

"Deal," he smiled. "You do realize I would never make you do anything you didn't want to, right?"

"I know, Ben. That's one of the things I like about you." She smiled.

Ava and Mark came out onto the porch just then, in a flurry of giggles. They sounded like two teenagers.

Ava looked towards the lake. "Hey. We are just going for a walk along the shore for a bit."

"Okay." Abbi nodded, a look of concern on her face. "Don't be too long if you can help it. Your brothers should be setting up the fireworks shortly." She wanted to say, *Hell no! You aren't going anywhere with that player*, but she had to bite her lip from speaking her mind. Ava was an adult. Abbi had no right to tell her what she could and could not do any longer.

Ben saw the concern on Abbi's face as she watched them walk away.

"Love don't worry. Mark isn't that stupid. Besides, he respects you too much."

"Mhm, let's hope not," she replied, absently.

A few minutes later they heard, "We're going to set up the fireworks now," Lane said, waving one in the air as he and his brother walked past with the dogs in tow.

"It's going to be a killer show this year. We spent over two grand on these," Luke added.

"Nice! If you need a hand, just yell," Ben offered.

"Sure thing," Luke nodded.

Kim ambled out onto the porch, followed by Greg and Nancy. She jerked a thumb towards the house. "The drug store dropped off a bag for you, Ben. And Abbi, some flowers were in the middle of your laneway. The delivery guy brought them up to the house." She wrinkled her nose in distaste.

"Flowers?" Abbi and Ben both asked, equally shocked. Puzzlement etched across Abbi's face, while Ben's showed a murderous look.

Kim noticed at once that Ben was glaring at her. "Hey, don't shoot the messenger. If it's any consolation, it looks like they were trampled on a few times."

"It's not you Kim, that I'm pissed with."

Getting up, Ben stalked into the house, followed quickly by Abbi.

Hurrying behind him, Abbi plowed into his back when he abruptly stopped before the table. Holding onto his arms to steady herself, she peeked around him. There, sitting in the middle of it was a dozen long-stemmed roses, laying on a newspaper. Kim had been right. The once beautiful petals were bruised and crushed; an envelope lying in the middle, nestled among the leaves smudged with what looked like blood.

Ben looked at Abbi, a foreboding furrow on his brow. He stepped closer to the table. Reaching out, he went to take the envelope.

Should I touch it, or should I call the police? ... To hell with it, it may be nothing. Maybe the wind had just blown them into Abbi's yard. He snatched the envelope and tore it open. Abbi waited anxiously.

"Son of a bitch!!" He ran a hand through his hair and started to pace the floor.

"What!" Abbi cried in alarm. "What is it?"

He cast a soft look in her direction. "Abbi no. You're not seeing this."

He had to protect her at all costs and the first way to do that was protecting her emotions.

"Ben. Let me see it." She held out her hand, waiting.

Mechanically, he watched his own hands as he folded the note. Shaking his head, he looked at her.

"No, I'm sorry. I can't do that. This is something that doesn't concern you... yet." He stuffed the paper in his pocket. He had to get Mark back here now and find out exactly what his brother told him.

"Yet? What does that even mean?" She spat the words out.

"I'll let you know, when I know."

"Fine, be stubborn." She turned on her heel and marched towards the back door.

Ben let her go. He had to. Otherwise, he would have given in and shown her the note. He watched as she made her way down the steps and into the yard. He turned to face the table once again and carefully rolled the newspaper around the flowers. He needed to get rid of them before she came back and the garbage can wouldn't work, she would just root through it when he wasn't around.

Opening the front door, he closed it behind him with a soft thud and looked around. He figured the weeds were as good a place as any and stalked across the front yard, crossing the road. With one last look behind him, he tossed them in the brush along the road, newspaper, and all.

Standing there with his hands on his hips, he turned back towards the house and glanced at the lake beyond. He knew he did the right thing, but he had to talk to Mark, and now. Taking his cell phone out of his pocket, Ben dialed his number and waited for the call to connect. His thoughts turned to Abbi. If she had seen it, she'd be a basket case right now if he had given in. How else would she have reacted if she had read it? Words that looked like they were etched in blood, five simple words...

'I'm coming for you Abbi.'

Chapter 24

It was a beautiful night for a walk. The water was gently lapping on the shoreline; gulls were flying back and forth, and Mark was kicking himself again, for selling to Ben. He had been a fool, staying away from such a beautiful place all the years he'd owned it.

He looked at Ava. "So, how do you like living so far away from your mother?"

"I hate it. We only get to see each other a couple of times a year now. Like I understand why she wanted to leave home, but damn, so far away is hard, you know?"

Mark nodded. "Yeah, I can understand that."

After the shock wore off from meeting him and realizing that both Ben and he were actors, Ava had turned out to be cool. He was amazed at how much he liked her. It had him wondering what was up with the Peterson women. It was like they were witches or something. Bewitching everyone they met.

Bewildered, he shook his head and glanced out towards the water, noticing a boat not far from the shore. *'Pearl Lake Yacht and Boat Rentals'* was written on the side.

"I didn't know you could rent boats like that around here." He jerked his chin towards the lake.

Ava glanced at where he was looking. "Yeah, only recently though. Like in the last year or so."

"Maybe I'll check it out while I'm here. When are you heading back home?" he asked.

"Well, I haven't mentioned it to Mom yet, we've been so busy. But I have the next two weeks off. Now I'm not sure I'll say anything though... with Ben being here and all." She wrinkled her nose.

"Why not?"

"Well, you know, I don't want to be in the way. Say, do you think Ben is serious about her?" she asked. "I... Never mind. Forget I asked that. It's probably against the man code, 'bros before hoes' to discuss things like that."

Mark stopped. He grabbed the sleeve of her jacket, stopping her in her tracks.

"Honestly, it's fine." He smiled. "I've known Ben for a few years now, and I know he'd expect me to answer you. He's just that kind of guy." He paused, thinking his words over carefully. *How much does she already know?* "Like I said, we have known each other for a while. I met him around the time he and his ex, split. He made a promise to himself, never to take any relationship for granted, ever. Which he never did, but you know some women, if you're not in their face 24/7 they feel neglected," he said, glancing at her. "Erm... um. Sorry got carried away there for a minute." He chuckled. "Anyway, he wanted to make sure the next one he had would be his last."

"Just spit it out, will you?"

"I'm getting to it, gee don't you know how to relax?" He laughed. He loved her spunk. "Yes, he's serious about her. If he weren't, he wouldn't be here. I can guarantee that." He started walking again. "He's had women falling at his feet.

Beautiful, gorgeous, stunning women. And do you know what he does?"

She shook her head.

"He steps right over them and keeps walking."

"Well, that's a dick move if I ever heard one," Ava said, frowning.

"No, you don't get it. These women pounce on him if he stops. Hell, some even grab his di.... Ah... well, you know!" Mark said, nodding, his brows raised.

Her brows shot up in response. "Oh! I see. Um... Well, it makes perfect sense then."

She fell silent as she looked at the boat again. It was no more than fifty feet from them now. She shielded her eyes, trying to make out the person at the helm. They looked familiar but she couldn't put her finger on it for the life of her. She waved, but they were so intent on watching her mom's house they didn't notice her.

Mark stopped and pulled his cell phone from his back pocket and looked at it.

"It's Ben." He hit the talk button. "Hey buddy, what's up?" he wrinkled his brow as he ran the tip of his tongue back and forth across his bottom lip as he listened to him. "*What?*! No, no, there wasn't anything like that when I came over." Mark glanced at Ava and frowned. "Yeah, we will be right there in..." he gave Ava a questioning look, she held up one hand, "... five minutes. Yep, we'll be quick, we can see the house from here.... M'kay... Bye."

"What was that about?" Ava asked. A sudden chill had her stuffing her hands in her pockets, oddly enough the breeze was warm.

"Well, your mom is pissed at Ben, and someone left some flowers in the driveway, dead ones with a nasty note. Come on. I have to talk to Ben."

"You were just talking to him." Ava pointed out.

"Yeah, but in private."

"You could have just told me to walk ahead, you know," she said testily. "And why is she pissed at Ben?"

"Will you just clam it for once and hurry it up." He laughed to soften his words.

"Sure, race you there." She took off at a jog.

Mark shook his head as her laughter carried to him on the wind.

THEY LOWERED THE BINOCULARS slowly as the boat floated soundlessly on the still waters of Pearl Lake. It was soothing really. Knowing that one day soon, they would live just a few hundred yards from where the boat now sat.

"Interesting. Very interesting... So, Ben, you didn't like the little present I left for my Abbi?"

How dare he touch them! And to throw them into the brush as if they meant nothing...as if they were trash!

"I hope Abbi was able to see them before that bastard removed them from the house."

'Ah, no worries. He will soon be out of the way... very soon, indeed.'

A feeling of pure elation coursed through their veins. Knowing that in less than 48 hours, when her family was heading back home, she'd be free, free of her family, free of his parents, but more importantly free from Ben Quinn.

Turning the helm, they directed the boat back towards its base. They would wait...It would be all over the news in no time that the great Hollywood actor was found dead.

BEN HUNG UP THE PHONE; he had to find Abbi. Tell her how sorry he was before Mark and Ava returned. Jogging across the front yard, he ran alongside the house to the back, looking at the porch to find it empty. Glancing down towards the lake, he saw her sitting there with his mum and Kim. His dad was helping Luke and Lane set up the fireworks.

He walked up to them, stopping short of the back of Abbi's chair. Mark and Ava were still not there.

"Hey, buddy." Kim called to him. "Why don't you sit?" she said, half-standing to offer him her seat.

He saw Abbi tense. "No, you stay there. I'll just sit over here," he said, crossing the circle around the fire pit. He sat in the lounge chair right across from Abbi.

Plopping back down onto her chair, Kim glanced at sister and did a double take. Abbi was shooting daggers across the way at Ben. Getting up, Kim said, "Alrighty! I'll just start a fire then. So, what's new with you?" Kim asked, glancing at Ben while she piled logs in the pit.

Kim felt terrible about the flowers. She should have just thrown them away; they were hideous. And even if they weren't, no one ever sent her sister flowers. Was someone trying to cause trouble between them? But who if that was the case? As far as she knew, only the people here knew that Abbi and Ben were in a relationship.

Ben cleared his throat before answering Kim. "Nothing much." He sighed, staring at Abbi. She wouldn't even glance his way. Just kept talking to his mother as if he weren't even there.

"Mum, when are you and dad heading back to England?"

"Oh, I was just telling Abbi here, that we have decided to travel a bit. Head towards Montreal or the East Coast, perhaps. Oh, I have the most brilliant idea! Why don't you and Ben come with us, dear?" She smiled, her face lighting up as she laid a hand on Abbi's knee. She sent a wink to her son.

*You sly woman...*Ben flashed his mum a smile.

"Ah, uh..." Abbi looked at Ben, a smile on her face. She remembered just then that she was still mad at him. Furrowing her brow, she gave him a dirty look and turned to his mother. "Thank you for the invite, Nancy, it is sweet of you. But I must decline. I'm afraid I've put my book on hold long enough. I really need to get it done. Ben might tag along with you though." She smiled sweetly in his direction.

He rose his brows in shock; she really was pissed at him.
Well enough of that.

He got up and went around the outside circle of chairs. Standing before her, he scooped her up and tossed her onto his shoulder. She screamed to be put down. But he didn't. He carried her off towards the house as she pummeled his back with her hands. With all her squirming, he was starting to lose his grip on her. Moving his hand, he tucked it in between her legs, accidentally grazing her warmth.

"Oh, my!" She gasped as the fight fled her.

He stopped and put her down on the porch step.

"That was so unfair just so you know," she muttered.

"I'm sorry." He went on apologetically." I never intended to do that; you were slipping. I just grabbed." He touched her face. "Abbi, I'm sorry… for everything. I shouldn't have withheld that note from you." Looking away, he dropped his hand. "But I had a very good reason to. I did it to protect you. But I realized this is something you need to know."

"You could have let me be the judge of that, you know."

"I know, I just didn't think. I reacted, okay? Forgive me, please?" He raised his eyes to her.

Nodding, she was interrupted from answering, as Mark and Ava ran up to them out of breath.

"Whew! Man am I out of shape." Mark bent over, sucking in a lung full of air.

Ava poked him in the ribs. "That's cuz you're not used to outrunning girls," she laughed.

"No, no, you're right! But I won, didn't I?" He wheezed.

"Ha! I let you win."

"I hate to interrupt your exchange here," Ben said, motioning back and forth with his hand. "But we need to talk, Mark, like right now!"

He looked at Abbi and took her hand in his. Feeling her chilled skin, he grabbed a blanket from the nearby chair and draped it over her shoulders. "No more secrets. Come on. The rest of the family needs to hear this as well."

"What's going on, Mom?"

"I have no idea," Abbi answered, as Ben guided her to the lake. "But I think we're about to find out."

"Lane, Luke, Dad. Can you come to the fire please?" Ben called out as they approached the others.

Everyone took a seat in various states of confusion, waiting for Ben to tell them what was so important.

"There have been some strange things going on around here lately, before you all arrived." His eyes settled on Abbi's face. Everyone present could see he was in love with her. "Abbi has been getting calls from an unknown number for, how long?" he asked, looking at her.

She shrugged. "Oh, I don't know, for about six months or so."

"...Six months?" Amazed, Ben looked at her and wondered exactly what else had been happening before he had arrived.

Abbi squirmed like a bug under a microscope. "What? ... It happens."

He looked at her in disbelief and wondered how she could be so trusting and naïve.

"Right." He glanced around at everyone. "Aside from that. She's heard laughter and music coming from what she thought was my house. Thinking it was me when I was likely asleep, as I had just arrived from England."

"Okay, so what does all of this mean?" Lane asked.

"At first, I thought the paparazzi had found out I was living here. But as things keep going on, I know it's not them." His mouth set in a grim line.

"How do you know that?" Greg asked.

"Dad, you know how they are. They are relentless, yes, but they are also in your face. If it were them, we would be seeing photos online already and they would be camped out in the yard."

Mark nodded. "That's true."

"And last week, there was blood on my porch, a lot of it. That night, coming back from the clinic, Abbi was driving and almost hit Molly who was sitting in the middle of the road." He nodded to the dogs lying flat out on the lawn.

"Oh, my goodness!" Nancy cried out, covering her mouth as the image played through her mind.

Greg reached out a hand and patted her leg.

"She was in bad shape, dirty and bloody. We took her to Mack, he patched her up and gave her some meds. But he determined the gash on her side was from a scalpel."

"*What?!*" Mark spat out.

"Yeah." Ben nodded. "I know right?"

"What kind of sicko would do such a thing?" Luke asked, a look of disgust crossing his face.

"A dangerous one," Lane supplied.

"After that, I surmised, they were trying to warn me off." Ben glanced at Abbi and softly said, "That will never happen. I asked Abbi what had happened to the person who had been stalking her before."

"What did happen to him, Abbi?" Kim asked.

"I went to the police and had a restraining order put on him. After that, I moved here, and I never heard from him again."

Ben saw she was on the verge of losing it. He wanted to pull her over to him and sit her in his lap. But he didn't. Instead, he got up and sat on the ground at her feet. She parted her legs, allowing him to rest his back against the seat of her chair. He felt her place a hand on his shoulder. Reaching up, he held it in his, tracing circles on her palm.

"Until now," Mark piped up. "Ben called me a few days ago, Tuesday, wasn't it?" Mark looked at him for confirmation.

"That's right," he said nodding. Ben laid his head back looking up at Abbi. "I went on your computer and found his name," he said, gazing into her eyes. "I'm sorry about that."

She answered him with a watery smile. She leaned forward, kissing him softly, as a tear rolled down her cheek.

Mark cleared his throat. "Ahem....?"

They both looked at him.

His eyes were large as silver dollars as he stared back. Rolling his eyes, he said, "As I was saying, Ben called me giving me as much info as he could from your files, Abbi. My brother is a cop. He worked his magic and found that your stalker left his last known address years ago. But there was a hit a month ago. The cops pulled him over in Springbank."

"That's what, a 30-minute drive from here?" Kim asked.

"Forty-five," Abbi murmured.

Mark raised his hands with fingers splayed. "I know what you're thinking but there is no guarantee that this is Jacob Randal doing all of this, but it is a possibility."

"What did your brother suggest we do?" Greg asked.

"He said that she could get another restraining order. But needs proof that it is him. His current address is in Ottawa, that's a fair distance from here. I'm really having doubts, that it's him," Mark said.

"To be honest... I have to agree with Mark," Abbi said. She could feel Ben move uncomfortably against her. "I say that only because the pattern is different. This time, this person seems... I don't know, sneakier." She paused, she had to tell them. "Jacob was never afraid of telling me what he wanted to do with me. He sent me flowers and gifts. This person almost seems more.... calculating...." She trailed off.

"Okay mom, I get where you're coming from, but who else could it be?" Ava asked, concern etching her brow.

Abbi rubbed her forehead and sighed, "I don't know, maybe a local?" She motioned a hand towards the water's edge. "Someone who is bold enough to sit not a hundred feet from the shore."

Ben added, "Someone who is brazen enough to walk in this yard and leave mashed up flowers with a note." He didn't want to say what was on that note and added, "Someone who knows their way around a boat."

"Boat, you say?" Mark asked.

Ben nodded and jerked his chin towards the lake. "Yeah. A week or so ago, there was one just sitting there 100 feet away."

Mark was thinking about the boat he and Ava saw on their walk. "Guys. Was there writing on that boat?"

Ben looked up at Abbi. "There was, wasn't there?"

Nodding, she tried to picture it in her mind. "Yes. I just can't remember what it said now."

Ava knew where Mark was going with his line of questioning. "Was it, 'Pearl Lake Yacht and Boat Rentals', by chance?" she asked.

"That's it," they replied in unison.

"How did you know?" Ben asked.

"On our walk earlier. There was a boat not more than 50 feet from the beach," Ava said pausing. "I thought I recognized the person, I even waved, but they were too busy looking off."

"Looking off at what, Ava...?" Ben questioned. He already felt he knew the answer.

"The house," Mark supplied. "They were looking at this house."

Chapter 25

A hushed silence fell over everyone sitting before the fire, each one lost in their thoughts. Abbi moved her legs from either side of Ben. Getting up, she settled herself on the ground beside him, sharing her blanket with him.

"Come here," he said, tucking her close by his side. He could feel her shivering against his body as he brushed his lips against her temple.

"But what did the note say?" Greg asked. Ben closed his eyes, wishing his dad hadn't asked.

Taking a deep breath, he whispered, "Move here, love." He patted the ground between his legs. Before he said anything, he wanted to make sure she was in the safety of his arm. He wrapped the blanket around them both, enveloping her in his warmth "Okay?" he whispered. At her nod, he began. "The note said five words that looked like they were written in blood."

Ben felt her body tense from head to toe. He brought her closer to his chest. "It said... I'm coming for you, Abbi."

His mother gasped while everyone else swore, everyone except Abbi. She just trembled in his embrace. He hugged her to him tighter.

"I didn't want to tell you, you know that, right?" he murmured softly in her ear.

She nodded, hugging him tightly. "It's okay. It's better to know and expect something to happen than be oblivious," she whispered against his neck.

Thank God he had me move down here with him.

If he hadn't, she'd have shot out of her chair, running blindly, screaming her fool head off.

He was her protector, her haven against all storms; she realized that now. She trusted him more than she'd ever trusted anyone in her entire life.

The loons suddenly made their nightly appearance. Hauntingly calling out their song, it somehow seemed fitting to Abbi. For at that very moment, all she wanted to do was cry along with them.

"Well, now that that's all out in the open, why don't we forget about all of this until tomorrow and have a hell of a good time," Kim said, standing up.

Ava took her cue. "Sounds like a plan to me. Let's get the booze Aunt Kim," she said, looping arms with her aunt. "Mark, give us a hand, will ya?" Ava asked, jerking her head towards the house.

"Absolutely!" Rubbing his hands together, he sprung up out of his chair, following them to the house.

Luke and Lane went back to setting up the fireworks; they needed to work fast, before the dark settled in.

Nancy and Greg decided they would sit on the porch to watch the show. They called for the dogs, taking them with them as they headed towards the house.

"Hey dad, can you make sure you shut the dogs in, please? Don't want them running scared from the noise," Ben called after them.

"Will do son," Greg responded, giving him a slight smile. Ben nodded his thanks.

Abbi hadn't moved a muscle since he revealed the contents of the note. He gave her a gentle squeeze.

"How you are you feeling?" he asked, worry in his voice.

She tilted her head up to meet his gaze, looking him straight in the eyes, she failed at giving him a reassuring smile. "Like shit."

He chuckled at her honesty. Sliding his hands over her back, he said, "You don't feel like shit, in fact, you feel pretty damn good.".

She leaned her forehead on his. "I don't know what I would do without you in my life. Until I met you, I was merely existing. No matter what happens, please know that you are so, so very important to me and you always will be." Despite putting on a brave face, her voice cracked on the last few words.

She wanted to feel alive again instead of the shell of a person she was slowly becoming. With tears that threatened to spill at any moment, she softly kissed him on the lips.

He broke off the kiss, taking her face in his hands, he searched her eyes. "Abbi. Please don't talk like that. Don't think something will happen, okay?"

One tear slipped slowly down her cheek.

"Abbi, I'm serious."

She turned away to conceal her emotions.

"No, don't do that. Look at me."

When she did, he gently wiped the trail from her cheek. "I will be here for you, always. I would go to the ends of the earth for you. You know that don't you?" he asked softly.

She shrugged. She knew nothing anymore.

He licked his lips. He was nervous as hell, but it was time to tell her. "Abbi, you own my heart. Do you understand what I'm trying to say to you?"

She looked at him, wiping her eyes with her sleeve.

"I'm in love with you, Abbi."

She stopped mid-swipe.

Did I hear him correctly?

Her brows shot so high they almost disappeared into her hair. She blinked rapidly. "Come again?"

He chuckled, "I said...I'm in love with you. More than I love the very air that I breathe," he murmured.

Ben started to sweat when all she did was stare at him with a glazed look.

"Are you sure?"

Sonofabitch, I overstepped my boundary.

"Right!" He pursed his lips. "Was it too soon?" He nodded his head vigorously. "I said it too soon, didn't I?"

He felt like an idiot.

Suddenly she was blubbering like a fool, as tears streamed down her face and snot bubbles formed at her nose.

What the hell is wrong with me?

She risked a glance through the wave of tears, half expecting him to set her aside, a disgusted look on his face and get up leaving her to sit and wallow in the dirt, alone.

Ben just sat there with a confused look on his handsome face. He didn't know whether to join her in crying or laugh his ass off at her. He thought it might be better if he just offered her his sleeve.

"Here love, use this." He held out his arm.

"No. I can't." She sniffled, shaking her head. "I'll get snot all over your sweater."

He smiled and shrugged his shoulders. "It's fine, I can wash it."

She wiped her face on the back of his sleeve; runny nose and all and heaved a heavy sigh. "I don't know what it is about you. But you have a knack for making me cry." She chuckled.

"Don't forget blushing too."

She smiled. "Yeah, that too."

Feeling awkward now, he returned her smile. "So, yeah... do you feel any better?" he asked. He didn't dare mention the word love to her again. She likely would fill the lake with her tears if he did.

In response, she wrapped her arms around his neck, and planted a kiss on his mouth.

A throaty groan escaped past his lips. She was put on this earth to drive him insane; he'd finally come to that conclusion. He deepened the kiss as he held her face in his hand. It felt so long since they had kissed this way. It was only a day or so but felt like an eternity since he had tasted her sweet lips.

Pulling away from him, she murmured, "No, you didn't say it too soon. You said it at the perfect time." She saw the relief wash over his face.

"Do you mean—?" It scared him to say the rest of it.

Reaching out a hand she touched his lips. Tracing the curve of his mouth with a finger she gazed into his eyes, eyes that showed him how much she loved him. The moment he saw it, his own darkened in response.

She nodded.

He covered her mouth with his, drinking in her sweetness. In a moment of madness, he just about laid her on the ground in front of the fire, forgetting that their families were there. He took her by the waist and plopped her on the ground beside him. "You need to stay there for a bit," he said, breathing heavily.

She hooted with laughter, but finally said the words he so longed to hear.

"I'm in love with you, Ben. I think I was the moment you caught me in Mack's," she smiled, remembering back to that day. "At first I thought you were an ass."

He laughed at her admission. "What? Why would you think that?"

"Have you looked at yourself in the mirror? Guys that look like you, are generally assholes... just saying.".

"I don't know how to feel about that," he replied, in shock.

"It's not how you look, but what you look like, if that makes any sense."

"Gotcha," he said, shooting her a wink.

"Would you really go to the ends of the earth for me?"

"Absolutely, without a doubt. Abbi, I would do anything for you. If you want me to quit acting, just say so."

She was stunned. She couldn't believe he'd even suggest that. "No. I could never ask that of anyone. That's your career, your life," she said, shaking her head.

"I too thought that myself once... until I moved here. I fell in love with the area right away. But acting will always be there waiting for me to go back, just like England, you know?" He pulled her back onto his lap, and in the circle of his arms. "And then one day I woke up, and I realized..." he paused, lifting her chin for her to look at him. "What's keeping my heart here is you. I mean it... just say the word, and I'm done." He looked at her with such sincerity; she knew he meant it.

They could hear Mark and the girls approaching from behind them, stopping them from discussing anything further. Abbi reluctantly pulled herself up from the comfort of Ben's embrace. Standing, she offered him a hand up and noticed him wincing in pain when he put his weight on his arm.

"Are you okay?" she asked.

"Yeah, just a little stiff is all."

Honestly, it was more than just a little stiff. It was hurting like the day he had injured it. But he refused to admit it; she was worried about enough already. He didn't need to add to it.

She knew it was more than that, she could tell by the look on his face. "I'll go get those meds that Doc dropped off."

"No. I'm fine. Just need to loosen it up a bit," he said, rotating his shoulder in circles. "I don't like taking anything stronger than what I have been." He needed his wits about him; he'd be of no use to anyone, especially her if he were flat on his ass.

She laid her hand on his forearm. "I can just cut one in half?"

He stroked her cheek; he couldn't deny her any longer. Leaning down, he gave her a quick kiss. "Alright love for you. But only half."

Abbi nodded, "I'll be right back."

He watched her run off towards the house.

"So, Ben. What are we going to do about this creep hanging around?" Kim looked at him, her eyes full of worry.

"Well, I for one, am staying here until they catch this guy. I've already called the shop and told them I'll be off for a bit and left Marissa in charge," Ava said.

Mark looked at her. "Wait... what do you do again?"

"I already told you... don't you listen? I own a spa... remember?"

"Oh right! Well, it was kind of hard to listen when your hands were all over me." Mark looked at her like the rake he was.

Ben let out a bark of laughter. "Whoa!!! What were you two doing?" he grinned, looking between the two of them.

Kim chimed in. "Ava! What the hell?"

"Massage people, I gave him a massage." She threw a hand in Mark's direction. "This fool thought he could do a somersault and twisted the wrong way."

Ben shook his head, grinning. "Man, some things never change with you, do they?"

"Never, Benny boy, never!"

"Hey, guys you about ready for the fireworks?" Lane asked joining them.

"Yeah," Ben said, glancing around.

He had that feeling someone was watching again. He looked out across the lake. Distractedly, he said to Lane, "Your mom just ran into the house for a minute."

A hint of light directly across from where he stood caught his attention. Not a light but more of a quick flash or a... reflection?

"Perfect. Gives us enough time to finish up." Lane turned, yelling as he walked to relay the message to Luke.

ABBI WENT OUT ONTO the porch. Stopping, she looked at Nancy and Greg.

"Are you two okay up here?" she asked, laying a hand on Greg's shoulder.

"Oh yes, dear! It's the perfect spot!" Nancy answered, nestling into the blanket wrapped around her.

"Great, if you need anything, please help yourself to whatever is in the house. I'm just going to run this down to Ben." She held out her hand to show them the pill. "His shoulder is giving him a bit of trouble tonight." With a wave, she went down the steps, sprinting to the lake.

Nancy and Greg watched as she went. "I like her Nan, do you?" Greg glanced at his wife. Her stamp of approval was pivotal in their relationship with their son; he knew Ben would choose Abbi over them any day.

"Mhm," Nancy paused, looking over at Greg. "He couldn't have done better if I had picked her myself," she said, grinning while she took his hand.

MOONLIT NIGHT

BEN TURNED WHEN HE felt a hand run down his back.

"Here you go handsome," Abbi said, smiling as she held out her hand to him.

"Oh, almost forgot." She dug a bottle of water out of her jacket pocket, handing that over, too.

"Thanks," he said, popping the pill into his mouth. He followed it with a swig of water to wash it down.

"What were you looking at out there?" Abbi asked with a nod towards the dark lake.

"Ah... nothing." Ben motioned down towards the shore with the water bottle. "The guys are ready to set the fireworks off."

"Oh good, I can't wait!" Abbi smiled, taking the chair next to Kim.

Ben sat down on the ground once again in front of Abbi. He took her ankles, bringing them around his waist, he set to work massaging her calf muscles and felt her relaxing under his touch.

Kim nudged Abbi with her elbow, motioning for Abbi to come closer. Leaning towards her she whispered in her ear, "I'm thrilled for you. I'll be honest at first, I thought you were robbing the cradle." She held up a staying hand. "I know, I know! That's not your style, and you battled your demons to get to this point. But after getting to know his parents and Ben and the way he is with you; I see that it's for real. I just wanted to tell you that." Her eyes sparkled softly in the glow from the fire.

Abbi wrapped her arms around Kim. "Thank you. I love you, sis," she whispered.

Kim returned the hug and leaned back, looking into her eyes. "I love you too, baby girl." She waved her hand and wiped her eyes. "Enough of this wishy-washy shit." With tears streaming down their faces, both broke out in a burst of hysterical laughter.

Smiling, Ben laid his head back in Abbi's lap, looking up at the two of them as he rubbed her thigh. "What are you two going on about now?"

Leaning forward, she ran a finger across his bottom lip. Her lips followed with a soft lingering kiss. Oh, how she loved them...loved him. She lifted her head and looked into his eyes.

"Nothing, just girl talk." She smiled. "I love you."

"I love you more," he said, a dreamy look in his eyes.

"Not likely," Abbi muttered under her breath.

A small smile graced his lips at hearing her words.

She noticed how tired he looked as she took his hand in hers and thought it strange how cold it felt.

The first burst of fireworks lit the night sky catching Abbi's attention. They watched in awe as one after another danced and soared high above the lake, falling in shimmery trails onto the mirrored surface.

Abbi felt Ben's hand go limp.

That's odd, there is no way he can sleep with all this noise.

She peered down at him, running a hand along his jawline. "Hey sleepyhead," she said as the next set of fireworks zoomed into the night sky, lighting his face. "Ben?" she said, placing both hands alongside his face. Panic set in. She nudged him, "Ben! ... Ben!" Tears sprang to her eyes, running down her cheeks, splashing his face. "Please God, wake up!" she pleaded.

Placing a shaky hand on his neck, she felt his slow but steady pulse.

"KIM!!!" she screamed. "Help him!"

Kim looked down to see what Abbi was talking about. One look was all it took.

"Oh, shit!" Jumping up, she told Abbi to move back as she bent down in front of Ben.

Ava and Mark looked over to see what the commotion was.

"Ava! Call Doc, now!" Kim ordered.

"Mark! Luke! Lane! Come help me move Ben. We need to lay him down," she yelled.

Abbi scurried over taking his hand as they laid him gently on his back. Kim checked his pulse while glancing at his chest to see the slow rise and fall of it. "He's breathing. Does anyone have a flashlight?"

"Here," Mark said, holding his phone out for her.

Kim checked his pupils to see if they were fixed. "Damn it, they are," she muttered to herself. She then checked to see if there was anything in his mouth and stuck her finger in to flatten his tongue, to check his throat.

Abbi dashed away the blinding tears, watching as Kim turned Ben on his side.

"Abbi, run to the house and ask his parents if he's allergic to anything." She glanced up to see Abbi frozen. "Abbi, snap out of it!" Kim reached out and smacked her across the face.

That got her attention.

"Get up to the house and ask his mom if he's allergic to anything."

Abbi bobbed her head up and down. "Yes, yes, I can do that."

She had to tear her gaze from Ben, not wanting to leave him. She wanted to curl up beside him, hold him tight and tell him everything would be okay; like he did for her so many times before. Instead, she got up and ran as fast as she could to the house and flew up the steps, alarming his parents.

"Ben has had some kind of reaction, is he allergic to anything?" She panted, trying desperately to sound as calm as she could.

Nancy stood up in horror. "Oh, my Lord, where is he?" Without waiting, she hurried down the steps.

Greg took Abbi by the arms. "No, he isn't allergic to anything. Come on, let's go," he said, in a worried voice.

Abbi took off running back to Ben, passing by Nancy not stopping to wait for her. Her only focus was to get back to him.

Abbi knelt by his side, taking his hand.

"What's wrong with him?" Ava asked.

"Well, I'm only a nurse. But I would say he's been drugged," Kim answered.

"That can't be," Abbi found her voice. "He hates taking any drugs, he didn't even want to take over-the-counter stuff."

Nancy and Greg came up with Doc just then.

"Hey Doc," Kim said when she saw him.

"Hi Kim. What's the prognosis?" he asked, kneeling beside Ben as he put on his stethoscope. He held a hand up, signaling for silence. Finding his beat to be slow but steady, Doc looked up to Kim, nodding for her to continue as he checked his eyes with a penlight.

"His breathing is shallow; his heartbeat was slow but steady. Pupils are fixed," she looked at Doc. "If I didn't know any better, I would say he's been—"

"Drugged," Doc said, finishing for her.

"Yes. But he didn't take anything, did he?" she said, looking to Abbi.

Abbi started to shake her head but than a horrified look flashed across her face.

"Yes. His shoulder was hurting him earlier. Just before the fireworks."

Tears flooded her eyes when she knew she was to blame. Bugging him until he caved and gave in to her. It was her fault he was like this.

Doc turned around to face Abbi. "What did he take, Abbi? The pharmacy said he never picked up the script I sent you home with."

"I gave him a half of a pill. The ones you had delivered earlier today. The directions said to take two, but he didn't want any," she answered. Her face crumpled as she laid a hand on Ben's chest. She needed to feel him, to touch him.

Doc reached over Ben, taking her by the arms, he gave her a shake. "Where are those pills Abbi?" he asked with urgency.

"They're in the house."

"I need to take them with me for testing."

A look of concern crossed Doc's face as he glanced down at Ben.

Making a judgment call with no time to waste, Doc took a vial of Naloxone and a syringe out of his bag. Measuring the amount, he jabbed the needle in Ben's arm and jammed the plunger down.

"Why would you need to test them?" Luke asked.

"Because when Ben didn't pick up the initial prescription, I didn't bother getting the ones from Springbank brought in."

"So, they must have had them in stock after all?" Greg asked.

"On the contrary. They don't." Doc gave his full attention back to Abbi. "I never wrote another prescription for Ben, Abbi. And I sent no one out here to deliver them. Whoever did this... I suspect, they were targeting Ben."

Abbi shook her head in denial. *It just can't be. Who would do such a thing...?* With dawning horror, she knew Doc was right. She now knew that Ben was right all along too. A low keening started in her throat as she collapsed on him, hugging him to her. Willing him to wake up.

Abbi quickly sat back on her haunches and looked up to the heavens, tears streaming down her face. Her wailing screams could be heard echoing over the stillness of the lake.

"Luke, Lane, you," he pointed to Mark. "I'll need help to get him out to my van," Doc ordered.

"Where will you be taking him?" Nancy asked, her voice thick with worry.

"I'll be watching him at the clinic tonight," Doc said, looking up at her.

All four men picked up Ben gently. Hurriedly, they started across the long expanse of the yard.

Over his shoulder, Doc called out, "Kim, Ava. Get Abbi to my van, now! She needs to be with him, and someone grab those pills!"

DIRECTLY ACROSS THE lake was the perfect place, a front-row seat...so to speak to watch it unfold.

"My plan was a success I see!"

They lowered the binoculars, as a bubble of pure glee erupted from their throat while the sobbing cries of despair from their dear sweet Abbi, rang out over the lake. Clapping, they silently congratulated Ben Quinn on his stellar performance... his last one. A shame the world couldn't have seen it.

"Oh! Abbi darling, soon I will comfort you, holding you in my arms! Just a few more days and your house will be empty, just like your heart. I will fill that hole... I promise you that my dear!"

Chapter 26

Abbi had never felt so alone in her life, standing by Ben's bed. Both of their families had come. His mother, only leaving when she knew her son would pull through.

Abbi reached out to brush the hair from his forehead. Bending down, her lips quivered as she placed them on his brow. It pained her so, knowing what she had to do but she had her mind made up. She had to end this. A gentle squeeze on her shoulder had her straightening. Turning, she saw Doc standing there, concern for her filling his eyes.

"Abbi, I'll bring you a cot. You need to get some sleep," he said.

She nodded numbly as he quietly left the room.

There were no tears left, she had cried a river's worth. Now all she felt was guilt and emptiness. She let out a heavy sigh and took Ben's hand in hers. Running her thumb across the back, she traced each vein that stood out on his smooth skin. Trying desperately to burn the memory in her mind, knowing once he woke, it would be the last time she did.

She watched drop after drop of the IV bag flow into his veins. He was stable. He just needed to wake up, Doc had told her. The lab tests would take time to come back, but he was confident that it was a drug of sorts that put Ben into this state. Lucky for him, he hadn't taken the full amount; otherwise, it would have affected his liver or kidneys or worse. She shuddered at the thought.

"Here Abbi," Doc said, rolling a fold-up bed into the room. "It's not the best thing, but it's more comfortable than the chair."

"Thanks, Doc," she mumbled.

"Abbi. He will be fine. He's young... he's healthy and strong. He just needs to sleep it off. If I didn't think he would, I would have called for the air ambulance back at your place."

"I know. I just feel like it's my fault. If I hadn't persisted that he needed to take something for the pain, he wouldn't be laying here right now."

"Don't talk like that. You had no idea. The police will get to the bottom of it, I'm sure." He had his doubts about that but kept that detail to himself. "Get some sleep. I'll just be in the other room if you need me. If he wakes up, yell." He nodded and left.

Abbi turned the lights out, all but one over the sink. She walked over to the fold-up bed, undid the strap, and pulled the legs down.

BEN COULD HEAR SOMEONE groaning from far away. It took him a moment to realize it was coming from him. It felt like he'd been trampled by a moose. His body ached everywhere; in muscles he didn't even know he had. Try as he might, he couldn't open his eyes, they felt so heavy.

A faint breeze caressed his brow, as he felt himself drifting back into the darkness. His last thought was of Abbi.

ABBI WHIPPED HER HEAD around. Dropping the legs with a bang, she rushed to his side, peering at his face. She squeezed his hand, praying he'd open his beautiful eyes.

"Ben?"

She wanted so badly to crawl up beside him to hold him but didn't. Instead, she sat down on the chair and crossed her arms on the edge of the bed. She felt the tears sting her tired eyes while her gaze never wavered from his face. Burying her head in the crook of her arm, she cried herself to sleep.

BEN SLOWLY CAME TO. The scent of jasmine in the air told him that Abbi was nearby. He could feel her presence beside him, could, feel her small hand in his, but he had no clue where he was.

Am I in my bed or hers and why is she down by my hip?

Was it that rough of a night that he couldn't remember? The last thing he did remember was looking up at her. Her telling him she loved him. He tried to gather the strength to squeeze her hand, to see if she were awake; that small task took more effort than he could muster, and his mouth was so incredibly dry.

"Abbi?" he croaked.

He moved his hand to her hair, catching a silky curl between his fingers, he gently tugged on the strand. "Abbi. Love. Are you awake?" He was so bloody tired and itchy. He brought his hand up to scratch his face and stopped. Squinting at his hand, he saw a needle taped down to the back of it, a tube running from it.

His eyes followed its path to a stand nearby. He frowned at the IV bag.

How in hell did that get there and why?

He'd find out later, right now he had to do something, anything to quench his thirst. But really all he could do was think, and so he thought of his mum's pickled beets and felt the spring of saliva rush in his mouth.

"Abbi..." his throat felt like he'd swallowed a mouthful of sand. Sweat beaded on his brow as he reached out and weakly rubbed her hair.

Her head popped up; a bit of drool had dried to the corner of her mouth. "What....?" she looked at Ben through her hair. She leaped out of the chair when she saw him looking at her. Happy tears splashed from her eyes as she covered his face with kisses.

"Abbi..." His eyes pleaded with her. "Love, I need a drink."

"Yes, of course you do!" Rushing to the sink, she snatched a paper cup, filled it with water and returned to his side. "Here, let me help you," she said. Pulling the side tray close, she sat the water down, while she pulled on the mechanism to lift the head of the bed. "Is that high enough?"

At his nod, she grabbed the cup, bringing it to his lips. He drank it down in two gulps.

"Um... you should have probably just sipped on that." She smiled through her tears.

"Couldn't help it, my throat felt like a parched lake." He looked around the room. "Are we at the clinic?"

Abbi nodded. "Yes. Um... I'll go get Doc, give me a second."

"No, tell me what happened. I can only remember you telling me you loved me." A look of confusion crossed his handsome face. "I can't remember anything after that."

"Do you remember taking that pain pill?"

"The one you broke in half, yeah, I remember." His brows shot up. "You mean that pill put me here?"

"Uh." Abbi wrinkled her brow and looked at him. "Yes. I'm so sorry Ben."

As he reached out to her, Abbi backed away, catching the hurt in his eyes.

"I'm sorry. I did that to you." She hurried on so he couldn't interrupt. "You were sitting on the ground in front of me. You looked up at me asking what Kim and I had been laughing about." She started to pace as she recounted the events. "I told you nothing...that it was just girl talk." She paused, touching her lips at the memory of that last kiss they had shared.

"I told you I loved you and you said... I love you... more." Her voice shook on the last word.

"Right. It's true you know," he told her quietly.

She frowned at him. "So you say. Anyway, you looked so tired. We were holding hands, and I noticed how cold yours felt."

He watched the emotions play across her face as she recounted the event. A look of sorrow was there now, and it tugged at his heart.

He shifted over in the bed and lifted the sheet with a slight tremble and said, "Come here."

She resisted the urge for a millisecond. She couldn't help it. Not needing to be asked twice, she quickly climbed up beside him, laying her head on his shoulder as he tucked her to his side.

She looked up at him. "Where was I?"

He squinted in thought. "Ah... I said I loved you more."

"You're teasing me, that wasn't it. I remember, your hand was like ice." She shifted her gaze, staring at his Adam's apple. "The fireworks had started as we held hands. After five minutes or so, yours went limp." She looked up at him. "My first thought was that you had fallen asleep, but with all the noise I knew that wasn't possible." Tears started to well in her eyes as the scene replayed in her mind.

"Go on love, I'm here now," he murmured, brushing his lips across her forehead.

She closed her eyes and took a steadying breath. "I called to you, but you didn't answer. I tried again and still no response." She touched his neck right where she had felt for his pulse earlier that night. "I put my hand, right here," she said laying her hand against the steady, strong beat that was there now. She opened her eyes, tilting her head to gaze into his. "I felt for your heartbeat. God, it was so slow." She sniffed, swallowing the tears that threatened. Burying her face against his neck, she mumbled, "It felt like it was getting slower with every beat. I screamed for Kim to help you. She pushed me out of the way and started to work on you right away." She looked up at him again. "She's a nurse, you know."

Placing his cheek on hers, he nodded. "Yes, I know," he murmured, against her ear.

She laid her head on his shoulder. "Kim yelled to Ava to call Doc and told the guys to help her move you onto your back. She checked your pulse, your eyes and your mouth, and throat." She looked back up at him. "She smacked me across the face."

Ben chuckled. "She did, did she?"

Settling her head back down she muttered, "Yeah, she did." She wrapped her arms tight around him. "I froze. I didn't want to leave you. She told me to go ask your parents if you were allergic to anything."

He bit his lip shaking his head. "I'm not, at least nothing I'm aware of."

"That's what they said. After running back, Doc showed up shortly thereafter. Kim told him what she thought was wrong; he examined you and came to the same conclusion." She fell silent.

"Which was?" he asked, hedging for an answer.

She couldn't bring herself to say it, instead, she said, "Doc took a syringe, and stabbed it into a vial. He filled it and jammed it into your arm." She rubbed the spot where the needle had punctured his skin. "It was Naloxone." She looked up at him then. Laying her hand against his jaw, she could see the confusion in his eyes. She quietly said, "It's what they give to reverse the effects of a drug overdose." She took a deep, steadying breath. "Doc didn't send those pills to the house, Ben. When you didn't pick up the first prescription, he didn't bother with another one. Someone deliberately did this to you."

Tears streamed down her face now. The moment of truth was here. She had to tell him; she couldn't do this to him anymore. She couldn't allow anything to happen to him again.

She mourned for the loss that would come with it, but she had to let him go.

She lightly placed her lips on his, savouring their feel against her own. The taste of him mingled with her tears, ingraining it all for a memory. She'd forever love him; so much that she would let him go.

Ben felt a shift in Abbi's emotions. This wasn't just pain or guilt. This was something else she was feeling.

Leaning back, he broke off the kiss to look her in the eyes.

What is she thinking about?

Noting the look of despair on her beautiful face, it hit him like a blow to the balls. "Abbi. I know what you're thinking of doing and you can forget about it," he said, giving her a dark look.

"No, you don't," she shot back, and was shocked when she saw that look in his eyes.

Damn it, he did!

"Ben, you can't stop me—"

He cut her off. "Like hell, I can't. Neither one of us is going anywhere... I've waited my whole life to find this kind of love and I'm not walking away from it, understood?"

Abbi was getting mad. "Fine... don't then. But I can. I need to," she said, getting off the bed.

He scowled at her. "You would give up everything we have over something like this?"

"You didn't see what happened to you! You could have died, Ben." She jabbed her chest. "And it would have all been because of me. Don't you see?" She touched his arm and with quiet determination, said, "It's the only way that I can protect you..."

"No! I don't see. And it's not happening. This was an accident, okay?"

She snickered in disgust. "Ha! Oh no, it wasn't! And before you say it, it wasn't a coincidence either; someone has it out for you. That bottle had your name on it." She turned away from him and rubbed her throbbing temples.

Pulling out his IV, Ben shoved the covers back, swinging his legs over the edge he sat for a minute. He closed his eyes, his head swimming with dizziness. With the same determination as her, he slowly slid his feet to the floor.

Abbi spun around to face him and hissed, "Just what do you think you're doing?"

He ignored her of course. Pushing himself off the bed, he took the few steps to where she stood and took her in his arms. She was like a lit firecracker ready to go off at any second. "We will get through this." He added gently, "together."

He kissed her on the top of her head when he felt her relax within the circle of his arms. "I told you once I would go to the ends of the earth for you." He lifted her face to look into her eyes. "I meant it. If there's one thing in this world that is worth fighting for, it's love. You, my love, are worth it." He kissed her then as if his very life depended on it because in truth it did. If she did ever leave him, he would be nothing but a shell.

She responded by wrapping her arms around his neck and smoothing the hair that brushed his collar. She was foolish to think she could resist this man and even more so to think she could ever leave him. To push him away was insane.

He pulled back to look at her lips and started chuckling. "What's so funny?" she asked.

He touched the corner of her mouth. "You have a bit of something here," he said, rubbing the spot.

Good Lord! I drooled when I was sleeping, didn't I?

Reaching up, she felt the area his fingers were currently trying to smooth away. "For cripes sake!" She dropped her arms and stalked to the sink. Turning the cold tap on, she splashed water on the spot then for good measure her whole face. She grabbed some paper towel, patting her face dry, she looked to him. He was slowly making his way back to the bed.

Ben lifted the covers. "Come on, let's get some sleep before we go home."

"I have to let Doc know that you're awake."

"Leave him Abbi, let the man sleep. I'm fine, still a bit tired, a little itchy but otherwise I feel normal," he said, patting the bed.

She climbed up silently, snuggling up to his chest as he hugged her to him.

"Are you sure you're comfortable, I can sleep on the cot there," she said, motioning a hand towards the fold-up bed.

"You're not going anywhere. Get some rest. I love you sweet one," he breathed with a contented sigh.

"And I love you... more."

She felt his chest shake with laughter and realized he was right. Together they could get through this, being apart was not an option.

Chapter 27

"Hey guys, can everyone come and sit for a minute," Luke called from the dining table. "We have to hash out some stuff."

Once everyone was present, Lane cleared his voice to begin. "OK, so let's figure this out," he said, smacking a notebook on the table. Flicking a pen, he held his hand, poised to write. "Mom started getting phone calls, when?" He looked at Abbi.

"Oh, hmm. Like I said before, at least six months; a year tops... maybe." She glanced at Ben, knowing it would upset him with her admission.

He sighed, shaking his head, a dark look settled on his face as he raised a brow at her. He inclined his head towards her. "Really?"

"Yeah." She shrugged. "But in my defence, they were always unknown numbers."

Ben pursed his lips and nodded. "Right. Can I see your phone Abbi?" he asked, holding out his hand.

"Of course." She passed it to him and watched as he took the case off. "Do you have a pin?"

"Ah yeah. Hold on." She rushed off to her office and came back holding one high in her hand. "Here you go."

"Thanks."

Abbi settled in her chair and watched the tiny tray open when he poked it into a little hole on the side of the phone. He took the card out and bent it in half. A little too late, she grabbed his arm. "What did you do that for!" She was stunned at the audacity of him.

"Good thinking, Ben." Lane said and looked at her. "Mom, you will need to get a new card, your phone is useless for the time being, only 911 will work."

Abbi stared at Lane like he was an alien from another planet for siding with Ben.

Ben took her hand, leaned towards her, and held the bent card in his fingers. "I did that because this, can trace you."

"Oh," she said, flatly.

"Yeah." He dropped the card onto the table.

"OK, what else do we know?" Lane continued.

"Shortly after I moved in, you heard music and laughing you said, right?" Ben looked to her for confirmation.

"Yes. That was before we met. I didn't know you had moved in yet. I thought your house was still empty." She looked at everyone gathered around the table, Abbi felt the need to explain. "I tripped over the bottom step and landed on my face."

Ava snickered. "How long has that step been waiting to get fixed?"

Kim hooted. "Since the day you moved in at least. Looks good on you."

"Yes. Well, someday I'll get around to it," Abbi said, and froze.

The sound of a yelp coming from the backyard had everyone turning their head, all except her. She had heard that cry of pain before. Getting up, she went to the back door to see Lucy lying on the porch while Brutus and Molly played in the yard. A little too rough she supposed. The dogs were otherwise fine. But that cry of pain....

She was lost in her thoughts as she walked back to the kitchen; to the day she met Ben at Mack's. She had been so pissed off when she found out he had bought the place, that she had called Nigel. She had found it strange that when she'd gotten home, the animals were all waiting for her at the window, Brutus howling his head off.

She remembered she had gone outside with them, sitting down in a chair on the porch. That's when she heard the same yelping cry that Molly had just done.

Oh my God! No wonder Brutus is so protective of Molly...

It was her cries they'd heard that day. As she went back into the dining area where everyone was a wave of nausea hit her like a ton of bricks. Reaching out she grabbed the back of Ben's chair; she was about to hurl.

Racing to the bathroom, she made it as far as the tub. That's where Ben found her, throwing up.

"Abbi?" He was at her side, rubbing her back. "Are you okay?" He held her hair as she threw up a second time. When she was done, he got up and wet a washcloth. "Here, love."

Taking it from him, she mopped her face as she sat on the floor, her back against the tub.

"You okay now?" he asked, as he went down on his knees before her. She nodded shakily. "What was that all about?"

he motioned to the tub. A movement caught his eye. Raising his brows in disbelief. He saw Void, her stubby-legged cat, sitting in the tub at the far end patiently waiting for her to finish so he could get a drink. He gave Ben an expectant meow.

Grabbing the cat, he set him on the floor, giving him a gentle push towards the door. He turned back and took the handheld shower head and rinsed the tub. Going to the vanity, he opened the door under the sink and grabbed the cleaner and a sponge. He knelt before Abbi, taking a hold of her waist, he slid her over and out of the way. He methodically started scrubbing the tub, waiting for her to answer.

"Love?" he hedged.

"Yeah?" She looked at him blankly.

"You want to tell me something?"

"Yeah, Um. That night when we first met, before you came over with the flowers... I heard a dog screaming in pain from across the lake... like directly across." She grabbed his arm. "Ben. You were right all along. I think it was Molly..." She trailed off imagining the horrors that poor dog must have endured at the hands of pure evil. "And that's not all. There was a flash of light, too. I thought it was just headlights from the road flashing between the trees, but now I'm not so sure." She began to chew her lip with worry.

He stopped and looked at her, a thoughtful look on his own face. "Huh...."

"What is it?"

He licked his lips and frowned as he bent to rinse the tub. "The other night. When you went into the house to get the painkillers, I saw a light too, directly across from the house. More of a reflection, really."

"That's it! That's what I saw! Oh my God, how long have they been watching me?" She felt the sickness rise in her throat, shoving Ben aside she let it hurl again.

He pursed his lips. "Alright!" he said, tossing the sponge down to hold her hair back once more.

KIM LOOKED UP AS ABBI and Ben walked back into the kitchen. "You look like shit!"

Abbi made a face at her sister as she sat with a thud on the chair. "Thanks."

"So." Ben looked to the dogs that were now resting on the floor. "What we just discovered is that Molly here..." He motioned for her to come to him. "...was likely abused by whoever is doing this. Before it was just me thinking it, but now Abbi is sure of it."

Greg looked at Abbi. "What makes you think so?"

"When I heard her yelping a bit ago. I heard it the night Ben and I met, just before he came over. There was a light across the water and Ben just told me he saw one the night of the fireworks," she said, hunkering down into her sweater.

Ben explained. "It's more of a reflection really, like light hitting off a lens."

"Or maybe binoculars?" Mark asked.

"Yeah, or that," Ben nodded.

Lane tossed his pen onto the notebook. "Well, there must be more that's happened."

Everyone sat quietly, trying to think if they remembered anything out of the ordinary in the last year.

Looking at the table with a fixed stare, Kim said, "Well, there's the flowers and note."

"True, that is true," Nancy agreed.

Ben leaned an arm on the back of his chair and clasped his hands together. "Mark. Did you find out anything more about Jacob Randal?"

"Actually, my brother is doing a more in-depth search of the Ottawa area... calling the locals there. I thought he'd have gotten back to me by now but hasn't. I should call him."

Kim looked at him. "Uh. Yeah, you should! What the hell are you waiting for?"

"Of course! I'll just go do that." Mark got up and took his cell from his pocket. Dialing his brother's number, he walked outside onto the front porch.

"I'll be right back," Ava excused herself, walking out to the porch to join Mark.

"Could there be anything on that note that might give us a clue?" Luke asked. "Where did it go, where did the flowers go?"

"Those flowers did look like they had blood on them, maybe it's the person that's doing this," Kim said. "And what about the prescription Ben got? That had the drugstore stickers on it."

Shaking her head Abbi looked at her. "Doc told us before we left the clinic yesterday that he checked with the drugstore. A new employee had tossed some old labels in the garbage instead of shredding them. Whoever did it must have searched through it and found them. It would be easy enough to print the directions on it." She sighed and started bouncing her leg up and down. This was all becoming too much for her to handle.

Ben laid a hand on Abbi's knee. "I threw the flowers along with the note in the weeds across the road," he said, rubbing his hand back and forth across her thigh. "They might offer a clue. But even so, they need to be tested at a lab and that would take weeks if not months."

Mark and Ava breezed back into the house. "Okay, guys... Steve looked into it further and it looks like there is no way that it's Jacob Randal."

Ben frowned. "How can he be so sure?" He was positive that it was him.

Mark sighed heavily and sat down. "Because he's been in jail for 2 weeks. Sorry guys."

"Mom, have there been any strange cars around lately, anyone walking around?" Ava asked.

Abbi thought back. There was that car a few weeks ago parked beside the lake. And the boat, not that either was out of the ordinary, but both had been close.

"Abbi. When was your break-in?" Ben asked quietly. He had a theory, but he just wanted to be certain before he mentioned it to everyone.

"The end of February, the twenty-seventh to be exact. I had been gone for a week. I had to meet with the director for the movie to go over some key points."

She knew exactly what he was thinking when Ben looked at her in surprise.

"He couldn't come here. I had no choice but to meet him in Toronto," she explained.

He grinned, taking her hand in his to silently convey his understanding.

His brow furrowed in thought, Mark spoke up, "That's around the time shooting for the movie started. Abbi, do you have any enemies?"

Ben looked at Mark at the mention of enemies, he had a flashback. That was something he'd need to investigate in his own past. No doubt he had a few.

Kim smacked the table and burst out laughing. "Ha, ha, ha. Abbi have enemies? That's a hoot! Maybe Sally Schmit from 5th grade! Didn't you put glue in her hair when she pissed you off for stealing your boyfriend?"

Abbi giggled at the memory and nodded. "Yeah. I did. And then I braided it!"

Ben folded his arms across his chest and leaned back, a grin on his face. "How does that not surprise me?"

"She deserved it; we had only been dating for a week."

"You were such a rebel mom," Ava laughed.

"Yeah, well. That's all behind me now," she smiled. Not really. If Sally Schmit tried that today she might end up bald.

"Back on track here. So, no unusual cars or people around." Picking up his pen, Lane noted it in the notebook.

"What about the boat?" Luke said.

Lane glanced up at him. "Boat?" he asked.

"Were you not listening?"

"Yes, I'm listening but I was also writing shit down."

Luke shot a hand towards the lake. "Ben and Mom said there had been a boat out there. Right?" He looked them for confirmation.

"Yeah," Ben replied, as Abbi nodded.

"Don't forget the boat we saw," Ava added, looking at Mark.

"Right, you said it was a rental. What was the name again?" Lane looked up expectantly, hand poised.

Ava rubbed her forehead in thought. Snapping her fingers, she said, "Pearl Lake Yacht and Boat rentals."

"Good, so we have a lead, one of us needs to go over there and see if we can find out the name it was rented under," Greg said.

"I'll go." Ben volunteered.

Shaking her head Abbi was about to tell him no when Kim said, "Nope, you can't."

He looked at her with a raise of his brows.

"Whoever did this, thinks you're dead, remember?"

"I'll wear a disguise," he said, blinking at her.

Shaking her head, Kim said, "Sorry stud." She pointed to her face, drawing an imaginary circle over it. "No can do, no disguise will hide that face of yours. You need to stay on the downlow." She pushed her hand down to emphasize. "Like way down... low."

Noticing the look of panic on Abbi's face, Mark chimed in. "She's right, Ben. You need to stay here. Ava and I can go," he said, looking at her for encouragement.

Ava nodded. "Yeah, we were talking about checking it out to see what they have to offer; this is perfect reason to now."

Abbi didn't want her kids involved in this madman's idea of a good time. "I can't expect any of you to stick around," she said, looking at all of them, casting her gaze on each of her offspring. "You have lives to get back to in Windsor. Traffic will be insane. No, you guys need to go home," she added firmly.

"Mom, I've already told the girls I'm staying here for a bit," Ava said, coming over to hug her. "They will cover the spa for me."

Lane reached across the table to take hold of her hand. "I have to get back. I've got meetings all week Mom. Otherwise, you know I would stay," he said, gently squeezing her hand.

"We had a train package booked." Greg looked at Nancy. At her nod, he said, "But we will cancel and stick around."

"No, you can't do that!" Abbi protested. She got up and went to them "It's your first time in Canada. You don't want to be stuck at my house." She bent, giving them each a hug. "Seriously you two, go have fun, I insist." She knew they had booked economy; she made a mental note to contact the train depot to change their tickets to first class with the glass top roof. It was the least she could do for them.

Luke came over to Abbi and hugged her. "I have to fly out of Toronto in the morning."

"Where are you headed this time?" she asked, holding onto her oldest for dear life.

"Not far... just to New York for a few days." He squeezed her tight. "As much as I hate to, we will have to leave in about an hour or so if I'm going to make it to Toronto before dark." He looked at Lane. "Will you be ready by then?"

"Yeah, just let me finish this up and I'll be good to go."

"Aunt Kim, what are you doing?" Ava asked. "Can you stay, or do you have to leave too?"

"Sure, I'll stay. I've got a month off... or more, so I'm good... unless you guys want me to skedaddle," she said, looking to Abbi and Ben.

Ben looked Kim straight in the eyes. "I could never say no to the woman who saved my life," he murmured.

Kim blinked rapidly. "Oh. My. God."

Abbi knew exactly what Kim was feeling at that very moment. When he used that tone of voice with her, he had her melting, every damn time.

Kim started waving her hand in front of her face. "Wow!" she said, visibly flushed. Giggling, she glanced at Ben. "Do you have a brother somewhere?" She quickly turned to his parents. "Is he your only son?" she asked, her hand waving faster.

Nancy and Greg laughed at her. "Afraid so," Nancy said, nodding her head.

Jerking her head back around. A sneer on her lips, Kim rolled her eyes and mumbled, "Figures." She threw her head back and let out a cackle. "I'm too much woman for you anyway."

Ben chuckled. "I don't doubt that for a second."

Abbi stood watching Ben exchange goodbyes with his parents.

Their car was packed and ready for the trip to Springbank. There, they would catch the train where their adventure would begin. Abbi had already changed the booking, so they were in for a surprise when they arrived. It was the least she could do to pay them back for bringing such a beautiful human into the world.

Her boys had already left an hour ago amid a teary goodbye, and she was missing them the second they pulled away. She wanted them all to move up here with her when she'd made the move, but they had their own lives. She understood, it didn't stop her from wishing they would change their minds someday.

Greg and Nancy were pulling out while Ben waved to them as he walked back towards the house. He was careful to stay next to the house where no prying eyes could see him.

"Hey." She reached out a hand to him and smiled.

He took it and spun her around so that her back was too him. "Hey yourself, gorgeous," he growled in her ear as he nuzzled her neck.

"Now what do we do?" she sighed in contentment.

Even though they weren't alone, the house felt empty somehow.

"Oh, I have a few things in mind," he murmured. His lips sought out the sensitive spot behind her ear, while he drew her tighter against him.

"Mmm. I bet you do," she purred. She slid her fingers through his hair as he raked his lips across her skin to her throat.

The door opened just then. "Hey! Oh man! Can't you guys keep your hands to yourselves for one second?" Mark asked. "Like come on! Feel for the single people around here would ya?"

Ben laughed pulling away from Abbi. "Sure buddy. What did you want?" he said, steering her into the open garage doorway.

"Well. We decided..." Mark motioned towards Kim and Ava standing there.

"That it would be best for you to stay in the house." He pointed at the floor with both hands. "This house... unless of course Abbi objects. If that's the case, then we need to move you in the dark to your place."

"That's absurd," Abbi snickered. "Why would I object?"

"Indeed," Kim looked at Ben and smiled. She flashed her eyes to Abbi, now a full grin on her face, giving her a wink along with a thumbs up.

Abbi just laughed and shook her head. "You're incorrigible, you know that, right?" Abbi asked her.

Grinning like the Cheshire cat, Kim shot back, "I try."

Mark nodded. "Good, it's settled then. Us three will stay at Ben's."

"Abbi, you need to lie low too. The less you're seen outside, the more likely it will draw the perp out," Kim said.

Abbi nodded. "Nice cop lingo, you have going on there."

"I know, right?" she laughed.

"Come on, Aunt Kim. It's time we got out of their hair," Ava said tugging on her aunt's sleeve.

They all entered the house and scattered in different directions, each gathering up their belongings to take over to Ben's house.

Ben came to her, taking her in his arms, he jerked her to him. "Love. What shenanigans can we get into, I wonder?"

He took her breath away. A hunger she had never seen before in his eyes burned over her skin. She smoothed her hands down his chest. "I have a trick or two up my sleeve." She smiled sweetly.

Just you wait and see...

Chapter 28

"You know I could get used to living here," Kim said as the three of them made their way through the forest on the path to Ben's house.

"Yeah?" Mark asked. "I know what you mean. Here I had this place for three years and only came to it once maybe twice," he said, waving his hand at the house.

"What're you crazy?" Kim looked in awe at Ben's house. Abbi's place was a dump compared to this. She especially loved the fact that the lake was all around it except for the adjoining land between the two properties. Otherwise, it was as if it were on an island.

"I bet you're kicking yourself now?" Ava chimed in, gawking at the sight before them.

"Careful, watch the branch," Mark said, holding it so it didn't swat one of them in the face. "Well, after Ben moved in, I came up... a few weeks ago now and yeah, I was kicking myself. But I have since figured out that if I stayed, I wouldn't have met you fine ladies, now, would I?" he said, raising his brows.

"True, that is very true," Kim said. "Or we would have met under different circumstances, and we might have hated you," she laughed.

"Don't laugh, I hated myself too," he said, climbing the steps. Maybe it was age, but ever since meeting Abbi and her family, Mark felt like his wild ways were a thing of the past. He stopped, shocked at the revelation.

Whoa! Man, where did that come from? He glanced at Ava and realized he knew exactly where that came from.... the Peterson women were witches.

Ava pointed to the top step of the back porch. "EWW. What is that?"

Kim peered down at it. "Huh... that must be the blood Ben was talking about." Not moving, she followed the trail with her eyes, to where it had stopped at the door and pooled into a puddle. "Oh, hell no!" She stood and looked at the others, her face void of colour. "We need to catch this bastard now."

Mark nodded. "Sooner, rather than later."

Ava just stood frozen to the spot. "If someone can hurt Molly like that... given the chance, what will they do to Mom or Ben?"

Kim took the keys out of her pocket and slid it into the lock and tried turning it, it wouldn't budge. Turning, she said, "Well, they already tried it with Ben, lucky for him it didn't work."

Mark draped an arm around Ava's shoulders. "Hey, it's okay. There's five of us and only one of them... well, maybe. We don't have a clue how many we are dealing with."

Ava's face took on a horrified look at the possibility that there could be more than one person.

"Nice going, Sherlock! Now you've scared the crap out of her," Kim said the obvious as she reached out to comfort Ava.

"I'm sorry. But the reality is..."

"Shhush!" Kim pointed a finger under his nose, effectively cutting him off. Shaking her head, she said, "Nope, no. You will not finish that thought. Would you just open the damn door already?" She had to restrain her foot from kicking him in the ass.

THE ANIMALS FLOCKED to the kitchen at the sound of the can opener and Bird came soaring in, squawking his delight. The poor guy had been locked in his cage for the last few days while everyone was there.

"Ben, are you hungry?" Abbi asked, dumping the food into the dishes. She glanced towards him as she set them on the floor.

He was in a world of his own. Sitting at the table, her laptop in front of him, he was staring intently at the screen while he ran his finger across his bottom lip.

She went to the cupboard to get some peanuts for Bird then walked into the library and dumped them into the dish in his cage and checked to make sure there was enough water and seed. "Hey Birdie, come and get it."

Ben was doing some checking of his own. He couldn't stop thinking about Mark asking Abbi if she had any enemies. He had doubted very much that she did. But he wouldn't rule himself out for not having any.

"Hey, Abbi! Can you come here a minute, please?"

Turning on her heel, she went to see what he wanted.

He pulled her to his side. "Here, look. Have you seen this guy around here at all?" he asked, pointing at the screen.

She bent closer to get a good look and felt Ben take a hold of her hips, guiding her to his lap. Frowning, she thought he looked a bit familiar but couldn't place him. Abbi shook her head. "Hmm, no. Not that I can remember." She turned and looked at him. "Why?"

"You're sure?" He bit his bottom lip. "Look again, please."

She did and then asked, "Am I supposed to know him?"

"Does he or doesn't he look like the guy that bumped into you outside of the mall in Springbank?"

"Well, the guy had a winter hat and gloves on." She looked at him. "I found that a bit odd for this time of year." She looked back at the screen.

"His face Abbi... look at his face."

She turned her head to the side. "Now that you mention his face... yeah! It looks like him." At once, she felt him tense against her. "Why....?"

"MARK, CAN YOU SLOW down a bit?" Kim called from the back seat of Ben's car.

Kim wasn't used to riding in the back seat, especially in a little black sports car with only two doors and a hatch that she could never in her wildest dreams smash her fat ass through, if the need arose.

"I'm only going ten kilometres an hour! How slow do you want me to go, woman?"

She was squished in a corner with clothes spread out beside her. The road was so bendy she didn't want them scuttling on her. "Uh, five is good." She wrinkled her nose as she picked up a black article of clothing.

Is this stuff even clean?

She held it up between two fingers, turning it this way and that and realized it was a pair of men's boxer briefs.

Ben's boxer briefs... In horror she whipped them to the floor.

"Hey, can you open a window, it's getting a little...stuffy in here." Kim gasped and pulled her collar away to get some airflow going.

Mark glanced at Ava and raised his brows. His eyes growing large as he asked, "Is she always like this?"

"She's worse when she gets to know you better." Ava grinned out the passenger window.

Mark gave her a double take. "You're kidding, right?"

"Stop talking about me. I can hear you know," Kim said, getting hotter by the minute. "Ava, crack your damn window! Now, before I barf on these clothes here," she motioned with her hand.

That's all it took. Both front windows were down in seconds, as the car crept painfully slow toward the boat rentals.

"I'M JUST NOT QUITE ready to share what I'm thinking at the moment," Ben said looking into her eyes. "I need to be 100% sure before I say anything."

"Not even a hint?" She smiled.

"No Abbi, not even a hint," he said, dropping a kiss on her nose. He closed the laptop with a snap. "What shall we eat?" he asked.

"Funny you should ask," she said, getting up. "The food here is just about depleted. I could order a pizza or have Mack drop off something?" she suggested.

"Would he do that?"

"Yeah. He does it all the time, especially when I'm in writer's mode," she said, walking to the fridge to see exactly what they would need.

"I'll just get him to cook us up something for tonight and bring a few groceries for the next few days," she said. "What do you feel like eating?"

He raised a brow. "Tonight? You for starters," he murmured. A thrill of delight skimmed up her spine at his words.

"Uh...well, we'll see about that." She felt the heat rise to her cheeks.

He grinned. "How about burgers and fries? I could go for that. My first meal here was one of Mack's burgers."

"They're amazing, aren't they," she agreed, nodding her head. Picking up the cordless house phone she dialed Mack's number and started to rummage through the freezer, waiting for him to pick up.

"Don't tell him I'm here," Ben said, in a loud whisper.

She gave him a quick nod and sent a dazzling smile his way.

"Hey, Mack... I'm good! How are you?" Her smile turned into a laugh. "Yeah, that is so true. But what can we expect, right? It's tourist season!" She paused, listening. "Really?"

Ben thought she sounded surprised; her expression confirmed it as he watched her features change from amusement to a frown, all while she kept the happy, upbeat tone with Mack going.

She nodded. "Right?!... Yeah, I was calling to see if I could order some burgers and fries, and a few items to last me through the week. Awesome! For tonight can I get two burgers and two orders of fries. Actually, can you make the fries into poutine?" She smiled as Ben gave her a thumbs up. "No. I uh, plan on just eating the other one tomorrow, you know how I am when I'm writing... No, Ben's not here. His parents were down... yes... um, yeah. He went back to England with them. He's just gone... I guess."

Ben could tell she hated lying to Mack. He went over to her and rubbed the tension from her neck and shoulders. She sighed softly at his touch as she placed the grocery order.

"Great thanks, Mack, see you soon." She ended the call. "God, I hate lying to that man." Turning around she put her hand on her hip, a thoughtful look on her face.

"What is it?" Ben asked.

How was she going to tell him what Mack had just said? *If I do, he will charge out of the house the second it passes my lips...* "Nothing. Mack just said that business is picking up."

He looked at her, his brows raised in question. "And...? Is that unusual or something?"

"Um...No... not at all." No, she'd keep it to herself. For now, there was no cause to tell him about the man currently sitting at Mack's, eating a fried Bologna sandwich. A man, Mack referred to as a real loony... considering it was a warm sunny day, too warm to be wearing a winter hat and gloves.

She pasted a smile on her lips. "Mack said he will be here in about an hour. He's just waiting on a customer to leave."

Ben nodded. "Sounds good. I'll just do a little more research, if you don't mind?" he said, looking at the laptop.

"No, go ahead. I'm going to head out to the garage for a minute."

Opening the laptop, he waved a hand her way, already engrossed in the screen before him. "I'll be here," he said absently.

Abbi crossed the room to the short hall that led to the attached garage. She never used it, only for storage. Glancing around, she heaved a heavy sigh. There were boxes upon boxes piled high against the walls, along with furniture from the previous owners scattered around. Maybe she'd have a yard sale once everything was back to normal. That was if she could get everything in order first. She grabbed the closest box. Rifling through it, she saw the kids' Mother's Day cards and gifts made from their school days, falling apart, and faded with age. They would think she was nuts for keeping all of it. It certainly wouldn't be the first time they would think that; she chuckled as she closed the box and put it in the keep pile.

Moving a rug that had been tossed and forgotten, she unearthed an old cd player. It wasn't hers. She frowned looking at it as she sat it on a table. Plugging it in she hit the power button. "Well, it works."

Now to find something to play on it. Moving another box aside, she found CDs in an old milk crate. Sitting on the concrete floor, she flipped through them. She was an 80's music kinda gal. This stuff was all classical. She found one that she thought might do. Getting up, she took the CD out of the case as she walked to the player. She popped it in and hit the play button. A thundering of beating drums followed by the soothing sounds of a cello set the mood for her cleaning.

After a half hour she had most of the floor cleared. There were still a few boxes left to break down and one more to add to the others, but that was the end of the clutter scattered about. She glanced at her watch.

Mack should be here shortly.

She took the last box in her hands and cast an eye around the room to see where the best place to stick it would be. She walked over to where there was a mirror on the wall; an empty spot on the floor sat under it. Putting it there, she caught her reflection. She looked like a dusty mess and, wondered if she'd have time to hop in for a quick shower. Abbi decided against it. She couldn't miss Mack and she certainly couldn't let Ben open the door when he was supposed to be on the other side of the world. She frowned, staring out the window. She hated lying to Mack but what choice did she have; he was a talker... not an intentional gossiper, but he did let things slip.

BEN SNAPPED HIS HEAD up.

Is that music?

"That can't be what Abbi heard the day we met," he mumbled to himself.

He got up from the table to find the source. He hoped not, as it was coming from the garage. He had been so engrossed with searching the web that he hadn't heard her leave. He followed the sounds of the music and stopped. She was standing by the window looking out, her arms folded across her chest. And she took his breath away. Her clothes were dusty and her hair a mess with what looked like a cobweb in it. Yet, she was still the most beautiful woman he had laid eyes on. He glanced over and saw the source of the music. He moved to it and saw the milk crate full of CD's. Selecting one, he hit the open/close button on the player and swapped the disks.

Abbi turned when the music cut out. She watched as Ben changed the disks and held out her hand to him as he crossed the floor to her.

He took it while the sounds of a piano filled the garage. His other hand snaked around her waist, pulling her to him.

"Dance with me, love." He touched his lips to her temple as he brought their hands to his chest. "This song describes what I feel for you, perfectly," he murmured, gazing into her eyes.

John Legend's voice crooned out the song 'All of Me', as they swayed back and forth. Listening to the words, Abbi's eyes filled with tears. She wrapped her arms around his neck so tight, she never wanted to let go.

He rubbed her back. "It's true, Abbi."

She leaned back, looking into his eyes then leaned forward and kissed him softly. Knowing she didn't deserve someone as beautiful as him. She ran her thumb across his bottom lip. "I love you so much and I will no matter what happens."

"I feel the same way. Nothing will happen or ever change that. We will figure out who is doing this. Now please, stop thinking about it because baby, you're stuck with me." He smiled and nuzzled her neck, which caused an eruption of giggles to pass over her lips as the song slowly ended.

They both froze when they heard a bang on the garage door. "Abbi, are you in there?"

"Shit, duck down," she whispered. "It's Mack, and you're in England, remember?"

Ducking down, Ben looked around. *Just how is he going to see me?* There were no windows in any of the doors.

"Coming, Mack... I'll meet you at the front door," she yelled, hurrying off into the house.

Ben stayed put. While waiting for the all-clear from Abbi, he stood looking around and saw she had a lot of boxes to go through yet. He flipped open the flaps of one nearest to him.

Huh, a box full of her yearbooks, cool...

Taking one he glanced at the year... 1986. He put it back, looking to see if there were any from Abbi's high school days. He pulled one out from 1991.

That was the year before the boys were born, she was only 15. God, at 15 he was into cars and drama class. He couldn't imagine having to raise a baby at that young, let alone twins.

He flipped it open and scanned the names listed alphabetically. Running his finger down, he realized he didn't know if Peterson was her married name or her maiden name. Maiden. There she was, Abbi Peterson.

A young girl stared up at him from the page, a soft smile on her lips. She was older now, wiser, and more beautiful. He couldn't help but feel protective of the girl back then. He scanned the page, wondering if she had met her husband in school too. He could hear her coming through the short hall to the garage and was about to snap it closed when a familiar face caught his eye.

What the hell? ...

Frowning, he looked at the name. There was no way that could be his name. He peered closer. But it was him. All this time he had been searching on the web for any background info and here it was in Abbi's garage the whole time. In the black-and-white photo, there was a younger version of the man Ben knew, but not the name he had now. The very man that wanted the lead for Abbi's book. They never gave him a chance to audition. Tony, the director knew exactly who he'd cast if they wanted the part.

And Ben couldn't refuse it.

Chapter 29

"What do you mean you can't tell us who rented a boat a few days ago?" Kim snapped at the attendant.

"Ma'am, it's against company policy to divulge the names of our customers to ..." she looked down her nose at Kim, "... other people."

Mark grabbed Kim by the arms and dragged her out of the way. Giving the attendant his most charming smile, he said, "Look." He dropped his eyes to her name tag. "Deloris. She meant nothing by that," he said, trying to calm the situation. "What she meant was, how much would it be to rent a boat for say... ten minutes?" he inquired, pulling his wallet out of his back pocket.

Deloris rolled her eyes, "We don't do ten-minute rentals. If you want to step foot on a boat, it's a minimum hourly rental, which is $100.00 plus tax," she replied snootily, then looked them up and down, giving them a look as if they couldn't afford it.

Kim gasped in shock.

"We'll take it." Ava smacked two $100 dollar bills on the counter. "But we want that one," she said, pointing out the window to the largest boat sitting at the dock.

Deloris changed her attitude quickly at the sight of the bills, "Certainly. I just need you to sign right here." She passed a clipboard over to Ava who signed with a flourish.

Snatching up the keys off the counter, Ava said to the others, "Come on."

Pointing at Deloris, Kim couldn't help but get the last word in.

She raised her brows. "Just an FYI. That's robbery!" she yelled, scurrying out the door after Ava and Mark.

MARK WAS BUSY STEERING the boat, aiming straight for Abbi's house. He wanted to know how easy it would be to see inside from 100 feet out.

"So... what exactly are we looking for again?" Kim asked for the tenth time.

"Anything," Ava answered. She bent down, wrinkling her brow in disgust at a squashed dead bug. "Anything that could be a clue."

"Well, it's kind of pointless, isn't it? I mean, they would clean the boats between customers, you would think," Kim mumbled, searching the floor for anything that didn't fit.

Ignoring her, Ava went down in the cabin below. Opening doors and drawers as she went.

There has got to be something here...

There was. A horrid smell. She couldn't quite discern where it was coming from. Glancing around, she spied a wastebasket under the sink and pulled it out then peered into it. She jerked her head back and gagged. Blindly turning on her heel, she stumbled up the steps taking two at a time. "Look," she said, shoving the basket under Kim's nose, as she dry heaved. "What is it?"

"Ava, what the hell?" Kim wrinkled her nose in disgust and backed away. "What is that God awful smell?"

Carefully setting it down, Ava too backed away. "I don't know. It smells dead, whatever it is."

Mark glanced over his shoulder, the smell wafting to him now. "That smells like shit. Ava, dump it out."

Ava's eyes snapped to his face. "Here? Like... on the floor?"

He shrugged. "Yeah sure... why not?"

Ava looked at the basket with revulsion as if it were a snake.

Balancing on one foot, she tipped it over with her boot, standing it upside down. Then for no reason at all, she kicked it like it was a soccer ball. The trees came alive from birds taking flight, as her screams of disgust shattered the stillness of the lake.

"Holy Montana!" Mark ducked as the basket sailed over his head, landing with a plop in the water.

"What the *hell* is wrong with you...screaming like that? I almost pissed my pants!" Kim hissed.

"I'm sorry! It's just gross..." Ava bent over examining the contents. "Oh... It's just rotten hamburger." She snatched up a crumpled piece of paper stuck to the dried blood on the cellophane and scrutinized it.

They were 100 yards out from Abbi's shoreline, and it was just as Mark thought... a perfect view. He could see everything in the yard and on the porch. But not in the house; that would likely change at nightfall. Killing the engine, he walked to Ava, and looked over her shoulder, squinting to read what was written on the paper. "What does it say?"

"I don't know." She frowned. "It looks like it's written in blood. Um, didn't Ben say the note mom got, looked like it was too?" she scowled, looking up at Mark.

"Let me see that." Kim snatched it away. Shaking her head, she tsked, "Whoever wrote this has terrible penmanship. It says... I'm coming...." She brought it closer to her eyes, "... for you Raven Black." Her face was screwed with confusion when she looked at the others. "Who is Raven Black? How many people is this person after?"

Mark stood there shaking his head. Disbelief on his face, he pointed at the note. "I know that guy."

"You do?" Ava felt a rush of relief at the possibility of a lead.

He gave a quick nod of his head. "Yeah. He wanted Ben's part in the Jasper Killings."

"We need to tell them. Can you get closer to the shore?"

"Yeah, sure. Ben has a dock over at his place." Mark started the engine and in less than a minute, they were pulling up to the dock.

"We can't stay long. This thing has to be back soon," he said, wrapping the line around a post. "Come on."

All three of them ran along the shore to Abbi's yard, their shadows long, as the sun made it's decent as they made their way to the back porch.

Just as Ava raised her fist to pound on the French doors, Mark grabbed her arm.

"Wait! Don't do that!" he whispered loudly.

"Do what?"

"Shh, keep your voice down!"

"Why?" Ava shook her head, her eyes growing large. With a raised voice she asked, "What the hell is your problem?"

"They might be, you know... busy." He gave her a look.

"Busy at what?"

Rolling her eyes, Kim reached around her niece to pound on the glass herself and piped up, "Sex, Ava. They might be getting it on is what he's trying to say."

Mark folded his arms across his chest. "Tell me... is everyone in your family so inconsiderate?"

"Only when assholes are threatening us." Kim grinned.

ABBI PEEKED INTO THE garage. "Hey handsome, the coast is clear. Mack just left."

"Abbi, look." Ben came to her with one of her old yearbooks. "Look who it is."

She took the book in her hands and glanced to where he was pointing. She looked at Ben and nodded. "Yeah, that's Roland Eddy. What about him?"

She turned around and headed back into the kitchen. Ben followed, going to the table.

"It's him," he said, and grabbed the laptop, sticking it in her face.

She looked up from the screen. "No, that's Raven Black."

He groaned in frustration. "It's the same guy, Abbi. Look, I'll show you." He sat the laptop on the table. Using his hands, he covered everything in the photo except the man's face.

Abbi sat down, holding the yearbook beside the screen for comparison. She laid the book down, got up and walked to the counter to get their food.

"Okay, I see it now. So, what does this mean?" She looked at him as she grabbed the forks. "Well?" She asked, after he didn't respond. Opening the fridge, she took a bottle of ketchup and grabbed two cans of pop. He watched her as she walked towards him with her hands full.

"Well, I had a theory, but I'm not so sure now." He sighed, taking his food from her.

"Which is?" She sat down and opened hers. Taking a bite of her burger, she stared at him.

Holding up a finger, Ben took a mouthful of poutine and groaned in delight. He pointed to the food. "This is better than that place in the mall."

Abbi smiled. "Mack is a man of many talents that's for sure."

"Now quit stalling Ben and tell me, what's your theory?"

"Well. When Mark asked if you had any enemies... it got me wondering if I did." He chewed thoughtfully. "Mack needs to branch out, has he thought of franchising?"

"Already asked him. I even told him I would back him, but he isn't interested."

Nodding, he said, "Right, fair enough."

She looked at him through her lashes. "Do you have any enemies, Ben?" She couldn't imagine why he would.

"Um... Yeah, most likely." He didn't want to come right out and say yes... because of the film. No doubt, she'd blame herself for that.

"Roland Eddy?" she hedged. She needed to know. Roland had always had a crush on her. Throughout school, he'd asked her out on a date. She kindly declined, but that never stopped him from asking. After she found out she was pregnant, she left school, never going back. She had no idea what happened to him.

Abbi watched as Ben licked his lips and leaned back in his chair, he was stalling.

"Ben, just tell me. We are in this together, remember?" she repeated the words he had told her so many times.

Pushing his food away, he sighed heavily, choosing his words carefully for her sake.

"Well, I can't be certain." He reached to take her hand. "But Raven Black wanted the part that I got—"

A bang on the back door had the dogs racing through the house to the French doors in the living room, growling and barking as they passed by.

"Who the hell is that?" Ben said, shooting out of his chair to see.

"Get back. We don't know who it is." Abbi rushed to see who it was, relief flowed over her as she saw.

"It's okay, it's Kim and them." She unlocked the door and swung it wide. "Come on in."

"Hey, Abbi. Ben around?" Mark asked.

She saw the look of concern as he scanned the room.

Coming around the corner Ben said, "Yeah, right here mate. What's up?"

"Good... we need to talk." He looked pointedly at Abbi.

"It's fine. Abbi and I were just talking about what's going on."

"Good, because we found something," Kim rushed on.

"So did we." Ben motioned for them to follow him into the kitchen.

"Us first." Kim interrupted Ben before he could say a thing. She snagged a fry from Abbi's food and stuffed it her mouth.

"Alright, what do you have?"

"Well," Kim swallowed loudly. "First off. Dude, you need to clean your car out." She wrinkled her nose at the memory of his boxers in her hands.

"Kim!" Ava and Mark hissed in unison.

"Alright, alright! I'll get to the point." She took a deep breath. "We went to the boat rentals and talked to Deloris," she said snidely. "Whom Ava paid two hundred bucks to... I might add." She shot Ava a disapproving look.

Mark made a sound in his throat. "What Kim is getting at; is we took the boat out on the lake. Ava found the vilest smelling garbage you can ever imagine." He looked at Abbi. "Your daughter kicked it at my head!"

"I did not!" Ava shouted. "I merely just sent it flying... your way."

"Yeah... lucky for you, the meat was on the floor. If that had splattered on me, we both would have gone for a swim."

Abbi was getting more confused by the minute. Closing her eyes and counting to ten she held her hands up. "Hold it. Would someone mind getting to the damn point of all this?"

Kim took a deep breath. "Okay, here it is. In the garbage pail, there was a pack of rotten hamburger... hence the smell. On the package was this..."

She pulled the note out of her pocket, triumphantly holding it up for them to see.

"Written in what I ... or.... we think was the blood from the meat, and the same blood used for the note from the flowers."

Ben slipped his arm around Abbi as he took the note from Kim. With their heads together, they read the message.

"So, whoever this guy is, he's not only after you two but he's also after Raven Black." Kim gave a satisfied nod. Turning, she gave high fives to Mark and Ava. "Hey, maybe we should team up and become P.I.'s. Yeah?" She grinned, nodding at them. Both winced and shook their heads no.

Ben looked at Abbi. She read the self-doubt in his gaze.

"Go ahead. Tell them what you came up with." She encouraged. She had a hard time believing his theory. But she knew she trusted him more than anyone in the room.

"Um, that sounds like a possibility, but...." He removed his arm from around Abbi's waist and walked to the table. Taking the laptop, he turned it around. "Look familiar, Mark?"

Mark walked over to stare at the screen. "That's Raven Black," he nodded, tapping the screen.

"Right," Ben said, sitting it down. He grabbed the yearbook.

"Now, look at..." Ben stabbed the photo of Roland Eddy. "...him."

Mark looked at the page, his mouth agape, brows rose in surprise. "No! There's no way, man! That can't be!" Following Ben's thinking, Mark was horrified.

Ben nodded. "Yes, that's exactly what I'm thinking."

"What are you two going on about?" Kim asked. Frustrated, she took the book from Ben and looked at him. "Who are you talking about?"

"That guy right there!" Mark pointed over her shoulder at the photo.

She looked at Ben with an arched brow. "You mean Roland Eddy?"

"Yeah," Mark responded. He looked at Ben. "You know, I always thought something was off with that guy. Man, I don't believe this," he said, throwing up a hand.

"I'm not following," Ava frowned.

"Hey, Abbi, wasn't this the guy that sent you flowers, and you threw them away?" Kim glanced at her questioningly.

"Yeah... I did," she stared blankly. She'd forgotten all about that. He had them delivered to her in a beautiful crystal vase.

Blood-red roses, twelve to be exact. She thought their dad had sent them for their mom. But that hadn't been the case. When she found out they were for her and from whom, she promptly threw them away. She didn't want to encourage any attention from him and neither mentioned it to each other. She liked him as a person, but that was as far as that went.

"Will someone please fill me in on what the hell is going on?" Ava demanded.

Ben looked at Ava and pointed to the computer screen. "This guy wanted my role for your mom's book." He pointed to the yearbook that Kim held. "And that guy. Roland Eddy who went to school with her, is the same guy."

Now Abbi knew what Ben was about to say earlier. He hadn't finished his sentence when they had heard the knock on the door. She cleared her throat. "Am I correct in assuming." She looked at Ben. "Raven Black was mad you got the part without auditioning?"

He nodded in response.

"And now he's here, to make sure you can never take another one away from him again?"

Ben looked up; he thought a moment. "Yeah... I think it's more than just making sure I'm out of the picture."

Taking a hold of her shoulders, he lowered his voice. "Abbi, it's more than that. He wants you. The phone calls, the flowers, and the note." He rubbed her arms. "The break-in," he softly reminded her. "Me..." He pursed his lips in indifference. "I'm just an inconvenience. One that would better suit his agenda, if I were out of the way for good."

She shook her head. It was absurd.

"Mom, did you think to look at the video when Ben's drugs were delivered?" Ava asked. "Maybe the guy was stupid enough to bring them himself."

"Why the hell didn't we think of that?" Ben asked Abbi, his eyes brightening. Smiling, he turned to Ava. He grabbed her by the arms. "Ava, I could kiss you."

She closed her eyes tight and braced herself. "Please don't," she squeaked.

Ben laughed as he promptly smacked a loud kiss on her forehead.

"Hey, what about me?" Kim asked, pointing to her face. He took her by the arms and promptly kissed her on the forehead too.

She let out a soft sigh. "I need to find a man like that," she said, giving Mark a side glance.

Mark's brows shot up as he held his hands up defensively. "Oh. No, no, no. You're way too much of a woman for me."

"Damn straight I am. I would eat you for a snack." She snorted with laughter.

Dropping a quick kiss on Abbi's lips, Ben tugged on her hand. "Come on, let's go check out the video." Turning to the rest standing there awkwardly, he raised his brows. "Aren't you guys coming?"

They all hurriedly followed Ben into Abbi's room. Abbi pulled out the laptop from the drawer, put in her password, and searched for the date.

"Who answered the door when they came?" she asked, eyes fixed on the screen.

Kim raised her hand. "That would be me."

"Did he look familiar at all to you?" Abbi asked.

"Not really. I wasn't paying much attention though." She made a disgusted look. "I was too busy staring at the shitty flowers he was handing me."

"Around what time was that?" Mark asked.

"Well, it was after supper, so I would say around seven," she answered.

Abbi typed in the search button for the time. The screen jumped to it at once; they waited and watched as the video played on the screen.

"What was he driving?" Ben looked at Kim.

"Hmm, now that you mention it... he was walking. At the time I thought nothing of it."

Abbi sped up the recording a bit. She was going to click the mouse again when Mark pointed at the screen.

"There!" he said.

They all leaned in to get a better view. A man came into view, walking and glancing around as if he was searching for someone. He was carrying something in his hands as he cut across the front yard. He made a beeline for the house, went up the steps, crossed the porch and rang the doorbell.

Abbi sat transfixed. Staring at what was in his hands. A small white bag and twelve long-stemmed, bruised and beaten roses.

"That's him!!" Kim yelled. "That asshole lied to me; he had the flowers the whole time!"

"Precisely!" Ben said grimly.

"Man, you have skills! I don't know how you figure all this stuff out. Every damn time, too!" Mark said, smacking Ben on the back.

"So now what do we do?" Ava asked. "Do we call the police?"

Ben looked at Abbi. He noticed she seemed withdrawn.

"I'll call my brother, with any luck he can come here and help us figure it out," Mark answered Ava.

Ben gave Mark a pointed look and tilted his head in Abbi's direction.

Glancing at Abbi, Mark followed his hint.

Ben, he gave him a nod.

"Great, but what do we do now?" Ava asked again.

Draping an arm around both Ava and Kim, Mark guided them to the door. "Right now, we take the boat back and leave these two alone," he said, as he escorted them out into the hall.

'OH, MY DARLING ABBI, I just know that we will be perfect together! I will mend your broken heart... silly girl falling for Ben in the first place was your one flaw. But I can overlook that. I just need you to leave your home. Seeing how you somehow blocked my number... I can't call you now, can I? ... Nor can I walk up to your door. No... that wouldn't do at all...'

Chapter 30

Ben closed the laptop with a snap. Placing it on the bed beside her, he knelt before Abbi, taking her cold hands in his. She was sitting still, lost in her thoughts.

"Abbi. Look at me," he whispered.

She looked down at him and saw the love shining from his eyes. She lifted her hand to run the backs of her fingers gently along his jawline and thought back to when he was lying on the bed at the clinic. So pale against the whiteness of the sheets. She felt so helpless and guilty at the same time...

But not this time.

This time she was mad and getting madder by the minute.

Ben saw the anger building in her eyes. He saw the fire coming back. "We've got this, love," he said. Standing, he tugged on her hands. "Come on. It's dark out. Let's go for a walk."

"Do you think that's a good idea?" she asked, with concern.

"I do. Yes. It's a beautiful night out. We'll just go in the backyard." Giving a sharp whistle he called for the dogs. Abbi snatched up a blanket from the window seat as they headed to the door. The dogs scrambled into the room, each one trying to be first out the door.

They made their way along the porch, down the steps to the middle of the yard. Ben took the blanket from her and laid it out on the ground. "Sit," he said softly.

The light from the full moon bathed the yard with its glow. Abbi sat, but glanced around at the shadows, imagining all sorts of creatures there. She wouldn't feel safe until he was at her side. She patted the spot beside her. "Join me?"

"You need not ask me twice," he grinned.

"Ben, what are we going to do?"

"Shh, not tonight. Tonight, let's just forget the world," he murmured to her softly.

She nodded then laid her head on his shoulder, but she had to know. Frowning, she looked at him. "But what if—"

His mouth on hers cut her off while his hands cradled her head. He deepened the kiss as he laid her gently on the ground; his other hand searched for the hem of her shirt with an urgency. Finding it, he touched her warm skin.

Shuddering from the touch of his hand, Abbi pulled the snaps of her blouse free. She lay there in her bra under the moonlight as Ben raked his eyes over her.

God, I'll never tire of her beauty...

He wanted nothing more than to make love to her right there, under the full moon but not for the world to see. He trailed a row of kisses from her belly button to her lips. He gave her one last plundering kiss before trailing his lips to her ear.

"Not here, love," he murmured huskily. She wrapped her arms around his neck as he picked her up and carried her towards the house. His mouth never leaving hers.

Taking a breather, Abbi leaned back, "Ben put me down, it will be faster if I walk," she giggled.

He stopped in his tracks. His gaze dropped to her lips, slowly he bent his head to touch them again. "You're right," he said, tearing his mouth away to set her down.

"Come on." She grabbed his hand leading the way back to her bedroom.

The dogs were all waiting, dashing in as she opened the door.

"We forgot the blanket, I'll go get it," Ben said.

"Don't worry about it." She tugged his hand and stopped. "On second thought. Maybe it's better if you did, do you mind?" she asked.

"Sure, be back in a second." He took off out the door.

Abbi rushed into the bathroom. Pushing down the plunger, she twisted the taps to fill the tub and dumped a generous amount of Epsom salts along with bubble bath. She turned to light the candles scattered around the room and paused to listen. Ben wasn't back yet.

She walked through to the back door, looking to see if she could see him. There he stood, folding the blanket staring out across the lake. Relieved, she went back to the bathroom, stripping her clothes as she did.

Ben was looking to see if there were any lights across the lake. Seeing nothing, he started back towards the house. When he and Abbi were out there, he had the feeling of being watched. He most likely imagined it.

Opening the door, he walked into silence.

Huh. Is she already sleeping?

Tossing the blanket on a chair his foot caught on something. Looking down he saw Abbi's shirt laying there. A few feet away her pants, where she had kicked them off. His brows raised at seeing her panties lying a few feet further. Rounding the corner at the closed bathroom door, he found her bra wedged between it and the frame. He slid the pocket door open, her bra falling forgotten to the floor; his breath caught in his throat at the sight before him. There she was lounging in the tub. Her head resting against the back; her hair falling over the edge.

As he walked towards her, he saw her eyes were closed as the whirring of the jets slowly churned the water into frothy bubbles. Bathed in candlelight, her skin glistened. The heady scent of jasmine in the air mingled with the bubbles that barely covered her breasts, was intoxicating to him. He stood silently. He wanted to dip his head to suck on one nipple, just one, bringing her to dizzying heights of pleasure with his tongue.

She must have sensed him there for she opened her eyes. She smiled at him. "Hey handsome, care to join me?"

Images of doing just that flashed through his mind. He felt like jumping in fully clothed, taking her in his arms and giving her a pleasure so intense like she had never known before. He grabbed the neckline of his shirt and pulled it over his head, rolling it into a ball he whipped it to the floor. He could feel the heat from her gaze scorching a path over his skin.

Abbi reached out to touch him. Taking a step back, he waved a finger at her. "Uh, uh."

He reached for the waist of his jeans. Unbuttoning them, he slowly pulled the zipper down, gazing into her eyes as he did, seeing them go from hot to fiery in a single heartbeat.

I should have thought this through a bit more... she thought, catching her teeth with her bottom lip. She was to be seducing him and here he was doing it to her. She loved watching his muscles ripple under his skin and wanted to touch him, any part of him she'd be happy with. But he denied her. He'd rather torture her by making her watch as his hands slowly undid his jeans. Her eyes followed as they dropped to the floor in a heap.

He stood there for a second, just watching her watch him.

Abbi licked her suddenly dry lips. The excitement building up in her made her wonder if it would always feel this way with him... as if every time was the first time.

Her heart raced as she watched him pull his boxers down. Her eyes went at once to his erection.

Good, God! Can one have an orgasm from just looking?

Ben cleared his throat loudly. "Abbi?" He held his hand out to her. She didn't take it. She just kept staring at him. "Love?"

He took a step closer to the tub and put his hands on the side of it, he leaned down and looked straight into her eyes.

She looked at him then and smiled softly. "Hi."

"Hi, yourself," he said, then placed a soft kiss on her lips. He deepened it, his lips clung to hers as he climbed into the tub and pulled her to him as he leaned back.

Abbi wrapped her arms around his neck and laid atop his hard body; she was fighting a battle within herself. She desperately wanted to sit on him, but she also wanted this moment to last forever.

Tearing her mouth from his, she slowly backed away. She needed to distance herself or the wantonness in her would win. Looking him in the eyes, she saw confusion replace the desire.

What is going on with her? One minute she is more than willing and the next she is backing away as if she is bored?

"Did I do something wrong?" he asked her.

In answer, she ducked her head under the water.

Great, she is bored!

Abbi came up sputtering, wiping water from her eyes.

"Are you going to answer me?" Ben asked, wondering how she could turn off like that so quickly.

"Yeah. It's simple really." She paused, running her foot along his leg to his inner thigh, up his stomach to his chest. "You drive me insane. I can't control myself around you."

The desire sprang back into his eyes. "Really?"

"Yes. Really." She frowned. "You make me feel like a wanton sex-craved—"

She couldn't finish her words because his hand snaked out, taking hold of her foot. He brought it to his lips lightly kissing the inner arch, trailing kisses up to her ankle along her calf. He lowered her leg into the water and guided it around his waist, only to do the same with the other as he pulled her by the waist to him. Their slick bodies pressed together, his breath, hot, fanning over her already heated skin.

She sucked in a breath when she felt his teeth nip her neck, followed by his tongue, soothing the sting away.

Breathing heavily, he murmured against her neck, "And you don't think you do the same to me?"

Abbi couldn't control it any longer. The thought of their lower bodies so close to each other. His lips, his breath, and his teeth on her skin. All had her shuddering a release as she held tightly to him, moaning her pleasure. She was just coming back to her senses when he grabbed hold of her hips and lifted her. She gasped at the sensation of him filling her as he eased into her warmth. Raking her nails across his back, she arched her head as his lips scorched a trail along her throat. She shoved her hands into his hair, holding onto his head as it dipped to one nipple, and slathered it with his tongue. Abbi was feeling so many emotions at that very moment that she was unsure what to do; he had her frozen.

Good Lord, I feel like ripping his hair out...

She moved her hands to his shoulders and braced herself as she slowly raised her hips. Tightening herself around him, she silently sent a thank you to the Gods that be, that all those Kegels had worked. She lowered herself onto him, but a millisecond later, she just about shot up and out of the water when his shaft encountered... "Oh. My. God." A guttural groan escaped past her lips, as a mixture of such intense pleasure and pain shot through her body.

So that's the g spot...

Water sloshed over the sides of the tub in time to their lovemaking as Ben took hold of her hips, lifting her just to pull her down on his shaft, again and again; until they soared ever closer to the edge of the universe. With one final thrust, he joined their lips, swallowing her groan of pleasure to meet his.

He could feel her shaking as she collapsed in his arms.

Is she going to cry every time we make love?

Concern had him leaning back, searching her face. "Abbi, are you okay?"

She looked at him and smiled, a bubble of laughter escaped past her swollen lips. "See what you do to me?" she asked, laughing as she wrapped her arms around him.

He nuzzled her neck. "God, I love you woman."

She leaned back, placing her hand on his face, and looked into his eyes. He could see the love there for him.

"I love you too. More than you will ever know." She softly kissed him on the lips.

Abbi looked around the tub at the candles she had placed. One lone one still proudly burned, casting low shadows on the walls, the rest, snuffed out from the waves in the tub; thank goodness she had the foresight to have a drain installed in the floor. Untangling herself from him, Abbi stood up and stepped out of the tub.

Ben had to resist the urge to run his hands over her body when she arose like a nymph from the water. It didn't surprise him when he felt the quick flare rush to his cock already. She had that much power over him, and she didn't even know it. Living without her would be impossible, he knew that. After this business with Raven Black, he'd ask her to move in with him. The problem was, the way he traveled all over the world, would she want to.

Abbi crossed the room and grabbed two fluffy bath towels from the shelf. She wrapped one around her head and the other around her body. Taking another one, she turned to Ben. He was watching her every move, a thoughtful look on his face.

"Isn't the water getting cold?" she asked. She shook the fold out of the towel then held it up for him to step into.

"It is," he nodded. Ben pushed himself out of the water and stood, taking the towel he wrapped it around his waist as he stepped out of the tub.

Abbi towel dried her hair as she walked to the vanity and picked up a brush.

"Abbi?" He walked up to her, placing a soft kiss on her shoulder, he looked up at her reflection.

"Mhm?" she answered back, catching his eyes in the mirror while she brushed her hair.

He stood for a minute, his lips pressed to her skin, not sure he knew how to ask her.

The look on his face had her laying the brush down and turning to face him. He was scaring her. She put her hand on his chest and asked, "What is it?"

"When this is all over..." He paused.

What does he mean by 'this'...?

He saw the panic in her eyes. "No... God no! I didn't mean us!" he said, taking her into his arms. "I meant this deal with Raven Black..."

She shook her head frowning. "Then what is it?"

"Would you want to move in with me?" He glanced around. "We can build on a bathroom just like this."

She walked to the tub and flipped the drain lever. She was not expecting that at all! She couldn't deny that she didn't think about the possibility someday, if they were still together, they might. She was sure once he left for filming, he'd find someone else. But if that didn't happen then they might live together, but this soon?

She bent to pick up his clothes. Tossing them over her shoulder, she walked into her bedroom. She stopped and looked at Ben. "What would I do with my house?" she asked, picking up her bra.

Rubbing his ear, he said, "Uh... I didn't think of that, to be honest."

He noticed she seemed unusually preoccupied with their clothes. That was the third time she folded his jeans.

I get it, she's worrying again about us...

Walking to the bed, he dropped his towel. "We can discuss this more tomorrow. Abbi, love... put down the clothes." He pulled the sheets back and crawled into the bed. "Forget those, come to bed?" he asked, holding the sheet for her to join him. She tossed his jeans onto the pile and marched over to her dresser.

"What exactly are you doing?" he chuckled.

Pulling out an oversized t-shirt and a pair of granny panties, she looked at him and said, "I'm getting dressed. I can't sleep in the raw..."

How has he not noticed that by now?

"... what if a spider crawls... you know, up there?" She motioned with her hand and giggled at how absurd she sounded.

He threw his head back, a howl of laughter escaping past his lips. His eyes shone with amusement. "I promise you; I won't let any spider crawl up there."

"How can you possibly promise that?"

"Come here, and I'll show you."

She went to the bed and climbed in. Lying flat on her back, she pulled the covers up to her chin. Raising her brows, she looked at him expectantly. "Well? I'm waiting."

"Face me," he said as he laid his other arm across her pillow. "Here, put your head on my arm and I'll show you," he murmured.

He shouldn't have said it using that tone of voice. Her insides were turning into molten liquid again. Any moment she'd be dripping like a broken faucet. She scooted closer and laid her head on his arm as he slid his knee between her legs to the junction of her thighs. She gasped, as his thigh moved against her crotch. "Oh my."

He had created a barrier that no spider could ever pass but it didn't matter. If one tried to, it would most definitely drown, anyway, she thought. His hand gently stroked her back and despite trying to stay awake, her eyes simply wouldn't allow it. As she drifted off, she heard him say, "Goodnight, my sweet one."

Ben laid there with Abbi, holding her in his arms. The soft rise and fall of her chest pressed against his, told him she was asleep.

He waited for ten minutes. Ever so gently he kissed her forehead. Sliding away from her, he crawled out. He had hated to leave her alone in the bed, but he had to come up with a plan to fleece Raven out... before it was too late.

Chapter 31

Abbi woke with a start. She reached out for Ben, only to find the bed empty. Rolling over, she squinted at the clock on the side table and groaned. It was 11:00 am, she never slept that late. She could hear voices coming from the other room. Frowning, she threw the covers back, swung her legs over the edge, and bounded to the bathroom.

"ANY IDEA HOW WE'RE going to lure him out?" Kim asked, frowning at Ben's chart. "What the hell is this gibberish?" Ben had noted the timelines of Abbi's contact with Roland/Raven since grade school. At least the ones he'd known of. "You think he's been stalking her all this time?" She scratched her head and squinted at him. "While he was acting, even?"

"Look I can see that you're doubting it but." He put his hands on his hips and nodded. "Yeah. He started in the 8th grade. I searched through Abbi's old yearbooks."

He selected one out of the dozen that lay on the table; all the years Abbi attended school. Stepping close to Kim, he held it in his hands. Pointing to the 'Autograph' section, he said, "From what I could gather it started here. 'My dearest Abbi, I'll count the minutes until I see you again.'" Cocking his head, he squinted. "Is that something a kid in 8th grade would say? They never dated, did they?"

"Oh, hell no! He wanted to. She shut him down every time. Good thing too, he's a psycho." She laughed.

Abbi breezed into the kitchen just then. "Hey you two." Putting an arm around Ben's waist, she reached up and kissed him.

"Morning Abbi," Kim mumbled, distracted. She was trying to figure out what their next plan of action should be.

"Morning, love. You slept well; I trust?" He asked with a sexy grin.

She nodded, returning a smile. "I did," she said, walking to the cupboard to grab a mug. Pouring coffee into it, she looked at Kim, "Where are your partners in crime, Kim?" She added sugar and cream and raised expectant eyes at her sister. "Kim? Where are Mark and Ava?"

"Oh! ... They went to Mack's, to see if he heard anything." Kim drummed her nails on the table. "Say, Abbi. Would you be bait?"

Abbi looked at her with huge eyes. "Pardon me?"

"Like hell, she will!" Ben snarled.

Kim raised her hands defensively. "Relax! It was just a thought."

Intrigued and ignoring Ben's outburst, Abbi asked, "Bait as in how?"

Kim looked between her sister and the man that Abbi loved. There was no way she was getting in the middle of that. They were standing ten feet from her, staring at each other, but she could feel the tension mounting between them.

Hell, to the no!

"Out with it, Kim," Abbi said, never taking her eyes from Ben's.

Ben stared Abbi down. "Don't you dare Kim."

"Uh, would you look at that! My phone is buzzing my boob at this very moment." Reaching into her bra, she produced her phone.

Bringing it to her ear, she slowly got up and made her way to the door.

"Ava! Sure, I can meet you guys at the store. Be right there!" She stuffed it back in her bra, desperately trying to escape out the door. "Gotta go, guys," she waved, slamming it behind her. She had no idea where Ava and Mark were, because she had been talking to air. As she set off across the yard, she thought how lucky it was that neither Abbi nor Ben had noticed her phone was upside down.

"Abbi, you're not putting yourself in harm's way," Ben said softly. He was leaning back against the counter, watching her drink her coffee. "I won't allow it." He folded his arms across his chest.

Abbi spit her coffee out. "Excuse me?" She wiped her mouth on her sleeve. "Did you just say you wouldn't allow it?"

"Yeah. I did." He nodded his head. "Do you have a problem with that?"

Her eyes flashed daggers at him, "You're damn right I do! Do you have a better idea?" She calmed down when she realized he was only concerned for her safety and not trying to give her orders. "Honestly, this is getting old. It's been going on far too long." She sighed and looked down at the floor.

Immediately Ben felt like an ass. "Love... I'm sorry." He reached to take her hand and pulled her to him, holding her in his arms. "I don't want him even breathing the same air as you do. Do you understand that?"

She nodded. She felt so helpless. "What if I was with Mark?" She looked up at him. "Maybe seeing him with me will bring him out?" She could tell he was weighing the possibility that it might work. "And if his brother is with us, even better."

He slowly nodded. "Yeah. I guess."

"You can come too, just wear a disguise, right?"

"Yes. It might work."

"I know. We will throw a party. A huge BBQ and invite everyone from the village." She broke free from his embrace to grab a pen and paper and started writing a list out. She stopped and pointed at him. "You most definitely will fit in with a disguise!"

He went to her. "Yeah, this could work, for sure." If anything happened to her, he wouldn't hesitate to kill Raven. "I'll be watching you from afar. You just make sure you're never alone." He caught her chin in his hand and rubbed his thumb across her bottom lip.

"I won't be." She kissed his thumb before turning on her heel to grab her phone. Punching a number in, she brought it to her ear. Frowning, she lowered her cell and looked at it, "Dammit! I need to get a card."

He pulled his out of his pocket and handed it to her. "Here. Use mine."

"Thanks, babe." She grinned, dialing a number from memory.

He chuckled. "What are you doing now?"

She held up a finger to him and spoke into the phone. "Kim! Get your butt back here and bring Ava and Mark, too. We are going to throw a BBQ. Now please, get over here so we can plan it!" Hanging up, she turned to look at Ben. He was gone.

"Ben?" She walked towards the living room, pausing at the open French doors. He was standing out on the porch with his hands in his pockets, watching the dogs chase after a squirrel.

Abbi walked to him and placed a hand on his shoulder. Feeling him relax under her touch; she laid her head against his back. "This will work," she murmured.

He turned around to face her, his hands reaching to pull her close. "It better," he said, grabbing a fist full of her hair.

She pulled back, searching his eyes. Her own, softening as she saw the glisten of tears in his. "Hey, what is it?" she said, tears springing to her own.

He shook his head as his tongue darted out to wet his lips. "Nothing."

She took his face in her hands. "Ben. Tell me... please."

He wrapped his arms around her tighter and swallowed the lump in his throat. "Abbi. I swear to God... If something happens to you, it will be the end of me..." He dipped his head and kissed her with such sadness.

She felt like her very soul was being ripped from her body. The tears slipped down her cheeks; she couldn't help it. She knew what he was feeling all too well as he leaned his forehead against hers.

"Love. If he touches one hair on your head. With God as my witness, I will kill him."

She was scared, not because she was worried about herself, but because she knew he'd follow through. She shook her head. "Shh! Don't think like that. Nothing will happen. I'll play you off as my new boyfriend... Sven." She smiled through her tears.

"Hey... hey... hey! Let's get this party planned!" Mark yelled from the side yard as the trio rounded the corner.

Filing onto the porch, Ava noticed that her mom had been crying.

Has Ben been bitching her out? From what Kim had said, they had been on the verge of a fight when she'd left earlier.

Ava looked at Ben and noticed the redness of his eyes. She was shocked to see him just as upset as her mother. "Mom, Ben, are you two, okay?"

Ben gave a brief nod, not saying a word.

"Yeah, we're okay, honey," Abbi said, hugging her. She looked around at her family, which now included Mark. "I'm just happy you're all here."

Kim was so relieved they had worked things out between them that she rushed to give Abbi a hug. "We got this, baby girl," Kim whispered into her hair. Pulling away she said, "Soon you and your man here..." she jerked a thumb at Ben, "... will be so bored for lack of excitement, you won't know what to do with each other." She laughed.

Ben snickered. "Uh, I doubt that."

Kim shook her head. Would she ever stop sticking her foot in her mouth? "Wrong choice of words!" She turned to go into the house and muttered to herself, "Damn. I need to find a man like that."

Everyone took her cue and followed her into the house.

"My brother is on his way, as we speak." Mark raised his brows up and down at Kim. "I could set you two up on a date."

"Does he have an accent and look like a Greek god," Kim asked, seriously.

"Nope. But he's a cop."

"Hmm." She nodded her head. "I'll consider it," she said, and started cackling. "Hah.... I crack myself up." Pulling out a chair, she sat. "Okay, enough of this crap. Let's plan," she said, folding her hands on the table.

"How many people are we talking?" Ava asked, pulling out a notebook from the drawer.

Abbi sat down on a chair at the table. "Everyone from the village."

"Everyone?" Mark pulled a chair out and sat next to Kim. "Don't you think that's a little too much?"

"No." Abbi shook her head. "I want Roland or whatever he calls himself, to feel like he's welcome to come. The more people here, the more likely that will happen."

"That is true," Ava said, writing it down.

"What about Ben? What are we going to do about him?" Kim asked.

"Well, I thought we would disguise him." Abbi bit her lower lip. "I don't know how, though."

"Well, you could put a dress on him and call him granny." Kim smacked the table, laughing at the visual her joke made.

"Or we could just put a wig and hat on him," Mark suggested. He looked at Ben. "I think there are some costumes in the attic over at your place."

"All I know is that I will be beside Abbi all day, or at least try to be," Ben told them. Taking her hand in his, he brought it to his lips.

Kim gagged. "You guys make me sick. But, if you two ever break up. You know where to find me." She shot Ben a wicked smile.

Ben and Abbi responded in unison. "That will never happen."

"Damn it!" Kim muttered, frowning.

Ava spoke up. "Well, I for one, am thrilled for the both of you," she said, looking to them. "Ben, I seriously had doubts about you. But after getting to know you, I realize you're cool." She came around to stand behind his chair and hugged him.

"Hey now, don't be doing that!" Mark said.

"Jealous, are you?" Ava looked at him mischievously.

"Me?" He scoffed. "Why would I be jealous?"

"Thanks, Ava." Ben looked at Abbi. "I think I speak for both of us, that it means a lot."

"It does... more than you know," Abbi said, squeezing her daughter's hand as she walked back to her chair.

"Okay, how does this sound? Us three will run to Mack's and spread the word... grab the food while we are there. Is there anything else we need?" Kim asked, looking around the table.

Everyone shook their heads no.

"Great. In two days, this shindig will be good to go." Standing Kim looked at Ava and Mark. "Let's go, you two."

Everyone got up and pushed their chairs in. Mark looked at Ben. "I'll bring the wig and hat over later tonight."

"How about we just walk over there when you guys get back?" He looked at Abbi for confirmation.

"Do you think it's wise?" she asked. She didn't want to chance Ben being spotted.

"Yeah. It will be dark. Besides, I don't know about you, but I'm getting a bit stir crazy, myself." He sighed, following the others to the door.

"Yeah, I am too," Abbi said.

"It's settled. We will pop by later." Ben held the door open for them. "Give me a ring when you get back, will you Mark?"

"Will do, buddy."

Ben stood watching them for a bit, the same thing kept running through his mind... *this better work*. Because he feared if it didn't, one way or the other, he would lose Abbi for good.

Chapter 32

Ben raised his hand to knock on the door, the other held onto Abbi's. The dogs were running, noses to the ground, sniffing every nook and cranny that they could.

Abbi glanced down at the porch, noticing the bloodstain had disappeared. She tugged on Ben's hand, getting his attention. She pointed to the floor.

"It's gone."

"Huh, I wonder—"

The opening door interrupted his words and caused him to glance up. Mark stood there and noticed Abbi looking at the porch floor.

"Yeah, there was some leftover paint in the shed," Mark said. "Had to do a couple of coats, but it's good as new now. Oh, and I painted around your BBQ too," he said, smiling.

Ben's face lit up. "Thanks, mate. I was wondering if I could get the paint to match. Looks like it did." he said, as they crossed the threshold.

Mark laughed. "It did. But you know this is your house, man... why did you knock?"

"No idea. I guess I've just been at Abbi's so much lately, it felt wrong not to."

Kim came in from the back patio door. "Hey, guys. Nice night out there for a stroll."

"That it is," Abbi agreed, casting her eyes around.

"I never came across it, so where is the attic?" Ben asked.

Mark waved a hand for Ben to follow. "Come on, I'll show you."

Abbi stood looking around the house, catching every detail that she missed before.

She loved it. Always had. Well at least the outside. But could she live here now that she had made her house a home?

"What are you looking for, Mom?" Ava asked.

She spun around on her heel and looked to where her daughter sat at the table. "Um... nothing. Just looking at the house," she said.

Wondering if Bird would have free rein here Abbi looked up at the ceiling and frowned. There was a walkway directly above her. *How in the world did I miss that before?* She jerked her chin up. "How do you get to that?"

Ava and Kim swung their heads to look up.

"Oh, that's the hallway upstairs. The staircase is in the front foyer," Ava said, writing in a notebook.

"What?" Abbi blinked rapidly. She pointed to the door that she and Ben just came in. "Is that not the front?"

"Nope, I'll show you."

Abbi followed Ava through to the living room, the same room that she thought was the back room the guys disappeared in. Kim was taking up the rear.

"Wow, this place is a lot bigger than I realized."

True she had only seen the kitchen, laundry room, and the bathroom before, and of course Ben's bedroom, but still. It just went on and on.

They climbed the stairs to the second level. To the left at the top was a room with a drop-down staircase.

Ava tossed a hand, "That's where the guys are, and this way... is the master and spare bedrooms." She turned to the right and headed down the hallway.

Waist-high glass sides allowed a view to the lower level. She looked over the edge to see the kitchen and dining area below on one side and the living area on the other. She was falling more in love with it with every step she took.

Could I live here? Maybe the better question to ask is, should I live here...

They came to the end of the walkway. A door to the right stood open, revealing a medium-sized bedroom with windows facing the lake, on the left was an identical room. Straight ahead, they stepped into the master bedroom. She raised her brows when she saw it. The king-sized bed was breathtaking. The bed itself was high off the floor. Steps led up to it on the sides and the foot as if it were on a pedestal. It was something that one would see in a castle it was so grand... almost over the top.

"Ben asked me to move in with him..."

"What?!" Ava looked at her in shock.

"Mhm," Abbi nodded. *Yeah, I could see myself living here.* As much as she loved the bed, it would have to go though. Her luck, she'd roll out of it and crack her head open on the stone.

"Well, are you?" Kim asked. "What will you do with your place if you do?"

Abbi sighed. "Not sure to be honest to both your questions." She walked over to the windows. Just like the other bedrooms, there was a wall of them overlooking the lake. But unlike the other rooms, these went from floor to ceiling.

"Do the windows open?" She looked at Ava.

She knew her mom would love them the minute she saw them. Walking over to a picture on the wall, she slid it over to reveal a panel. Pressing a button, she smiled. "They sure do."

Abbi was in love. She could feel the warm breeze on her skin. Yes, she could see herself living here. She was lost in thought, still gazing out the window when two strong arms wrapped around her waist that pulled her back against a chest of steel.

"What are you thinking about?" he murmured, near her ear.

Nuzzling her neck, Ben felt her grow tense in his arms. "Don't worry sweets. I sent them downstairs."

It amazed her how he could read her so well.

Relaxing, she tilted her head, thrilled at the touch of his mouth. She gave a blissful sigh. "I think I love the house almost as much as I love the owner." She grinned at his approving growl.

"Oh really? Well, I heard the owner is... you know... an ass." His lips spread a blazing trail to the sensitive spot just behind her ear.

"Yes, the owner has a nice ass." She laughed at the memory of that conversation. Turning to face him, Abbi said, "As a matter of fact. The owner has a nice everything." She kissed the exposed skin of his chest where his shirt was open. Gazing into his eyes, she softly said, "The owner couldn't be more perfect to me if he tried."

"We all have flaws, Abbi. Not you of course, but the rest of us do," he said, grinning down at her.

"Perhaps we're both a tad blinded, hmm?" She kissed him then. He felt perfect to her. No one had ever treated her so tenderly or made her feel so cherished in her entire life. Her husband, who had vowed to love her, showed revulsion at the sight of her scars, and stretch marks. Yet this man saw past them, touched them as if they weren't even there. No, he was perfect. He was her rock in a sea of insanity.

Ben had to pull away from her, he wanted nothing more than to toss her onto the bed and make her melt. But no, that wouldn't do with the others downstairs. "So, what do you think?" he asked, putting some distance between them.

"I'm thinking this place is a lot bigger than I first thought." She chuckled.

"Yeah, it's big. But that bed..." Ben gave it a sneaky look.

"Uh-huh," Abbi said. She didn't know what he thought of it, but the more she looked at it, the more she found it to be horribly out of place. The bed itself was great, just not the rest of it.

He shook his head. "Sorry if you like it, Abbi, but it's gotta go."

"Thank God. I thought maybe you wanted to keep it. All I can picture is me—"

He swung his gaze to hers and raised a brow in question. "Falling and cracking your head on the steps?" At her nod, he smiled. "Right, that was the first thing I thought of too." He took her by the hand. "Okay, let me show you what I have in mind." He directed her to the spare bedroom.

"This is where I thought we could build a bathroom like yours." He looked at her for approval.

"We could put the tub here." He stepped in front of the windows. "... a corner tub though, big enough for the both of us." He threw her a sexy smile. "And the shower could go over there." He pointed to the opposite wall. "And in here...." He walked to an open door and flicked the light on, revealing a massive walk-in closet. "We could have the sink, toilet, and a towel closet." He folded his arms across his chest and smiled. "What do you think?"

She could tell he had thought about this for some time. "I think..." she paused and looked around.

He hurried on. "Or we could build on and redo a few rooms downstairs. You could have the master as a library/office... the windows in there would allow for natural lighting. Also, the breeze in there is amazing." He was rambling on; he knew but she wouldn't say anything. He was readying himself for her flat-out refusal.

"Ben, whatever you think... its fine with me."

The smile faded from his face. "Well, that isn't very helpful," he replied.

"We could live in a train car for all I care, as long as we're together," she told him. "If you wanted to move back to England... say it and I'll start packing. I won't be happy about it, but I would leave in a heartbeat if you asked... that is if you wanted me to." *Shit! Maybe he wouldn't want me to...* She, of course, had to think of that after the fact. "But just so you know. Where I go, so do my animals. If it means me having to hire a private plane so they can ride in first-class than that's what I'll do." She held her breath. She knew he loved the animals as much as she did, or at least she hoped he did.

"I have no plans to move back to England, Abbi. This is where I want to be. With you and your animals. Either here or at your place, I don't care."

She was so happy; she sprinted the few steps to him and laughed as he caught her in his arms. Wrapping her legs around his waist, she took his head in both hands to plant a wet kiss on his lips. She was so relieved. Not that she hadn't meant every word she'd said, but she didn't want to fly clear across the world. Unwinding her legs from his waist, she slid down the length of him. She could feel the swell at the front of his jeans against her as her feet touched the floor. That thrill of excitement shot through her again, spreading like wildfire. "Let's go home," she whispered breathlessly, holding out her hand.

"My sentiments exactly, love." He gave her a knowing smile, as he shut off the lights.

They were walking down the stairs when she stopped and turned to him, frowning. "What will I do with my house?"

"Mark said he will rent it or buy it, whichever you want to do."

Shocked, she lowered her voice to a whisper. "Mark? You're kidding, right? He just sold this place to you and now he wants my place? Will he live in it though? I can't just leave it empty, as he did with this one."

"Yeah, he's determined... says he's a new man. Funny, but I believe him, this time."

Continuing down the stairs, she said, "OK. I'll ask him about it." She'd almost forgot the reason why they were there. She glanced over her shoulder. "Did you get your disguise?"

"Sure did." He grabbed a clear plastic bag off the last step.

She looked at what he held in his hands and asked, "Is that a ponytail?" She wrinkled her nose as she stepped onto the floor of the front foyer. It looked like a dead squirrel that had seen better days.

He chuckled. "Yeah. I'm dressing like a biker. Think I'll pass?" He asked, sticking the wig on his head.

She waved a hand in front of her face. "Uh yeah. But that's gross. What is that smell?" she gagged.

"Mothballs," he answered, with a grin.

"Hey, you guys wanna join us? We're watching a movie with Mark in it," Kim snickered.

Mark and Ava were sitting on the couch while Kim was in a recliner. All three had their eyes glued to the TV.

"Thanks, but we are heading back," Ben answered.

"Suit yourselves."

They said their goodbyes and quietly left through the front door.

As they were walking on the trail back to her house, Abbi couldn't help but wonder what else was in the bag. Taking it from Ben, she asked, "What is the black leather looking thing?" It was too dark for her to tell.

"Oh. That's a vest," he said with a laugh. "You'll get to see my chest all day."

"Great!" Awesome... All the women won't be able to keep their eyes off him... Just what she needed.

Ben put his arm around her shoulders. He knew that tone; the doubt was back, rearing its ugly head again. But why now? He had no idea. But one way or another he'd find out.

"So, Mark was telling me they spread the word about the party. Kim told Mack to tell everyone it was potluck. You okay with that?" he glanced her way, as they came into her yard.

"Yeah, it's fine. Mack will probably bring enough to feed a small army," she said with a shaky laugh as she went up to the steps of her house.

He nodded and noticed her fumbling with the lock, "Want to tell me what's bothering you?" he asked, taking the keys from her trembling hand.

"Nothing. I'm fine." At his glance, she added, "Really, I am." She tried desperately to act normal, she was failing miserably.

He looked at her, noticing her agitation. "Abbi..." he said her name in a deep warning voice as he pushed the door open. Letting her enter first he added, "I know when something is bothering you."

She went directly into the kitchen. She felt the sudden urge to clean something... anything. Picking up the animal dishes, she took them to the dishwasher. *Damn! He's got to be tired of my constant worrying that he will leave... Hell, I am!* Biting her lip, she risked a glance in his direction. He stood there in the middle of the room, waiting for her to respond. Sighing, she finally said, "The same thing as usual...." She grabbed a detergent pod from under the sink, tossed it in and shut the door, setting it to on.

Turning to face him, she leaned her back against the counter, gazing down at the floor. "I don't want other women gawking at you, okay?" She looked up at him, "Especially younger ones."

"Fair enough," he said, turning towards the hallway.

Fair enough? That is it? What the hell kind of answer is that? "Where are you going now?"

Stopping, he turned to look at her.

"To bed... want to join me?" he murmured in that voice that always made her melt.

She stepped away from the counter and followed him. "Fine... sometimes you're impossible, you know that, right?" She nearly collided into his back; he'd stopped so abruptly.

He turned and bent down and wrapped an arm around the back of her knees. He scooped her up onto his shoulder amid her gleeful laughter.

"Ben put me down!"

"Watch your head, love," he said, swinging her around, as he headed towards her bedroom.

"How can I watch my head when my eyes are looking at your glorious ass?"

He said nothing as he plopped her onto the bed.

Abbi had to close her eyes to the vertigo this man created, as she felt him lay beside her. His body spooning to her side, she opened one eye and looked at him. There he was his head propped on one hand, staring at her face intently, desire in those beautiful eyes.

"Hi. How you are doing?" he murmured, raising a brow in question, a soft smile on his lips.

She was suddenly breathless. "Um, hi... good. You?"

He covered her legs with one of his. "Good, good," he said, grinding his lower body into her hip. "Fantastic actually," he murmured, inching his face closer to hers.

Whispering against her lips, "Now that that's settled..." His voice dripping with lust he added, "... Let me show you how impossible I can be." His lips soft at first intensified with every beat of her heart. She moaned, opening her mouth to his seeking tongue. Ben couldn't get enough of her as she tugged on his shirt, pulling it free of his jeans. He broke away long enough to pull it over his head. His lips returned, blazing a trail to her neck, nipping her there. He felt the shiver of pleasure ripple through her body. Hearing her cry out his name when he moved away from her, caused his cock to pulsate.

She opened her eyes to see him staring at her with such an intensity; she thought she did something wrong.

She raised herself slightly off the bed. "What?"

In answer, he pushed her gently down and reached for her shirt. Slowly he worked each button loose, his eyes never leaving hers.

Abbi shimmied out of her pants, as he continued to work the buttons. She was about to go over the edge with just the look he cast her way and was about to rip the damn shirt off when he set the last button free. Laying there in her bra and panties, she waited for his next move. But something felt off. There she was ready to jump his bones, and all he wanted to do was sit and stare at her?

Ben was deliberately taking his time. He wanted this moment to last forever. He knew Abbi was champing at the bit, but she was just going to have to wait. "Roll over," he murmured, using the tone that he knew drove her crazy.

She did as he asked. Propping her chin upon her arms, she waited. *What the hell is he doing?*

He placed a gentle hand at the back of her neck when he saw her attempt to look over her shoulder. "Uh, uh, my love."

She was getting weirded out and was about to tell him so when she felt his lips touch the back of one knee.

Ben gripped the waist of her panties and pulled them down as he trailed soft kisses up her leg. Further they traveled to her butt cheek where he lightly nipped her soft skin. He revelled as she sucked in a quivery breath when he darted his tongue to the spot, soothing the sting. He pulled her underwear free with one hand as the other traveled up the back of her leg. Ben slipped it between her thighs at the gentle swell of her butt, his fingers dipped and searched out the pearl he knew was there. His lips continued to travel upwards to the dimples at the small of her back, his tongue tracing the circles there, while his fingers found what they were looking for. He heard her soft moan; as her legs clenched together, trapping his hand. He inserted his thumb, could feel her warmth tighten around it, while his fingers lightly feathered her as he kissed and nipped his way to her neck.

Abbi couldn't help but bite her lip as a moan escaped her throat. She just about ate the damn pillow she had been resting on when he'd slipped his thumb into her wetness, his fingers ever so softly teasing her even more. She felt his warm breath at the back of her neck while she rode his hand as his lips nuzzled her ear. *Dear God! This man is...* She couldn't even think of a word as he brought her to the edge of the universe.

Ben could tell she was close to climaxing. "Let my hand go," he whispered hotly against her skin.

Is he crazy? She reluctantly did as he asked when his lips touched just behind her ear. She felt him kneel on the bed, spreading her legs with his knees. There was no way she could.... She couldn't even formulate a thought.

Ben laid on top of her. "Are you, okay? I'm not too heavy, am I?"

Good Lord! NO! ... Her mind screamed. She couldn't even speak. Instead, she shook her head vehemently, loving the feeling of him draped over her.

His shaft felt like satin as he slowly entered her. That did it for Abbi. She was already soaring upwards in a dizzying, soul-shattering climax.

Knowing she had orgasmed, Ben waited, until she was coming off the high. Even though he knew before this night was over, she would have another, he didn't want to ruin the moment for her. When he felt her returning, he knelt on his knees and grabbed her by the hips. Jerking her upwards towards him, he rammed forward and bent forward over her back, his mouth finding her shoulder he nipped it with his teeth.

The sensations she stirred in him, blew his mind. He covered her breast with one hand, teasing the peak while the other continued it's feather touch on her clit. Matching him stroke for stroke, Abbi turned her head towards him, her mouth searching for his. He kissed her swallowing her cries of ecstasy as together, they went over the edge. Unable to move; she had never felt so utterly spent in her life. Ben gathered her into his arms and pulled the blankets around them.

Abbi tilted her head up at him. She kissed him on the neck. "You're right. You are impossible."

His gaze dropped to her swollen lips, gently he kissed them. "Am I now?" he murmured.

She felt like she was liquid. She could barely keep her eyes open, smiling she nodded. "It was impossible to know your next move."

"Get some rest, my love." He chuckled; his arms tightening around her as they both drifted off to sleep.

Chapter 33

"A party! Oh, how I love parties. I must make an appearance, no doubt about that. She always knew how to win me over. I know she's throwing it for me. She must be well on the way of being over Ben."

IT WAS A BEAUTIFUL sunny day with clear blue skies, perfect for a BBQ with friends and family. Too bad there was a dark cloud hanging over it. Abbi kept scanning the crowd, wondering if Roland would show, as did the others. True to his word, Ben was never more than ten feet from her. She gazed at him, thankful she had her shades on, otherwise she wouldn't have been able to do so, at least not as often as she liked.

Her brow wrinkled. There was a woman a little too close to him in Abbi's opinion. Her nerves were shot enough already and was having a hard time controlling the urge to walk over to intervene. She watched the red head size him up. Any minute she would make her move. Would she be able to just stand by and watch? Ben must have seen her behind his shades and quickly escaped, making a beeline to Ava. Abbi breathed a sigh of relief as she watched the ponytail on the wig bounce with every step he took. Hearing her name called, she spun around.

"Abbi, girl!" Mack said, approaching with a bowl in each hand.

"Mack! It's great to see you!" Abbi took the bowls from him and placed them on the already laden table.

"How're you doing?" he asked.

She bobbed her head. "I'm good."

"You hear anything from Ben at all?"

She glanced down at the table, not daring to meet his gaze. "Ah, no. I haven't."

He shook his head, tsk-tsking. "That's too bad... I thought you two hit it off."

She sighed. "Yeah. Well, these things happen."

"Mack! How are you?" Kim asked, approaching from behind him. She held up her hand, "Before you answer that... Abbi, Mark needs you in the kitchen for a minute." She jerked her head towards the house.

Abbi frowned. "Oh? Oh! Right! ... Okay. I'll talk to you again soon, Mack. Enjoy yourself." As she walked away, she could hear them talking about the tourist.

<hr />

BEN HAD TO ESCAPE, fast. If he'd stayed there, the redhead would have blown his cover. He couldn't go to Abbi, so he did the next best thing.

"Ava, kiss me," Ben hissed, close to her ear.

"What!" She turned to him, confused as hell. "Ew. No!"

"Redhead, six o'clock," he nodded.

She turned around to see which redhead he was talking about exactly.

"Don't look!!" He grabbed her by the arms. "That is Lorna Parker."

She raised her brows. "So?"

"The actress." At her blank stare, he continued. "If she gets too close to me, which she was, she'll recognize me."

Ava gave an exasperated sigh.

"Well, I couldn't very well go to Abbi, now, could I?"

"Why would she be here?"

"How should I know? Just pretend we are together or something."

"Oh, God! Do I have to?" Ava griped.

"Yes!"

"Just so you know." She grimaced and puckered up. "I'm not enjoying this."

"Neither am I... Now get a grip, it will be over soon." He wrapped her in his arms. "Just relax, you're stiff as a plank. God, here she comes!" He leaned her over his arm and dipped his head, aiming for her mouth.

KIM WAS STILL CHATTING to Mack, her eyes roaming the yard in search of Roland as she sipped her drink. She did a double take.

What the hell? ... Who in God's name is Ava kissing?

"Holy shit!!!" She started choking on her vodka and O.J.

Mack smacked her on the back. "Are you okay, Kim? Should I go get Doc?"

"No!" She gasped. "I'm fine, Mack. Just swallowed a bug... I think."

She scrutinized Ava and the mystery man as the two parted and headed towards the house... holding hands.

Kim's eyes narrowed. *That isn't a man. That's Ben!* ...

"Excuse me, Mack," she mumbled, absently.

She stalked after the pair. Kim was on a mission to find out what the hell was going on.

MARK LOOKED UP AS SHE stepped into the kitchen. "Abbi. Good, you're here. This is my brother, Steve." He waved a hand at the man standing beside him.

"Hi Abbi, nice to meet you." Steve nodded.

"Thanks for coming, sorry it's under these circumstances," she mumbled.

"No problem. Has there been any sign of Raven?" he asked, looking at Abbi, then Mark.

She shook her head. "I haven't seen him. To be honest, I don't even know if I would recognize him. I saw him briefly about a month ago, wearing a hat and winter gloves, but I didn't get a good look."

Steve pulled something from a folder he was holding. "No worries. Here's a recent photo," he said, passing it to Abbi.

She scanned the photo. An older version of the boy she had once known stared up at her. She shook her head.

"What is it?" Steve asked.

She looked up at him. "I just don't understand why. Why would he risk everything?" She passed the photo to Mark.

"Simple... He's infatuated with you. Has been for some time to my understanding?" He looked at Mark for confirmation.

"Yeah," Mark replied. "Well, that's what we suspect anyway."

Ava and Ben came into the house just then, with Kim hot on their heels.

"Hey, you two! Just what the hell was that?" She yelled, jerking her thumb towards the yard.

Ben walked to Abbi's side and looked at Kim. "That was a public display of affection," he answered dryly.

"What happened?" Abbi's eyes shot to his. *Was it Roland?* ...

"Lorna Parker is what happened," Ava supplied. "Ben made me kiss him."

Mark frowned "Really?"

Kim was waiting for the impact of Mark's fist to connect with Ben's jaw; it didn't happen.

"What the hell is she doing here?" Mark asked. He sent Ben a quizzical look.

Ben shook his head. "No idea. But it can't be good."

"Hey, Ben." Steve nodded in greeting.

"Hey, man. Thanks for coming." Ben said, holding his hand out.

Steve shook it, and asked, "What exactly happened out there?"

"Wait... who is Lorna Parker?" Abbi asked.

Mark was about to speak when he caught Ben's slight shake of his head. Turning his head to the side, Mark gave Ben a dark look. "She has a right to know Ben," Mark said, trying to reason with him.

Ben glared at him, knowing he was right. He turned to Abbi; his eyes softened. He licked his lips. "Abbi. You saw the redhead who was coming towards me?"

At her nod, he continued. "Right. That is Lorna Parker. She and I dated, very briefly. Nothing happened between us... not that she didn't try." He watched the emotions play across her face. He hated to continue, but he had no choice. "It upset her when I broke it off and she vowed to get me back."

Abbi didn't know what to do next. Hearing those words was almost her undoing. "Excuse me," she mumbled, making a hasty retreat to the bathroom.

ALL THREE DOGS WERE lying on the floor, when she sailed into the room, all jumped when she slammed the door shut. Leaning back against it, she slumped to the floor in a heap, hugging her knees to her chest. Brutus came to her and let out a big sigh as he rested his chin on her knees.

"I'm a fool, boy. I knew this would happen, but did I listen to myself?" She muttered to him, burying her face in his fur. Ben was more concerned with his ex being there than Raven, it seemed.

Had he secretly invited her? Why else would she go to him in a disguise of all things?

She jumped at the knock on the door. "Go away," she mumbled.

"Abbi open the door." It was Kim.

"No. Just go away!" she yelled.

"Oh, for cripes sake, Abbi, open the damn door," Kim yelled back.

"It's open."

Kim turned the handle, pushing on the door to open it. She found that it wouldn't budge more than an inch. "Move your ass!"

Abbi scooted forward, sliding Brutus as she did. "That's as far as we're moving."

Kim felt like a sausage being squeezed out of its casing as she shoved herself through the opening. She stumbled into the room and almost fell flat on her face when her foot caught on the throw rug by the tub. "What the hell is wrong with you?" Kim asked, accusingly.

Abbi's eyes bugged out of her head. "Me? What's wrong with me? His ex is back," Abbi hissed. "Don't you get it? She's here to win him back! I don't stand a chance." She shook her head.

"How can you be a writer when you're that dumb?" Kim asked.

Abbi just stared at her.

"Do you honestly think he'd call his ex and have her come here to meet him? Give your head a shake, Abbi."

She glared at her sister as Lucy came over and settled herself in her lap. "What am I supposed to think?"

"Not that. The guy is crazy for you. How can you not see that?"

"It won't last you know," Abbi bit back. She laid her head on her knees. "He will find someone younger, someone, prettier..." she mumbled miserably.

"Will you piss off with that age bullshit? Have you seen the women out there? He could have any of them, but no he chooses you! Someone who is giving herself a pity party on the bathroom floor! If he wasn't interested in you, why is he still here?"

That was a good question. She had brought him nothing but grief since meeting him.

Kim squatted in front of her and reached a hand to lift Abbi's chin. Looking into her eyes, she said, "Ben is the best thing that has ever happened to you aside from your kids, Abbi. Accept it, embrace it and most of all be thankful you found each other." As she stood up, she added quietly. "Most people never find a love like that, don't let it go over something so stupid for God's sake." She offered her hand, Abbi took it and stood up. She gave Kim a hug. "I've been an idiot."

Kim scoffed as she turned the doorknob. "Nah. You're just crazy."

The dogs took off like rockets when she opened the door and Kim jumped. With a laugh, she said, "Oh! You scared the crap out of me."

Abbi looked around her to see Ben leaning against the wall waiting for her. He smiled at Kim.

"Thanks." He stepped forward and hugged her.

"Oh! All right! I'll gladly accept that," Kim giggled. Wrapping her arms around him, she sighed as if she had just found the key to eternal happiness.

MOONLIT NIGHT

He kissed her on the forehead and thanked her again before letting her go.

"Lord, have mercy." She fanned a hand in front of her face and pointed at Abbi. "Don't you screw this up." Turning, she held onto the wall like a drunk as she headed back to the kitchen.

"Hi," Ben said, looking at her. He reached out a hand to stroke her cheek, slipping it to the back of her neck, as he pulled her to his chest.

"I'm sorry. I jumped to conclusions. I shouldn't have done that," she quietly said.

He breathed in her intoxicating scent and rubbed her back. "Abbi, I'm here because I love you. With every breath I take, I take it for you. Wild horses couldn't drag me away from you.... Please, stop doubting us. Stop doubting me."

She nodded. "That was the last time, I promise."

He kissed her, so tenderly, she thought she'd might start to cry when he pulled back to look at her. "You know what? This wig needs to go." He pulled it off his head.

"Ben, you can't. He will recognize you."

"He's already here, Abbi. Mark told me; Steve spotted him ten minutes before Kim opened the door."

"Even more of a reason for you to wear it," she said.

"It's fine. I'm not hiding any longer. The cops are watching from a distance. Steve called in the local force. They're out on a boat, watching his every move."

She looked like she was ready to bolt.

"Abbi, nothing will happen to you. I'm here. He won't get within twenty feet of you. Okay?"

"It's you I'm worried about Ben. When he sees you, he's going to flip, and you know it. Hell, we all know it."

"I hope he does," he said, airily. "Sorry, it's been a long time coming. Steve and Mark have a plan. It's time I filled you in." He reached in his pocket, revealing a small box with a wire in his hand.

ABBI SCANNED THE FACES there, with every step she took, making her way slowly to the bar at the water's edge. She wasn't too sure about this plan as she made her way through the backyard. For starters, she felt everyone could see the wiretap under her shirt. Ben had put it on her, making sure it was well concealed. He explained that the police needed to hear Raven confess to anything that they suspected him of doing. She was to mingle among the crowd and never be left alone.

BEN WAS STANDING AT the side of the house, Brutus, and Molly by his side. Every so often they would bring him sticks to throw. It at least kept him occupied while he was to stay out of view until Steve gave him the signal. He wasn't entirely sure he could stay put. That would mean waiting until Abbi was over half a yard length from him. He was itching to make a mad dash to her right at that very moment. But no, he had to wait, going too early, could scare Raven off. But if he waited, it would mean he'd be out of reach to protect her if something went wrong. To hell with it, he was going. Calling the dogs to come, all three set off across the yard.

ABBI GLANCED AROUND as she made her way towards the lake. She saw that most of the people invited were still there along with a few that weren't, all down by the water's edge. The closest person to her right now was Ben, and he was clear across the yard by the house. She never regretted having such a large yard, until now. She had no idea where Raven was in the sea of people. She still found it weird to even refer to him by that name, but the more she thought about it, the more he resembled the bird he so aptly named himself after.

She could see the boat offshore where the police waited, ready to spring into action when the need arose and Steve and Kim were sitting at the fire pit, talking. Abbi chuckled to herself. Mark must have introduced the two like he said he would. Ava and Mark were over by the bar, talking to Lorna.

Wait... Why would they be talking to her?...

Of course, as soon as that thought came to mind, her foot caught on a tree root that was hidden in the grass, causing her to stumble. Abbi felt a hand grab her from behind, catching her from falling flat on her face.

"Abbi, darling. Be careful." An unfamiliar man's voice, cautioned.

Tightness gathered in her chest as she slowly turned around.

Oh God, did he feel the wired box under my shirt?

She felt panic rising with every breath she took.

"Uh... I'm sorry. Have we met?" she asked, a smile plastered on her face. She hoped she sounded unbothered despite her racing heart.

He seemed taken aback as if she should have known who he was. He laughed. "Oh, don't play coy with me, darling. It's Roland, from high school. Raven Black, the actor now." He grinned, like the fool he was.

"Oh! Roland! Yes! You have changed so much. I didn't recognize you." Her fake smile faltered.

"I just wanted to say, how sorry I am to hear about the passing of Ben Quinn." He hurried to explain. "He was a colleague of mine. I knew he was a... friend of yours. It was bound to happen... just a matter of time. He should never have been cast for the lead role in your book."

Abbi was stunned that he would even mention Ben's name. "Who told you about Ben?" Tears of anger sprang to her eyes. Here she was face to face with the madman that tried to kill him. She felt a very strong need to scratch his eyeballs out of his head.

"Oh, no, don't cry." He shushed her, like she was a child. "It's all over Hollywood, of course. He overdosed on drugs... morphine I believe the rumour was."

He placed an arm around her shoulders. "Come, darling, I'll tell you all about it." Turning her, he started to direct her to the side of the yard near the bushes.

BEN SAW EVERYTHING happen. Abbi falling, Raven catching her, and he knew he'd never make it in time to get to her side. He called on the next best thing. "Brutus, go to Abbi!"

That was all the dog needed to hear. The gentle beast darted to his mistress.

SHE GAGGED AT HIS TOUCH and shrugged his arm off in revulsion. "No!" But she recovered quickly and smiled. "Sorry. Something isn't agreeing with my stomach. It's fine, we can talk here."

"But it's more private over there." He pointed to the stand of trees. "In case you need a friendly shoulder to cry on."

She shook her head. "Nope! I'm good."

"Abbi, nothing will happen. You're safe with me," he smiled, charmingly.

She felt like she was going to vomit. If she did, she'd be sure to aim it at his hateful face.

He started to tug on her arm, in an attempt to guide her away.

"I said, no!" She wrenched her arm free, taking off towards Kim and Steve's direction. She hadn't even taken a step before she felt his arm snake around her waist and lift her off the ground as the other came around to cover her mouth. Her eyes desperately sought out where Ben was waiting. He was gone!

Great, this lunatic is going to take me, and no one will ever be the wiser.

Hope welled up inside her as she heard a low warning growl of an approaching attack. It was Brutus. A howl of pain erupted in her ear just before she was dropped to the ground. She quickly scrambled away, turning in time to see Brutus sink his teeth firmly into Raven's backside.

"Brutus! Stand down," Ben commanded. He rushed to Abbi's side and helped her off the ground.

Raven stumbled back as if he saw a ghost. "Y... you... you're dead, I poisoned you myself!"

Ben sneered and flexed his fists. "Evidently I'm not." He so wanted to beat the shit out of Raven but restrained from doing so.

Ava and Mark came running up along with Steve and Kim. Abbi glanced at the lake and saw the police boat coming to shore; the officers piling out before it stopped.

"We have Raven's confession on tape, all of it," Steve said.

Raven lunged at Abbi. "You're too good for the likes of him." He pawed at her. When she jumped away from his advances, he resorted to calling her names.

Ben had had it with the guy. He grabbed him by the shirt with his left hand, and drew back with his right, smashing his fist into Raven's face.

Dropping to the ground from the force of impact, Raven screamed in pain. "You, sonofabitch! You broke my nose."

Once wasn't enough. Blinded by fury, Ben pounced on him, smashing his fist again and again against Raven's face. He thought of all the times Raven had terrified Abbi and wanted to cause him as much pain as he put her through.

MOONLIT NIGHT

"Ben! Please stop!" Abbi pleaded. Wide eyed, she turned to Mark. "Make him stop!"

Abbi's voice was the only thing that Ben heard through his rage. He grabbed Raven's shirt, and lifted him off the ground, their faces mere inches away. Ben sneered. "Consider yourself lucky that she stopped me," he said, and flung him away in disgust.

Mark moved into action a little too late, but he grabbed Ben under the arms, and tried to drag him away. Ben stood and shrugged him off and searched for Abbi in the gathering crowd.

She was by his side in a heartbeat, cradling his bruised and bloody hands in her own.

She looked at him with tears in her eyes. "Why did you go and do that?"

Ben brushed his lips against her temple. "He should've kept his mouth shut. There was no need to call you those names."

"Let's get you inside," she said, as she ushered him towards the house.

Steve noticed Raven getting up off the ground and saw that he was struggling to get something out of his pocket.

Pulling a gun out, Raven aimed at Ben's retreating back, but Steve tackled him to the ground before he could get a shot off. The gun flew, landing at Kim's feet.

Abbi and Ben, none the wiser continued to the house. When they heard a woman calling to Ben, they stopped. On the steps, Abbi glanced back to see Lorna trying to catch up with them, followed by Mark and Ava.

Ben looked at the ex from his past. "Not now, Lorna."

"Please. I just had to come here for myself, to see. Raven told me you had died," she said, with a cry.

He didn't have any fight left in him, putting an arm around Abbi's waist, he sighed. "As you can see, I'm alive, and well."

Lorna arched a brow. With a pointed look at where Ben had placed his arm, she said, "I see." Without another word, she spun on her heel, and she stormed away.

Abbi squeezed his hand at her waist. "Come on, let's get you cleaned up." Then led him into the house.

"Sit." She pointed to the table on her way to the bathroom.

Ben pulled the chair out with his foot. Sitting down hard, he looked at his hands. He wasn't sure if it was his blood or Raven's... both, he supposed.

If Raven had just kept his mouth shut.

They throbbed, but he'd do it all over again to protect Abbi. The things Raven had said to her, had called her, were not acceptable.

She came into the kitchen and set a first aid kit on the table. Ben watched as she hurried over to the fridge. He chuckled when he saw the bag of frozen peas that she wrapped in a towel. She had nursed his wounds more than his mother ever had needed to.

He sent her a lazy smile when she took the chair opposite of him. Taking his right hand in hers with her head bent, she looked up at him in the eye. "This will sting."

"Go ahead, love."

He gritted his teeth while she gently wiped the dried blood away with a damp cloth then watched her as she took a medical pad from the kit. Ripping it open, she soaked it in disinfectant. Her hand poised over his skin; she glanced up to see if he was ready. At his quick nod, she gently pressed it to his wounds.

Ben felt like he could have shot through the roof if it were not for her hand on his. The sting was so intense; he felt like vomiting. Sucking in a breath, he dared not move.

"I'm so sorry," Abbi softly said. She tried to be as gentle as she could, but try as she might, she knew she was causing him more pain. She quickly removed the cap on the antibiotic tube and squirted a generous amount on his wounds and carefully smoothed it with her finger. Taking a roll of gauze, she skillfully wrapped it around each finger, across his knuckles, and wound it around his hand, taping it in place. She studied her handiwork. "There how does that feel?"

"Better. Thanks," he said, flexing his hand. "The other is fine, just bloody, is all."

Getting up, she took him by the arm. "Come along." She walked to the sink and turned the tap on, shoving his hand under the running water she lathered it up with dish soap.

A knock on her back door, had her yelling, "Come in."

Ben looked around to see Steve with a uniformed officer standing there.

"Steve," he said, as he nodded to the cop.

Abbi turned and smiled a greeting to both.

"Hey, Ben." Looking to the man beside him, Steve said, "This is officer Vince Scott. We just wanted to let you two know that Raven Black is being charged with attempted murder twice, assault, assault with a weapon, and uttering threats. The list goes on, but that's the gist of it."

Kim came around the corner just then, laughing. "Man, that was great!" At their confused looks, she said, "Oh yeah! After you guys came in here. Your dogs went after Raven."

"What?" Abbi cried in alarm. She shot a concerned look at the dogs that were now lying on the floor chewing on a bone.

"Yeah, Steve tackled him when he pulled a gun, and he was—"

Abbi gasped. "Pulled a gun?!"

"Yeah. He was going to shoot Ben in the back."

Both Ben and Abbi looked at the cops for confirmation. At their nods, Kim continued.

"Yeah. Anyway, Molly went up to him, sniffed him, then she squatted... pissed right on his face," Kim cackled. "He tried getting up and kicking her... until Brutus bit his balls." She was now smacking her leg, howling with laughter as the tears streamed down her face.

Grabbing a fistful of paper towel, Ben dried his hand as best he could and laughed as the image flitted through his mind, Raven deserved everything he got.

Abbi looked at the two as if they were insane. "I don't find this funny at all."

Kim dismissed it with a wave of her hand. "Ah, you had to be there."

"Abbi, it's fine. Nothing happened."

"You nearly getting killed twice by the same man isn't fine with me Ben."

"And that's why he's being charged with what he is. Don't worry, he won't be getting out anytime soon," Steve told her.

The sound of someone coming through the living room had them all turning. It was another officer. "Vince, we are ready to roll." Nodding to everyone, he turned and left.

Tossing the paper towel onto the counter, Ben stepped forward, half expecting Vince to arrest him for assault. "Are you taking me in too?" he asked, ready to face the consequences.

"Yeah, no worries, we all agree your actions were justified," Vince replied.

Relieved, Ben thanked him as he shook the officer's hand.

"No problem," he said. He nodded his head to Abbi and touched the brim of his hat. "Ma'am."

"I'll walk you out," Steve said, following him.

"So now what, guys?" Kim asked her eyes still shining with mirth.

Abbi looked at her as Ben snaked his arm around her waist and nuzzled the soft spot just below her ear. His breath hot against her neck sent shivers up her spine.

"How does a bath sound... hmm?" he murmured. She leaned back, gave him a smile and a slow nod. They turned and started to walk the hall to Abbi's room.

"Hey! Where are you guys going? The party is still going on..." Kim watched as they went, their lips locked together the whole time. "Guys?"

The only answer she received was the soft thud of the bedroom door.

She smiled as she headed back towards the party. "Boy, do I need a man like *that*..."

The End

I hope you enjoyed Ben and Abbi's story.

Now here is a quick look in the continuation of their love story with the beginning of Moonlit Road.

Prologue

ABBI SAT IN FRONT OF her computer, just finishing up her last chapter.

Finally! She thought as she typed the last word. She sat back staring at the screen, thinking how only six months ago she had been struggling with every word she typed. Odd how life turns out.

Brutus' loud yawn had her glancing at him as he lay in the sun, Molly and Lucy were at his side. She got up, walking to the control panel for the wall of windows. She opened one, allowing the crisp air outside to come in. She marveled at the view of the lake they provided. It was a picture-perfect day, blue skies, brilliant sunshine, the fall colours were spectacular this year. She couldn't wait until it snowed. She could see it already in her mind. The lake frozen, the sun sparkling off the snow-covered pine trees. Ben had been right. This was the perfect room for her to write in.

They had used his bedroom until they had completed the addition. Ben got the bathroom he wanted. He claimed it was for Abbi, but she secretly knew differently. And she got the bedroom of her dreams. Not that she hadn't already had that, but this one was for them both this time. She smiled. How excited he was designing it all himself, with her input of course.

She moved into his home the week after her party. She frowned, thinking back to the BBQ... not realizing at the time, how close Ben had come to being shot. Thank God, Steve saw Raven's intentions. Otherwise, she very well could have lost him that day. The thought drove her nearly to the edge of insanity. If Raven had succeeded, she'd be the one sitting in a jail cell now. As it was, Raven's case was before the courts. The Crown Attorney was pushing for life. She just hoped to God, he got it, for all he had done... especially to Ben.

Oh, how she missed him! He'd been away for a month and a half now. He and Mark had been off shooting another movie. This time a comedy, both having a main role in it. That was another thing... Mark had convinced Abbi to let him rent her house. He told her he had two willing roommates to move in with him as well. So, it would never stand empty as this one had.

Ava and Kim both shocked the hell out of her when they announced they were staying in Pearl Lake. Ava had sold her spa in Windsor and opened a new one on the edge of the village in a gorgeous Victorian home. And Kim, she was helping Doc Spence at the clinic. Her reason for staying was she couldn't bring herself to leave her partners in crime. Abbi chuckled at the thought of what those three had gotten up to in the past few months.

Sighing, she looked at her watch. Just a few more hours... Ben would stroll through the door and take her in his arms. A thrill went through her body at the thought of it. Their flight took off eight hours ago from somewhere in South America. She had such an uneasy feeling whenever he was flying. He always reassured her that nothing would go wrong, but it didn't help any.

Hmm, I should know what country they are coming from. She'd just turned to look at the itinerary of their trip sitting on her desk, when she heard a car flying into the driveway. Ben, he must be home earlier than he thought! She rushed to the window, frowning as she saw Ava's car come to a sliding halt.

That's odd. Turning from the window, she crossed the room at a hurried pace. She all but ran the length of the walkway to the stairs, her foot touching the bottom step just as the front door flew open.

Ava stood there panting for a moment, her face pale.

"Ava? Honey, are you sick? What's wrong?" Abbi felt sick herself at that very moment.

Shaking her head, Ava sucked in a deep breath and said, "I tried to get here as fast as I could. Why didn't you answer your phone?"

"I was writing. I have it on silent. What's going on?"

Ava waved her hand. "It's all over the news. Turn on the TV," she said. Hurrying into the living room Abbi grabbed the remote, stabbing the power button on.

There before them on the screen was a live viewing of a plane wreckage. With a sinking feeling, Abbi sat down on the arm of the couch. "Ava... what are you trying to tell me..." Abbi knew exactly what she was trying to tell her. Her brain, however, needed to hear it, as her heart was in denial.

Ava turned to her mother, her tears streaming down her face.

"Mom," she went to her then. "Ben and Mark's plane went down twenty minutes after takeoff."

"Ben?" Mark swallowed hard. His throat felt like he hadn't had a drink of anything in a week. "Buddy... can you hear me?"

He lay still on the ground. Straining to hear anything. Only silence met his ears. Slowly moving, he tested each limb to see if anything was broken. His left wrist was the only thing that hurt like a bitch.

A loud screech broke through the silence causing him to jerk straight up. He sat, gazing around at his surroundings for any signs of life.

Where the hell is Ben? And why am I sitting on the ground in the middle of a forest?

He remembered now. They were on their way back to Canada when the plane started to shake and shudder.

Mark glanced to his left, seeing Ben with his cellphone in his hand. He looked at him, both knowing the peril they were in, knowing this could be the end. "I had to send Abbi a text to tell her one last time that I love her."

Mark scoffed at him, trying to reassure him that they would get through this... despite him having doubts to the contrary. "Man, everything will be fine. We will be back home in

no time. And you can ask her to marry you like you planned."
Mark put an arm around Ben then, both men hugging.

They felt the plane rapidly falling to earth. The air masks dropped, both grabbed for them, putting them on. Being frequent flyers, they knew the drill, as they ducked and tucked their heads between their legs. A sound of metal ripping and roaring wind was the only sign that it had damaged the plane as it grazed the treetops. Their section landed with a sickening crash of metal on branches.

The next thing Mark remembered was calling out to Ben. Panic started to set in with the realization that he might be the only survivor until he heard a faint groan.

Mark stood up looking around. Luggage, metal, trees, and bodies were strewn about him. He caught movement out of the corner of his eye. Rushing over he saw a woman still strapped in her seat. "Miss, are you okay?" Mark asked, concerned when he saw the gash on her brow, blood pooling into her eye. Looking around for something clean, he tore open the nearest suitcase. Grabbing a t-shirt, he ripped it into a makeshift bandage wrapping it around her head.

He unbuckled her from her seat and laid her on the ground, telling her to lay still.

He went to the next victim. Finding the man to be fine except for a few bumps and bruises, he learned his name was Hank. Together they started helping others.

After a while, Mark still hadn't come across Ben. He saw there was one more person needing help... and they weren't moving. He made his way over to them, seeing that they were wearing the same colour jeans Ben had on. Mark had to stop for a minute, steeling himself for what he may find.

He slowly went to the person. It relieved him to see that it wasn't Ben, but instantly he was filled with sadness. The person hadn't made it.

Mark hurried back to the others. "Hey, Hank. Did you come across a man, brown hair, about yay high? Speaks with a British accent?"

"No, sorry, I didn't..." Hank replied, earnestly.

"Thanks, man." Mark turned away, glancing around, in case he missed someone laying there. He stood with his hands on his hips. Worriedly, he muttered aloud, "Ben... Where the hell are you, buddy?"

ABBI DIDN'T HEAR AVA. She focused her eyes and ears on the reporter's sober tone: "The cast and crew of Stoned River's plane crashed shortly after takeoff."

Photos of the plane were now on the screen as the reporter continued. "It's confirmed that cast members Ben Quinn and Mark Donovan were to be on this flight that was en route to Toronto Canada."

Their photos were now on the screen. Abbi got up and walked to the TV. She laid her hand on Ben's photo, the tears now falling from her eyes.

"There have been some casualties, but at this time we aren't sure if they are among those who perished in this tragic accident."

Abbi put her hand down. She stood there looking at the TV.

Wouldn't I feel it if he were gone?

She didn't believe it. She refused to believe it after everything they had gone through... she would know.

"Mom?" Ava sniffled, putting a hand on Abbi's arm. "Are you okay?"

Abbi turned, looking at her. "Yes honey, I'm fine." Taking a steadying breath, Abbi knew what she had to do. "Ava, go pack a bag."

Ava gaped at her. Oh my God, she's lost it. Shaking her head in confusion, she said, "What?"

"I said... go pack a bag. We are going to that plane wreck. I'll call Kim. Both of you better be ready in a half-hour, or I'm leaving without you," she said, pulling out her phone.

She hated flying. Ben knew that. When he needed to go back to Madrid to finish up his scenes for The Jasper Killings, true to her promise, she begrudgingly went with him... Tears formed in her eyes as her mind replayed the beautiful memories that they made there.

She, of course, was drunk as a skunk on the flights there and back. Thank goodness he was there to take care of her. Otherwise, she'd never have returned to Canada.

She chewed her bottom lip, waiting for Kim to pick up. "Hi, Kim..."

"Hey, Abbi, did you hear..."

Abbi cut her off. They didn't have time for that. "Yes, I heard. Ava came by and told me. Can you ask Doc to stop by and check on the dogs for me? Better yet, ask him to stay here for a while? I have no idea how long we will be." She paused listening to the exchange in the background.

"Uh, Abbi... he wants to know... who is we?"

"Tell him, we as in, you, Ava and me. We are going down there to find them."

"She told me to tell you that 'we' is me, Ava, and her and... wait... what?" Kim yelled into the phone.

"Be ready in ten minutes. Ava is packing for you, as we speak." She hung up with Kim still jabbering.

She looked through her contact list. Stabbing the digits, she waited for it to connect.

"Nigel. Abbi Peterson here. I need you to find me a plane..." She listened... "No, not a rental. One for sale.... How soon? Oh, in about an hour I'll be in Toronto, can you make it happen? Great, and make sure a pilot goes with it... a very experienced one, please. Right! I'll get Ava to transfer the money on the way down. Thanks, Nigel" She hung up the phone.

Sending a prayer to the powers that be she swallowed hard at what she was about to undertake. Speaking aloud she said, "Ben..." She had to pause. The lump in her throat caused her voice to crack as the tears streamed down her face. She had to continue, maybe just maybe he would hear her voice. Heaving a shaky sigh, she cleared her throat. "I'm on my way. Please babe, be safe. I know you're out there, somewhere... you have to be."

She grabbed her keys, kissed each animal on the head, telling them to be good, and headed out the door. She knew she was crazy for doing this, but she'd be crazy not to. She refused to give up on the one man who had changed her life so completely... one who loved her with his very soul. Ben had once promised her he'd follow her to the ends of the earth. She just never told him that she'd do the same for him...

If you want to see what happens next, you can get your copy by clicking on the cover or link to the following page.
[Moonlit Road.](https://books2read.com/AQMoonlitRoad)[1]

---

1. https://books2read.com/AQMoonlitRoad
2. https://books2read.com/AQMoonlitRoad

Did you love *Moonlit Night*? Then you should read *Moonlit Road*[3] by Aquila Thorne!

What was to be a joyous occasion has turned into a tragedy. Abbi Petersen needs answers, and she needs them now. Her only option is to travel with her family to the plane wreckage in search of them.

Instead of the truth, what they find are lies and corruption. Distraught and at her wit's end, Abbi's only hope is a lonely old woman who talks to the dead.

---

3. https://books2read.com/u/bpwD5k

4. https://books2read.com/u/bpwD5k

When she sends Abbi on a wild goose chase in the Tennessee hills, her family thinks she has finally lost her mind. None of them believe Ben is out there, at least not alive.

Will she make it in time? Or will she have to face the unthinkable heartbreak of forever being alone?

Hello again! It's Ben. I wanted to let you know that this is the conclusion of my and Abbi's tale! Well, not quite yet, we do continue on with the series, we just aren't in your face as much! If you have gotten this far, we want to give you a big thank you! I'll bid you farewell for now as the lovely Abbi wants to have a word. Hey there! I hope we didn't bore you with our lives, pretty eventful some might say but there's more as we couldn't stop telling Aquila our story! I just wanted to say thank you as well to also warn that there are some touchy areas in this book that may trigger some people. Miscarriage is one, as well as death and ghosts. I don't want anyone diving in headfirst without a fair warning. With that said, I hope you're enjoying the series so far, this isn't goodbye, Ben and I will be in the series until the last book is done. Take care ~ Abbi and Ben.

Printed in Great Britain
by Amazon